Praise for *Candlelight*

"Susan Phillips's thoughtful, listening intelligence incandesces in this account of her practice of spiritual direction. The process comes to vivid life in her personal narratives of sessions with directees in God's presence. I was moved by the way Susan's insights grew in relationship with those she met with over months and years. I felt holiness creeping into my own life." —Luci Shaw, author, *Breath for the Bones: Imagination, Art, & Spirit* and Writer in Residence, Regent College

"Reading *Candlelight* is like watching spiritual direction sessions through a two-way mirror while simultaneously privy to the thoughts and feelings of the author. Invaluable for people doing spiritual direction or contemplating it. Provides discerning insights into the difference in form and focus between psychotherapy and spiritual direction. Likely to be absorbing reading for Jungian or transpersonal psychologists." —Jean Shinoda Bolen, M.D., author of *Close to the Bone* and *Crossing to Avalon*

"Some form of spiritual direction is to be found in all the world religions and in many tribal religions as well, but it is only recently that this function has come to be widely recognized in modern societies. As we grope toward understanding what spiritual direction might mean to us we badly need to know how it actually works today. Here Susan Phillips's book offers a signal contribution. She gives us not a 'how to' book but illustrations of spiritual direction in practice as no other book I know of does. By following the experiences of those she has directed over time and through deepening insight we get an understanding that no set of generalizations can provide. This moving book deserves close attention by all those concerned with retrieving the rich possibilities of spiritual direction today." —Robert N. Bellah, Professor of Sociology, emeritus, University of California, Berkeley, and co-author of *Habits of the Heart*

"Susan Phillips doesn't just talk about spiritual direction, she allows us to see her engaged in this ministry, providing a much needed glimpse inside the spiritual direction room, inside the lives of real directees, inside the mind and heart of a gifted spiritual director." —Elizabeth Liebert, author of *The Spiritual Exercises Reclaimed: Uncovering Liberating Possibilities for Women*, and Professor of Spiritual Life, San Francisco Theological Seminary

"While some books on spiritual direction emphasize theology and theory and others are more practical and applied, Susan Phillips offers us something quite unique. We are invited to peek into sacred spaces, absorb poignant stories and watch the candle shed light and sketch shadows. Instead of the harshness of pragmatic, prescriptive and programmatic approaches to spirituality, one is left with a deep and gentle sense that God is here with us." —Rod Wilson, President and Professor of Counselling and Psychology, Regent College, Vancouver, Canada

"More than mere flickers of insight, in this fine book Susan Phillips sheds the light of much wisdom that will encourage and inspire both the givers and the receivers of spiritual direction." —Richard Mouw, President and Professor of Christian Philosophy, Fuller Theological Seminary

"I have waited for just this book for a long time. Susan Phillips's *Candlelight: Illuminating the Art of Spiritual Direction* is a balanced and biblically faithful portrait of the journey into the place where thoughtful spiritual direction can happen. She avoids the entrapments of personal and interpersonal influences in which powerful leaders dominate others around them. Phillips understands that dangerous terrain and draws the reader toward the healthy place where our human stories can be shared and told in safety toward the goal of edification. I recommend this book for pastors, counselors and for all who want to understand ways to explore their spiritual natures." —Earl Palmer, senior pastor, University Presbyterian Church, Seattle, and author of *Love Has Its Reasons* and *Trusting God*

"*Illuminating* is the precisely accurate word for this brilliant evocation of spiritual direction in action. If I were permitted only one book on spiritual direction, this would be it." —Eugene H. Peterson, author of *The Message* and Professor Emeritus of Spiritual Theology, Regent College, Vancouver, B.C.

Candlelight

Candlelight

ILLUMINATING THE ART OF SPIRITUAL DIRECTION

SUSAN S. PHILLIPS

MOREHOUSE PUBLISHING
An imprint of Church Publishing Incorporated
HARRISBURG—NEW YORK

Unless otherwise noted, the Scripture quotations contained herein are from the New Revised Standard Version Bible, copyright © 1989 by the Division of Christian Education of the National Council of Churches of Christ in the U.S.A. Used by permission. All rights reserved.

"The Avowal" by Denise Levertov, from OBLIQUE PRAYERS, copyright © 1984 by Denise Levertov. Reprinted by permission of New Directions Publishing Corp.
"Anthem" by Leonard Cohen. Copyright © 1992 Sony/ATV Music Publishing LLC. All rights administered by Sony/ATV Music Publishing LLC, 8 Music Square West, Nashville, TN 37203. All rights reserved. Used by permission.

Morehouse Publishing, 4775 Linglestown Road, Harrisburg, PA 17105
Morehouse Publishing, 445 Fifth Avenue, New York, NY 10016
Morehouse Publishing is an imprint of Church Publishing Incorporated.

Cover art: Detail of an eighteenth-century icon of the Virgin Mary and the Christ Child in the private chapel of the Archbishop of Sinai, Saint Catherine's Monastery; photo by Hieromonk Justin Sinaites.
Cover design by Brenda Klinger
Back cover photo by Claudia Marseille

Library of Congress Cataloging-in-Publication Data

Phillips, Susan (Susan S.).
    Candlelight : illuminating spiritual direction / by Susan S. Phillips.
        p. cm.
    Includes bibliographical references.
    ISBN 978-0-8192-2297-8 (pbk.)
    I. Spiritual direction—Christianity. 2. Spiritual direction—Christianity—Case studies.
I. Title.
BV5053.P49 2008
253.5'3—dc22

2007048925

Printed in the United States of America

08 09 10 11 12 13   10 9 8 7 6 5 4 3 2 1

*With gratitude to the women and men who
have made God's grace visible to me, as we
met together in the candle's light*

Contents

PART TWO. JOURNEYING

PART THREE. FRUITION

Preface

Benedictine monk David Steindl-Rast declared that "the very act of lighting the candle is prayer."[1] He described lighting the candle in solitude as he prayed, and also the experience of lighting the candle in a church procession. When someone comes to me for spiritual direction, I light a candle and say, "We light the candle as a reminder that God is here with us." It is a prayer akin to the spontaneous candle-lighting of compassionate humanity and the liturgical lighting of candles for worship. The flame represents human yearning toward that which transcends and ignites our hearts.

We are a candle-lighting people. There are candlelight vigils whenever people gather in solidarity with others' suffering. When New York City and Washington, D.C., were attacked in 2001, people around the world gathered in public squares, lit candles, and prayed. When the tsunami hit Southeast Asia in the late winter of 2004, people around the world lit candles expressing compassion. When students die in attacks on schools, people gather at other schools, and light candles. Amnesty International's symbol is a lighted candle encircled with barbed wire, indicating the light of hope and others' care smuggled into the darkness of a person's imprisonment.

A directee has told me about the candles he has seen in Eastern European churches, Holocaust memorials, his own church and home, and in my office. He is certain "It's the same flame."

As we pray at the beginning of the spiritual direction hour, the flame wavers, grabs hold and runs down the wick to the surface of the wax where it wallows briefly, engaging our hope, and then gains strength as it remounts the wick. The flame remains through our time together, reminding us of God's presence as we open our hearts and minds. The candle forms a corona of light, and we are gently held in it. It also casts shadows, bringing to mind God's holy mystery as well as those parts of ourselves that lie in shadow.

I have never received spiritual direction from someone who lights a candle as I do, though I've heard that other directors do this. Perhaps I am inspired to light candles by my Episcopalian childhood, my young adult involvement with Amnesty, or my familiarity with psychotherapy and a desire to signal spiritual direction as a different practice. It may be that God's grace leads me to do so.

The candle cultivates both hope and humility. The light it represents is not mine. The directee and I wait before a divine director who spoke light into being, came to earth as the Light of the world, and continues to enlighten our lives. Candlelight draws our attention to God. This way of drawing our attention is at the core of spiritual direction. Spiritual directors do not direct like circus ringmasters, filmmakers, or uniformed directors of traffic. We direct attention toward the holy as we see and hear it in the life of the person sitting across from us.

More than twenty years ago at the University of California, Berkeley, I studied sociology and was part of a group of scholars funded by the National Institute of Mental Health. We read the great psychoanalysts, and I was struck by the soul work they did, wondering whether and how the Christian church offered soul care. During those years I also worked with volunteer counselors at my church and saw how they (and I as one of them) were changed by the responsibility of compassionate listening. In those years, the late 1970s and early 1980s, spiritual direction was unheard of in my Protestant Christian circles. I discovered it by reading the accounts of the desert and monastic sages of early Christendom and saw its imprint in the soul care given by later Christians, including anchorites, Puritan pastors, and missionaries. In their writings were traces of the transformative, grace-filled listening also evident in the practices of some psychotherapists and psychoanalysts and in the counseling work done by volunteers at my church.

What began then as an ember of interest in my graduate studies has grown into a fire in my life. Its heat and light inform my theology and mold my vocation. As many persons have pointed out, the word "amateur" means one who loves, and I love the art of spiritual direction. Having kind and skillful spiritual directors listen to me for nearly two decades has helped me to know God and receive God's love. The training I received in spiritual direction and my immersion in the work for many years have added fuel to the fire of my love for this manifestation of God's grace in human relationships.

Receiving spiritual direction has made me a better human being. I have seen that in others who have taken up the discipline of spiritual direction. Spiritual direction is entirely optional; it is not necessary for spiritual growth and flourishing. Those who receive it are not better than those who don't. But it can be a way we grow in grace, and it has been so for me and for many others. This book shows what I've had the privilege to see, through spiritual direction, in the lives of a few individuals.

Note

I. Steindl-Rast, *Gratefulness, the Heart of Prayer: An Approach to Life in Fullness* (New York: Paulist Press, 1984), 57.

Acknowledgments

This book tells stories from spiritual direction, and I am grateful to the nine people who have allowed me to tell their stories. When I told one of them that *Candlelight* was to be published, he wrote that he was delighted about "our book." It is, indeed, our book. I am indebted to these people whose lives illuminate the art of spiritual direction depicted in this book, for working with them has shed light in my life and on this writing.

All acknowledgments paint pictures of the communities that surround the author in the solitary task of writing. Several communities have buoyed me through the years of living, thinking, praying, and writing that have yielded this book. The community of New College Berkeley—faculty, board, staff, students, and friends—has helped keep my feet on the path of Christian discipleship and provided the rich soil of conversation in which to cultivate the thoughts that appear in these pages. Many who teach for New College Berkeley have been companions on this journey of faith and scholarship. Margaret Alter, David and Susan Fetcho, Sharon Gallagher, Laurel and Ward Gasque, Virginia and Walter Hearn, Margaret Horwitz, Bonnie Howe, Mark Labberton, Earl Palmer, Martha de Laveaga Stewart, and Robin Wainwright have all encouraged me by their collegial companionship during the years of *Candlelight*'s creation.

Other scholarly communities of support have been Regent College in Vancouver, B.C., Fuller Theological Seminary, Berkeley's Graduate Theological Union, the praying community of New Camaldoli Hermitage in Big Sur, and the staff and faculty of San Francisco Theological Seminary's Diploma in the Art of Spiritual Direction. From these communities, I am especially grateful for the encouragement of Thena Ayres, Jill Boyce, Tish Bulkley, Mary Rose Bumpus, Kay Collette, Jeffrey Gaines, Tom Glenn, Sam Hamilton-Poore, Arthur Holder, James Houston, Rebecca Langer, Bruce Lescher, Elizabeth Liebert, Curt Longacre, Tom McElligott, Deborah Arca Mooney, Marie Pappas, Soohwan Park, Sophia Park, Luci Shaw, Mary Elva Smith, and Katarina Stenstedt. In the field of spiritual direction and the broader care of souls, I also am indebted to Jean Bolen, Liz Budd Ellman, Frances Ann Hamblin, Kathy Miranda, Henry Ormond, Sandra Russum, Mary Ann Scofield, Chris Shiber, Barbara Williams, and many others who have guided, inspired, and, at times, corrected my thinking.

This book would not have been possible without the sustaining worship and community of the First Presbyterian Church of Berkeley, and people from the wider communion of saints and friends who have supported me with love and prayer. I thank Chris Anderson, Carol Aust, Lynne Baab, Jan Baeuerlen, Penny Barthel, Doug Bunnell, Jan Ghirardelli, Kathie Johnson, Linda Kamas, Susan Kegeles, Jeffrey Lazarus, Wendy Lichtman, Suzy Locke, Claudia Marseille, Becky McCain, Diana Mei, Kathryn Muhs, Jennifer Paige, Patti Pierce, Frances Reid, Valerie Ruud, Father Justin Sinaites, Sandra Ramos Thompson, Nancy Wainwright, and Debbie Whaley.

Several people have been kind enough to read this manuscript as I was writing it, and the completed book benefits from their wisdom. For their generous and wise companionship, I thank Maryann Aberg, Mima Baird, Mary Rose Bumpus, Diane Deutsch, Margret Elson, Virginia Hearn, James Houston, Jay Nickel, Carole Petiet, and Steve Phillips. I also thank Nancy Fitzgerald, my editor at Morehouse, for her skillful and calming accompaniment of me as I wrote.

Throughout the book's gestation my family has encouraged me. They were with me on Bay Island one afternoon a few years ago when I was startled to sense God telling me to "write Candlelight." (My first thought was of

Bill Cosby as Noah responding to God's instruction that he begin a large construction project: "Ark? What's an ark?") On that day my parents, Betty and Lloyd Sanders; brother, David; brother-in-law, Ted; sons, Andrew and Peter; and ever-loving husband, Steve, encouraged me to go off and wrestle with God's invitation. They have done the same for many days and nights since then. I am grateful.

Introduction:
Understanding and Seeing
Spiritual Direction

People express curiosity about what I do. They understand my educational ministry, but wonder about my listening practice. I spend many quiet hours listening to people—to what they say and don't say, to inflections, silences, laughter, weeping, aspirations, sorrows, joy, and longings. I listen for prayer. Some of prayer's manifestations were expressed by seventeenth-century poet George Herbert as "God's breath" in us, "the soul in paraphrase," the "heart in pilgrimage," "a kind of tune," and "Heaven in ordinary."[1] I have witnessed such prayers in my office. My listening is different from that of many professional listeners, in that I listen for how the holy penetrates lives. I am there to help people discover the ways their lives are imbued with spirituality. This is spiritual direction.

Spiritual direction is an ancient practice, manifested throughout history and across cultures in many ways. Because "praying is a historical constant of humanity," it is not surprising that people have always sought other people to hear and aid their prayer.[2] This historical constancy was brought home to me years ago when my family and I were vacationing in the Mediterranean and spent a day touring the island nation of Malta. There we visited both the place where St. Paul was shipwrecked and an excavation of one of the world's oldest temples that dates from approximately three

thousand years before the time of Christ. The Hagar Qim temple buildings are said to be among the oldest free-standing buildings in the world,
predating Stonehenge and the Egyptian pyramids. Following guides,
tourists poured through those ruins with their enormous rock lintels in
varying configurations on all sides. The sun blazed. I strained to catch the
historic echoes of intact buildings where ruins now lie, trying to glimpse
once vibrant paintings in cracked, faded fragments.

Our family stood with the tour group with which we had been island-
hopping. Encircling our English-speaking guide, we listened as her voice
pierced the cacophony of languages rising from the crowd of visitors to the
site. At one point she pointed to a rock wall with an opening and explained,
"That's where the listener stood. Before people entered the temple, they
told their regrets and hopes to the priestess." A psychiatrist from our group
joined me in lingering at the orifice, while the rest moved on.

Peering into the stone window, he observed *soto voce*, "The oldest profession," then, turning to me with a twinkle in his eyes, "or the second oldest." I knew he was a listener. I did not tell him I was one too—a spiritual
director.

The designation "spiritual director" is provocative. People react to it.
Priest, undertaker, urologist, chaplain, bodyworker, spiritual director—
those professions make people uncomfortable. People who work in them
enter areas of mystery, places of private suffering or joy, territory traveled
by every man and woman, often in solitude and silence, sometimes with
loved ones.

Psychiatrists often enter such places as well. However, talking cures are
not the primary focus of today's psychiatrist, whose approach to care is
more often medical and pharmaceutical. Many psychiatrists regard spirituality with skepticism. When I mention "spiritual direction" to some people, their faces react as though I have said "palm-reading" or "phrenology."[3]
I, too, have struggled with the label for various reasons. That struggle has
rendered me inarticulate more times than just that day on Malta.

Silence fell between the psychiatrist and me beside the ancient listening window. He and I regarded the stones. Were we, I wondered, each pro-
jecting our own experiences of listening for a living onto the relationship
that had existed between people and priestess five thousand years ago?

Gift, Art, Practice, and Profession

It is a privilege to listen to another person. Anyone who accompanies someone exposed and vulnerable must on some level register the magnitude of
trust. Sometimes listeners buffer their hearts with protocols and boundaries in response to the enormity of the experience and the awe it provokes.
The Maltese listener had a stone booth shielding her from view and the
other from eye contact. I often feel awe when I encounter the mystery of
another soul in intimate conversation. The other's vulnerability makes me
aware that any clumsiness on my part occurs in proximity to the tender,
open core of the one who trusts me.

The art of spiritual direction is cultivated through practice, by God's
grace. The gift (or *charism*) of spiritual listening may take the form of ongoing professional companionship. Many terms are applied here: art, practice, gift, and profession. Each tells us something about spiritual direction.

An art reveals our understandings of excellence, rests on skills that are
learned and shaped, and resides within communities of appreciation and
craft. Writing to artists, David Bayles and Ted Orland counsel, "As a maker
of art you are custodians of issues larger than self."[4] In the art of spiritual
direction, those large issues include theological matters as well as moral and
psychological ones.

A term commonly applied to the listening arts today is that of "practice," which connotes both the occupational form and the practical craft of
the art. Psychotherapists have practices, and they practice psychotherapy.
The same language is used today with spiritual direction and captures significant dimensions of the work. Practices shape us. People seek professional helpers hoping for salutary change in their lives. And we ourselves
are shaped by the practices in which we engage as practitioners. For example, teachers learn to teach better through teaching students. By teaching
they also learn about themselves, about humankind, and about what is
meaningful in life and relationships. In becoming teachers, those of us who
teach enter into an age-old community that carries traditions and understandings of what is good practice. These transcend and undergird any particular schools or communities of teaching in which we participate, linking
us with Socrates, Lao-tzu, Jesus, Maimonides, and others.

Spiritual direction, like teaching, is an ancient art and practice that adapts to the context of the culture in which it exists. Like teaching, spiritual direction is engaged in by some who are professionally trained, and by others who have learned the practice by receiving it and witnessing it, in apprentice fashion. "Craft is the visible edge of art," and some teachers and spiritual directors learn their craft in formal training programs that grant certificates or diplomas.[5] Spiritual direction is an unlicensed practice that in our day has many features of a profession, including the experience of the work as vocation, a calling that benefits society. Through the social organization of a profession, particular people meet other people's complex needs by using skills they have cultivated and in which they specialize.[6] Many spiritual directors offer their skills under the discipline of an ethic developed and maintained by peers through supervision and collegial networks, and some offer this service as a small part of their overall ministries.[7] Some spiritual directors request a fee for their services, some are part of larger organizations that compensate them for the work, and others see spiritual direction as a gift they offer freely to others.

The professionalization of spiritual direction is a subject of debate these days. Some of the benefits of this professionalization are wider availability, expectations of competence, and ethical accountability. Dangers include commercialization, focus on technique, and, most seriously, the loss of primary attention to God's sovereignty and grace.

In addition to skills, values learned by those who enter the practice of spiritual direction shape them as they participate in the community of practitioners. Practical wisdom is cultivated through the particular experiences of the practitioners, shaping each director as well as the profession.[8]

Tradition and Contemporary Expression

Wisdom is also transmitted by tradition. Spiritual direction is practiced by people in various religions and stands within those particular traditions.[9] The tradition of Christian spiritual direction rests, in part, on biblical examples and teachings. Paul encouraged the Roman Christians to shape one another through words of counsel and encouragement, assuring them that they could do so because they were full of goodness and knowledge.[10] Eli, in the Hebrew Scriptures, is an exemplar of spiritual direction. Though failing in sight and strength himself, he realized that God was talking to young Samuel. Eli advised the boy to wait for God to speak again and, if and when God spoke, to answer that he was listening.[11] Scripture has much to teach us about spiritual direction, and it enfolds us in the historic, global Communion of Saints through which this practice has been transmitted.

Spiritual direction rests on traditions of the church. Although, as Tilden Edwards writes, spiritual direction as a formal and named practice has "been rare outside of ordained ministry and vowed religious communities until the twentieth century," as an informal and often unnamed practice it has flourished for centuries among ordinary believers.[12] In his classic book *A History of the Cure of Souls*, John T. McNeill writes that those who undertake the cure of souls have not, in general, been members of the pastorate, but rather have been "a spiritual *élite*, a fraternity that spans the churches and even the religions."[13] The composition of soul-tenders throughout history, including the Maltese priestesses, is broader than the word "fraternity" suggests. In my view, the word "elite" applies today only in the etymological sense of "elite," in that spiritual directors experience themselves as having been chosen, elected, or called to this practice and remain in it only as long as that sense of vocation continues to be felt by themselves and by those who seek them. Spiritual directors today are part of a long and wide tradition.

Priests, ministers, and lay people have been soul friends and spiritual directors throughout Christian history within Catholicism, Orthodoxy, and Protestantism. In Puritan England three hundred years ago, a minister was advised "to identify himself with his consultants, sharing their sorrow and their tears, . . . be a good listener who guards their secrets, and, where the conscience is unduly disturbed, is not censorious."[14] Those values remain in the practice of spiritual direction today, whether practiced formally by ministers and trained spiritual directors or informally by lay persons and spiritual friends. The relationship is not hierarchical: We are brothers and sisters in Christ. Like Eli, the spiritual director helps the other attend to God, but may not have the direct and vivid spiritual encounter experienced by the directee. Spiritual direction is compassionate, attentive, and confidential. It welcomes the other into a safe, nonjudgmental sphere of self-examination in the light of Christian faith.

Spiritual directors are formed by the traditions, shared understandings, and commitments that constitute the practice biblically and historically. We also are shaped profoundly by those we serve through shared contemplative work. Sandra Schneiders, a scholar who brings definition and clarity to the field of Christian spirituality, claims that the study of spirituality is "self-implicating," meaning that the person studying spirituality affects the subject under study, and is, in turn, affected by it.[15] This observer effect has been recognized in all contemporary research. Even the physical sciences are shaped by the personal knowledge and appraisals of scientists and are guarded by their commitments to truth, accountability, practices, and communities.[16] This is true for those studying spirituality and for those of us who offer spiritual care.

Perhaps the observer effect carries particular weight in a field that attends to the experience of faith. Elizabeth Liebert, a teaching colleague at San Francisco Theological Seminary's Diploma in the Art of Spiritual Direction Program, writes, "When lived spiritual experience comes into the room, it makes the study of Christian spirituality immediate, transformative, compelling, self-implicating, and life-changing."[17] Her sentence refers to the classroom, but is likewise true for the room in which I see people for spiritual direction. Our own knowledge is molded by what we encounter, and that personal knowledge is in corrective tension with the tradition and its communities.

One way in which such correction can take place is through writing about our work with individuals, so that particular knowledge can interact with general knowledge about Christian spirituality and spiritual direction. Writing about practice is customary within the secular professional practices of psychotherapy, and has been called a "public airing" that "extends the claim of credibility beyond the cloistered pair that forms the narrative."[18] In spiritual direction, we are the pair before the real Director. In order to see the direction that is taking place, it is appropriate to see that direction occurring in both people's lives. A spiritual director said to me recently, "I just saw a directee and felt just as directed as my directee. Maybe more so!" This is often my experience, too.

Many people today are eager to explore their spiritual natures. A culture long immersed in the material and rational aspects of life has left many feeling that our psyches have been undernourished. We want to pursue our inklings of the holy, plumb the depths and capacity of our humanity—and some of us want to do this in the company of a trusted companion familiar with the territory. As a sociologist I am keenly aware that the social recession today in the United States, indicated by declining participation in civic life (for example, the well-reported attrition from bowling leagues), has left us with a longing for community.[19] Lives spent primarily at work and in front of television sets may be bereft of the experience of knowing and being known by others.

Psychotherapy has flourished as social life has receded, offering people the opportunity to know themselves better in the context of being known by another. A growing rapprochement has been achieved between the care of souls offered by religion and the secular profession of psychotherapy, two fields that until the 1980s were aloof from, if not antagonistic to, each other. While valuing the expert service psychotherapists can offer, today many Christians believe that the church has outsourced too much of its care of souls to psychotherapy, a profession that, on the whole, does not train its practitioners in theological matters. This is the context in which contemporary spiritual direction has spread from the confessionals of priests and cloistered communities into the broader Christian culture.[20]

Unlike much psychotherapy, which regards the therapeutic relationship itself as the fertile soil of personal growth, spiritual direction views the relationship as situated within the larger framework of God's gracious presence. Like the listener on Malta millennia ago, spiritual directors are with people as they prepare to enter the "temple," the place where they encounter the divine. The temple always has been the sheltered space for prayer. In the life to come, there may be no need for temples, but in our noisy world with its myriad distractions, we need focal places and practices that enable prayer. When a spiritual director and directee meet, two "are gathered" in God's name.[21] A temple for prayer is erected.

The temple can rightly be viewed as interior, since God dwells in our hearts. It also may be experienced as exterior, as when we step into a garden, a sanctuary, a worshiping community, or any place that gives us the sense that the holy is present. Spiritual directors are with people as they contemplate, turn their hearts toward God in anticipation of encounter, or remember how they have seen God in their lives. Reflection also brings to mind times of not attuning to God. The presence of a spiritual director helps another person articulate what is usually experienced in silence. As a directee confided to me, "Telling you about my experience gives it weight and reality."

Spiritual direction refreshes and teaches me, while taking me to the depths and heights of my own humanity and to the edge of my comprehension. What distinguishes this listening profession from many other listening practices is its explicit acknowledgment of God. Whatever I miss through inattention or ignorance, the person I work with may notice through God's grace. Spiritual directors say, "God is the true director." Therefore, we are servants of the holy, listeners with the job of being attentive to God, with and for the sake of another. Both director and directee listen for the One who promises, "Call upon me and come and pray to me, and I will hear you."[22]

Seeing Spiritual Direction

Although I know nothing about the beliefs and practices of the Maltese listener, I do know she sat inside a solid rock listening-booth that magisterially signaled the sacred. I have a book-lined, work-worn office in which most of the work I do is not that of spiritual direction. During the several hours each week in which directees and I engage in spiritual direction, I light a candle. Some directees have called a third chair in my listening space "God's chair." That chair sits to the side and between the person coming for spiritual direction and me, as though a third person were part of our conversation (which is, I believe, the reality). The candle sits on a Bible on that third chair. I light the candle at the beginning of the time together and extinguish it at the end. The flickering light encourages me. When confidence falters, it flames on. It testifies to a God who asks us to communicate and trust, to know and be known by the One always present and seeking connection. The candle symbolizes God's presence for those who bare their hearts near it. There is light and warmth, clarity and mystery, in the play of glow and shadow. The Bible on which the candle sits is a "lamp to my feet."[23] It signifies the faith tradition I stand in and rely on.

Both candle and Bible are directive, pointing to the One who directs us. They are directive in the way that spiritual direction is directive. Attention is turned to our experience of God. Spiritual direction is gentle, steady, and true, like candlelight. The stories you read will illuminate this art.

This book is an invitation to glimpse what transpires in the sacred listening space into which I welcome others. Some people frown, laugh, or shake their heads at the words "spiritual direction." The best way to answer the questions and address the preconceptions, I believe, is to show spiritual direction so that it can be seen. There are excellent books on its theory and practice, but the field lacks narrative descriptions of the actual work. My hope is that this book will allow a broad community of readers to reflect on these stories, and be refreshed by the glimpses of grace contained in them

Just as I enjoy and benefit from accounts of work in professions other than my own, so I imagine that some who are not spiritual directors or directees will read this book and enjoy sharing my experience in spiritual direction. Written here is what the art of spiritual direction is for me, not an ideal model of how spiritual direction should be done. In the conversations recounted in this book, the directive choices I made about what to attend to and what to say might not be the choices another spiritual director would make, nor were they necessarily the best choices. In most cases they seemed helpful, enabling the other to attune better to God. In all cases, something happened that lingers in my memory and has shaped my understanding of God's Spirit and people's spirits.

Although I teach and supervise spiritual directors and have practiced spiritual direction for more than a decade, I rarely see directors, other than my own director, at work. Like teaching and psychotherapy, spiritual direction is a caregiving practice that is done away from the observation and exemplary practice of colleagues.[24] In this book I offer some descriptions of my work, with the hope that they will reflect on the practice in ways that benefit spiritual directors and others interested in this art.

No actual word-for-word transcripts of the spiritual conversations are presented here. While guarding the privacy of people I have known over the years, I offer my recollections of our work together as well as reflections on how knowing them has stretched and transformed my own heart and life. Although the requirements of confidentiality, the renaming and thick disguise of directees, and the absence of detailed records may diminish historical precision, what is preserved and offered is personal, narrative truth affirmed by the permission to publish granted by each person represented on these pages.

We are formed and encouraged by stories. We learn how to live through hearing narratives of others' lives, as stories convey meaning and morality, embed memory, and sometimes promote healing as they engage our feelings. The word "narrative" is related linguistically to the word "knowledge." Narratives are a source of human understanding. They are not tidy. The stories in this book don't fit onto Procrustean beds of spiritual or developmental theory, but they are rich in what they offer.

The individuals you encounter have trusted me with their stories of seeking and knowing God. Now they are trusting me to share some of those stories. Even though these people are disguised, their allowing this book to enter the world is a courageous act based on hope that their experiences of God and journeys of faith will bless others. The book rests on their generosity, extended to the many people who ask them and me what spiritual direction is, what goes on in a session, how it changes hearts and lives.

As we are formed by others' stories, so, too, we are formed by our own. What we do shapes us, and how we find meaning in it shapes us as well. People who seek spiritual direction are choosing to engage in a discipline that will change them and change the way they tell their stories. They know God in particular ways, some ways unique to them, and some familiar to many people of faith. Spiritual directors, by skill and vocation, help people notice and cultivate ways of knowing and being known by God.

Each directee I have met with has taught me about God and discipleship. Together, facing each other in the candlelight, we form a "three-fold cord," intertwined with God and each other.[25] That entwining generates strength, warmth, and hope. What I see as people pray and turn toward God encourages me as I also pray and seek God. If my hope flags, I am encouraged by the hope I witness.

The Shape of the Book

This book is divided into three sections, marking the arc of the spiritual direction relationship. It tells the stories of nine people with whom I have worked and marks three periods of our relationship: Beginning, Journeying, and Fruition. Each of the nine people entered the work of spiritual direction at different places in their journey of life, hoping to grow spiritually, and ultimately granting me a long view over time of what that means. Most of them have now moved away geographically or moved out of our working relationship.

In addition to chapters showing the work of spiritual direction, there are also expository chapters, like this one, about the practice of spiritual direction. Some readers may prefer to focus their reading on the narratives alone, perhaps reading each directee's story continuously through the three sections, and then picking up another story at its beginning in Part One. Other readers may be especially interested in the more theoretical chapters, beginning each major part, which offer reflections on what takes place in spiritual direction over time.

The heart of the book lies in the stories of the nine directees, who are introduced in Part One, "Beginning." When the nine relationships began, some of the directees came to see me from lives of fulfilling religious activity with a desire for their spirituality to grow and find greater expression. They hoped that spiritual direction would help them channel their bursting enthusiasm. Some directees came to spiritual direction on the verge of admitting faith, while others came feeling they were on the brink of abandoning it.

Others came with heartfelt longings for God that had been obstructed by an impenetrable interior wall from contact with their officially "religious" pursuits and beliefs. Some of these people are religious professionals or seminarians who needed a place to be honest about their faith apart from their formal faith-related roles. Others lived in a religiously defined social world that had grown increasingly dissonant with their private experiences and convictions. All these people were able to benefit from a spiritual director who could look at their lives and see the whole. Both compartments (public religious life and private experience of faith) could then be explored as well as the separation and connection between them.

Those individuals who come for spiritual direction do so with various hopes and fears, but also with willingness to invest in this discipline. In response to the music of spiritual stirrings, they enter the dance. With the formation of the relationship, the work itself becomes an important part of the person's spiritual journey.

Often what happens in spiritual direction is that people learn to listen for God in their own lives and hearts, and in places previously assumed to be separate from God's governance. It is easy to slip into the assumption that God's dominion stops at the threshold of our lives and souls unless we open the door. We confine our spiritual experience to Sunday worship, for instance. It is true we can turn from God. But we believe in a God who is omnipresent, immanent as well as transcendent. There is folly in believing in such a God and then mentally confining that God's knowledge and power to areas outside the domain of our sovereign selves. It's as though we think there is a chlorine-free end of the swimming pool, a God-free zone in our lives. Not so. We affirm theologically that God is ever-present.

It also is true that God invites us to open our hearts to relationship. We can choose to turn our hearts toward God and to the sometimes searing illumination that God's grace brings to our inmost selves. Sanctification by grace is not an obliteration of self, but is rather a transforming fulfillment of ourselves. We engage the process by turning and returning to God, opening and reopening our hearts and minds. Even if our theological convictions tell us that God is the prime mover who initiates our every turning toward God, there is still significance in our intention to make that turn. We are invited to hear, knock, open our hearts, and trust that our desires and attempts to do so are of value.

Spiritual direction encourages an honest look at what grace illumines. It affirms that God is in our lives and hearts and can be encountered. Contrary to some romantic, ascetic notions of spiritual formation, expressed well in the closing line of a poem entitled *Self-Knowledge*, most spiritual directors today do not believe that it is necessary to "Ignore thyself" in order to know God.[26] Rather, I and many others stand with Protestant Reformer John Calvin in claiming that "true and substantial wisdom consists principally of two parts: the knowledge of God and the knowledge of ourselves. . . . The knowledge of ourselves, therefore, is not only an incitement to seek after God, but likewise a considerable assistance in finding him."[27] In modern times this view was well-expressed by Catholic author, Trappist monk, and spiritual director Thomas Merton, who wrote, "There is only one problem on which all my existence, my peace and my happiness depend: to discover myself in discovering God. If I find Him I will find myself and if I find my true self I will find Him."[28] Gradually, by the light of God's grace, we may be able to see beyond illusions that have obscured our true selves.

Understandings of self and God shift over time and through prayer. The midsection of this book, "Journeying," illustrates transformations I have witnessed as particular individuals have engaged in spiritual direction. Much good can be experienced in a short period of spiritual direction work, and nothing in the theory of the practice argues against brief work. I have worked with a number of people as they end one phase of life and are deciding how to enter the next. I work in Berkeley, a university town, and students sometimes will come to spiritual direction for a semester, an academic year, or the time they're in the crucible of writing a thesis or dissertation. We work for a few months, and then they move to another place and begin a new chapter of their lives. The work of spiritual direction helps them make prayer central to their decisions through a time of transition.

Helpful as short-term work may be, it is the steady pace and rhythms of ongoing work with which I am most acquainted. Such work yields an intimacy of prayer and conversation that, by God's grace, allows deep encounter with desire and fear, light and shadow, suffering and healing love.

Since prayer requires a willingness to be who we are, without pretense or sleight of hand, it's important to get to know who we are as we make room for God with us. People come to spiritual direction because the desire to know and be known is stronger than the fear of it. Yet it takes time to ease into "nakedness." Once our shields are down, we can see ourselves and be touched. We are rendered vulnerable, and, surprisingly, free. Many marvel at how much more freely we can move when no longer encumbered by protective devices. We see what life stirs within us when our energies are no longer focused on image projection or defense of our selves. We encounter

God's quiet presence as we open our hearts and listen, willing to be surprised by what is not in the religious script we have followed so closely in our lives of faith and prayer.

Maps and scripts, religious roles and *dramatis personae*, histories and landmarks, cherished images and names for God that come from Christian tradition enable us to learn from others who have sought to know God. These representations can play significant parts in the work of spiritual direction. They tell of the One we seek. They are humanity's record of the relationship. Yet that relationship is with One who is beyond our grasp, whose name is beyond our speech. That One is not bound by our constructions, nor controlled by our rehearsed words. God is the One after whom we "grope," the One in whom Paul and the ancient poets claimed we "live and move and have our being."[29] This all-surrounding God desires our rent hearts, not our rent clothing.[30] God invites us into a life-changing relationship that requires us to "choose life."[31] Jesus dares us to allow ourselves to be transformed at the cellular level by drinking "living water."[32] We are asked to stretch, reach, and open in faith. Faith is not a subject of study to be mastered. Day by day we are summoned beyond a safe theological "knowledge of description" to one of unpredictable "acquaintance."[33]

God desires our search and our desire. Throughout Scripture, representatives of the Holy One tell us to "fear not" and to be at "peace." The antithesis of fear is not certainty, but rather the vitality of relationship. Because this vitality is sometimes recognized through suffering, suffering and its meaning are a major chord of this work. The middle passage of spiritual direction vibrates with the choice for life and longing for relationship with the living God. Longing, choice, and transformation can be elicited by suffering, as is seen in the stories in this section of the book.

In the book's third section, "Fruition," I reflect on spiritual direction relationships as they have become exceptionally deep and mature in relation to God and God's grace. Most of these relationships have come to a formal end, but continue in our hearts. Although this book contains only a few stories, every person I've been privileged to know through spiritual direction has allowed me to see some facet of the magnificence and complexity of God's love.

The work of spiritual direction can be like gardening. Old growth and decaying matter must be removed to make room for new growth. There may be a season of seeming emptiness and barrenness when the spiritual landscape is desertlike and seems to signal the end of the road. A feature of deserts is that any movement, color, or change is evident against the dominant starkness. A breeze stirs sand, a flower blazes, perhaps a lark rises at the break of day. What emerges is robust and real. This final section contains stories of people with whom I have continued to work as they have undergone significant spiritual maturing. They are like trees planted by the waters of God's grace, even as they walk on the right path—a paradox seen both in Psalm One and in life.

This section includes one story of death, which may seem odd given the title "Fruition." Because this directee made me think about what is possible in dying, I hope you will be engaged in this way, too. I've worked with some people for as long as I have been a spiritual director, but most direction relationships come to an end. Some partings are circumstantial, as when a person moves to another city and finds a spiritual director there. Other people discern the need for another kind of work—usually psychotherapy or pastoral counseling—and drop spiritual direction for a season. Some partings are brought about by health, finance, or employment changes. Some people find other spiritual disciplines offer them what they had found, for a season, in spiritual direction. In spiritual direction there is often no sense of arriving at a place of natural termination. Just as there is no circumstance that necessitates spiritual direction, so there is no moment in the work that determines its end point. There are many of us who anticipate receiving spiritual direction for as long as we live, just as we intend to engage in a variety of other practices that help us pray and listen for God.

Not all partings bear the mark of fruition. This section contains stories that do. Closure can allow comprehensive review. The end of a particular trail brings the shape of the journey into view. The final sessions of a spiritual direction relationship provide opportunity to reflect on all God has wrought in a soul through the steady, prayerful work of contemplative listening. Some of these stories allow that sense of closure, although growth continues.

Fruition does not imply completion. It does, however, indicate a spiritual flourishing that has taken place in the lives of each of the nine persons you will meet. I have worked with many people over the years, and those described here are a few among many who have taught me about maturing in faith. These have been selected because I have known them well over several years, and their stories illuminate particular facets of spiritual direction.

Most of the people in this book are in midlife, but a few are younger. Age does not guarantee mature thriving, nor does youth preclude it. As historian William Bouwsma wrote, "The essential element in the Christian idea of adulthood is . . . the capacity for growth, which is assumed to be a potentiality at any age of life."[34] There are some commonalities to spiritual fruition, but, as with trees, there is much variety. We begin spiritual direction wherever we find ourselves in relationship with God. In the pages ahead you will see lives I have seen illuminated by candlelight.

Notes

1. Herbert, "Prayer (I)," *The Temple: The Poetry of George Herbert*, ed. Henry L. Carrigan Jr. (Brewster, Mass.: Paraclete, 2001), 45.
2. Perry LeFevre, *Understandings of Prayer* (Philadelphia: Westminster Press, 1981), 151.
3. Samuel Coleridge captures some of this concern in the following intricate sentence: "[R]eligion itself, if ever in its too exclusive devotion to the specific and individual it neglects to interpose contemplation of the universal, changes its being into superstition, and becoming more and more earthly and servile, as more and more estranged from the one in all, goes wandering at length with its pack of amulets, bead-rolls, periapts, fetishes, and the like pedlary, on pilgrimages to Loretto, Mecca, or the temple of Jaggernaut, arm in arm with sensuality on one side and self-torture on the other, followed by a motley group of friars, pardoners, faquirs, gamesters, flagellants, mountebanks, and harlots." Coleridge [1830], *The Portable Coleridge*, ed. I. A. Richards (London: Penguin, 1978), 390.
4. Bayles and Orland, *Art and Fear: Observations on the Perils (and Rewards) of Artmaking* (Santa Barbara, Calif.: Capra Press, 1993), 108.
5. Ibid., 99.
6. For an examination of the development of professions and contemporary understandings of profession, see William M. Sullivan, *Work and Integrity: The Crisis and Promise of Professionalism in America*, 2nd ed. (San Francisco: Jossey-Bass, 2005).
7. There is a growing literature on the supervision of spiritual directors. For example, see Maureen Conroy, *Looking into the Well: Supervision of Spiritual Directors*

(Chicago: Loyola Press, 1995); and Mary Rose Bumpus and Rebecca Bradburn Langer, eds., *Supervision of Spiritual Directors: Engaging the Holy Mystery* (Harrisburg, Pa.: Morehouse, 2005).

8. See Aristotle [350 BCE], *Nicomachean Ethics*, bk. 6, *Introduction to Aristotle*, ed. Richard McKeon (Chicago: University of Chicago Press, 1973) and Alasdair McIntyre, *After Virtue: A Study in Moral Theory* (Notre Dame, Ind.: Notre Dame University Press, 1981).

9. There are several books about spiritual direction in different faith traditions and/or different Christian traditions. See, for example, Gary W. Moon and David G. Benner, *Spiritual Direction and the Care of Souls: A Guide to Christian Approaches and Practices* (Downer's Grove: Ill.: InterVarsity, 2004); and Norvene West, *Tending the Holy: Spiritual Direction across Traditions* (Harrisburg, Pa.: Morehouse, 2003).

10. Rom 15:14.

11. I Sam 3:1–10.

12. Edwards, *Spiritual Director, Spiritual Companion: Guide to Tending the Soul* (New York: Paulist Press, 2001), 13.

13. McNeill, *A History of the Cure of Souls* (New York: Harper and Row, 1951), 330.

14. Winthrop S. Hudson, "The Ministry in the Puritan Age," *The Ministry in Historical Perspectives*, ed. H. Richard Niebuhr and Daniel D. Williams (San Francisco: Harper and Row, 1983), 198.

15. Schneiders, "Spirituality in the Academy," *Theological Studies* 50 (December, 1989): 677.

16. See, for example, Michael Polanyi's seminal work on this subject in *Personal Knowledge: Towards a Post-Critical Philosophy* (Chicago: University of Chicago Press, 1962).

17. Liebert, "The Role of Practice in the Study of Christian Spirituality," in *Minding the Spirit: The Study of Christian Spirituality*, ed. Elizabeth A. Dreyer and Mark S. Burrows (Baltimore: Johns Hopkins University Press, 2005), 95.

18. Arnold Goldberg, *The Prisonhouse of Psychoanalysis* (Hillsdale, N.J.: Analytic Press, 1990), 86.

19. See Robert D. Putnam, *Bowling Alone: The Decline and Revival of American Community* (New York: Simon and Schuster, 2000).

20. Some psychotherapists explicitly integrated their religious faith with their professional work even during the decades when it was considered professionally inappropriate. Today, there is growing acceptance of spiritual dimensions to psychotherapeutic work. While psychotherapy has become more spiritually attuned, spiritual direction has become more professionally organized in recent decades. The collegial organization Spiritual Directors International, with an interfaith membership, now has more than six thousand members, having begun with little more than a few hundred less than thirty years ago.

21. Matt 18:20.

22. Jer 29:12.

23. Ps 119:105.

24. I am instructed by the literature on reflective practice, including Gillie Bolton, *Reflective Practice: Writing and Professional Development*, 2nd ed. (London: Sage, 2005); Anna E. Richert, "The Corrosion of Care in the Context of School," *The Crisis of Care: Affirming and Restoring Caring Practices in the Helping Professions*, ed. Susan S. Phillips and Patricia Benner (Washington, DC: Georgetown University Press, 1994); and the journal *Reflective Practice: Formation and Supervision in Ministry*.

25. Eccl 4:9–12.

26. Coleridge, *The Portable Coleridge*, 216.

27. John Calvin [1536], *On the Christian Faith: Selections from the Institutes, Commentaries, and Tracts: I.1.Knowledge of God and Ourselves Inseparable*, ed. John T. McNeill (New York: Bobbs-Merrill, 1957), 3–4.

28. Thomas Merton, *New Seeds of Contemplation* (New York: New Directions Books, 1961), 36.

29. Acts 17:28.

30. Joel 2:13.

31. Deut 30:19.

32. John 4:10.

33. These are Bertrand Russell's philosophical categories which are also helpful in theological reflection. Russell [1910], "Knowledge by Acquaintance and Knowledge by Description," *Mysticism and Logic* (London: Allen and Unwin, 1963): 152–57.

34. Bouwsma, "Christian Adulthood," *Adulthood*, ed. Erik H. Erikson (New York: W. W. Norton and Company, 1978), 87.

PART ONE

Beginning

1

Shall We Dance?

The beginning of a spiritual direction relationship may be initiated by a phone call, correspondence, recommendations, or even some personal familiarity. Occasionally a former student of mine will come to me for direction. Some inquirers have read something I've written and seek me out. Sometimes someone I don't know who is part of my church community will be interested. Others simply get my name from a minister, psychotherapist, physician, or an organization that maintains a referral list of spiritual directors. Each new contact is a surprise, introducing me to a person who wants to grow in faith, seriously examine spiritual experience and belief, and, ultimately, become more alive. Even when there is no follow-up to an initial brief phone call, I am left with the delight of having encountered a person who is reaching beyond weariness, busyness, indifference, and trepidation in order to seek holy mystery. Several people I have listened to for only one hour, yet something in their story or perspective persists in my memory, shedding light on my own path in life.

Many years ago when I was training to be a spiritual director at Mercy Center, a Roman Catholic convent and retreat center south of San Francisco, there were practice requirements throughout the three years. At some point my classmates and I were told we needed to meet with directees. We were encouraged to let people know we were available free of charge while we were interns. I mentioned this to a few people. The deadline for having a directee approached, and I had no one asking to meet with me. My life was full with family and work, and I hadn't strategically worked toward this goal. No doubt cold feet were as much the problem as were full hands.

I had no idea if I had much to offer. Even if I could identify what I had to offer, the relationship felt too sacred to subject to marketing analysis and promotion. My spiritual direction professors had said that although spiritual direction is an art that can be learned, taught, and cultivated, it is also a *charism*, a gift from God. I sincerely hoped I had received the gift and that, God willing, the gift would be recognized by people who could benefit from meeting with me. My teacher Mary Ann Scofield asked, "Have you prayed about it?" Not much. But starting then I did, tentatively imagining that people might be ushered into my office by the hand of God.

First Encounters

To my surprise, that was what appeared to happen and has continued to happen. My first spiritual direction relationship, however, was short-lived and disappointing. The potential directee came from outside my religious tradition and with expectations I couldn't meet. She had been reading a series of captivating novels by Susan Howatch in which spiritual directors play significant roles. The focus of those novels is an Anglican cathedral town in England. The characters are, on the whole, complicated, educated, articulate people of faith. A number of them seek counsel from spiritual directors, who seem nearly omniscient. Like Yoda in *Star Wars*, they reveal deep knowledge of directees' innermost souls and exude complete confidence in their own powers to discern and proclaim. They confront, cleanse, and heal, often in short order, though they are also depicted as wholly human, engaging in their own faith struggles. In one of these novels, a spiritual director, Father Darrow, says to a directee he has met the previous day, "[God] has come to your rescue at last, and here in this village, here in this house, here in this room where you've hit rock-bottom, here's where your new life finally begins."[1] This fictional spiritual director with such brief acquaintance with his directee has more precise knowledge of God's action in a directee's life than I ordinarily possess, which has been frustrating at times, not only to me.

This first, Howatch-loving directee told me some things about her life and then asked me to tell her what really was going on in her life spiritually. I told her I would be happy to keep listening and tell her what I noticed, but that I did not have access to any knowledge about her other than what she chose to disclose. She was disappointed. It was clear I was no Yoda privileged with secret knowledge. I did not have a soothsayer's insight. Worse, I was not even a good host, being acutely self-conscious and ill at ease throughout the entire hour we spent together. The candle flamed as I sputtered.

As time has passed, I have come to know better what I do have to offer and am able to offer it confidently. People come with various expectations, and I do my best to welcome them, even if I cannot fulfill their stated expectations. Fears have ebbed while my trust in God's grace has increased. I myself am less and less on my mind when I meet with someone for spiritual direction. My job is to be host to a time of reflection focused on the other person's experience of the holy. I do not create the experience, nor do I have to understand it. I help the other person move more deeply into it, noticing what I can as we go, and trying to keep us on course toward the sense of God. From time to time I do sense the Spirit's movement when the other doesn't seem aware of it. If the awareness persists, I mention it to the directee as my experience and of possible value to him or her.

In early sessions, I want to learn that person's spiritual make-up: What is his language of spiritual experience? What kind of religious culture is she part of or coming from? How have they experienced the holy? I listen for that. Often people who come to see me are ready to talk about their experiences with organized religions, positive and negative, or about their tenets of faith. That interests me. But I am most interested in what has opened a heart, stirred the sense of hope and joy, immersed the other in a broad stream of peace, and inspired care in such a way that joy, grief, and action are possibilities.

God created us as human beings. I listen for the depths of humanity, believing that in those storied, embodied, sensate, emotional, intellectual, social, and spiritual depths lies the presence of God. An encounter with

God is not achieved by stripping us of our human nature, but rather by entering into it honestly, as Jesus did. As a new relationship begins, I listen for the ways God encounters the real person and how the person prays from the depths of his or her heart.

Hearts' Desires

Seeking spiritual direction is an act of courage and hope. The people who climb the three flights of stairs to my office for the first time have felt sufficient desire to know God better that they have come. Like the word "heart," "desire" is a word that most academic education has not addressed, yet it is core to the work of spiritual direction. Desire is a state of being in which we encounter the other. It is an opening out of oneself, a posture of reception and vulnerability.

In the soul work of spiritual direction, we strive to discern the desires of hearts and the conforming of those desires to God's desire. Desire includes both orientation and leaning toward. We may desire success or wealth or integrity. Desire itself is the opening outward, like the baby's mouth straining toward the mother's breast. There is an infinite range of objects of desire, and Scripture enumerates many of our hearts' unhealthy desires. The first mention in Scripture of the heart's inclinations describes a dissonance between human hearts and the heart of God: God sees that "every inclination of the thoughts of their [our] hearts was only evil continually . . . and it grieved him to his heart."[2] The General Confession of the Book of Common Prayer reads, "We have followed too much the devices and desires of our own hearts."[3] We often fail to attune our hearts to God's heart.

Much of Scripture and Christian theology is aimed at encouraging us to train our desires toward God. Theologian Belden Lane in writing about John Calvin notes that "spirituality, in Calvin's thinking, is a performance of desire shared by the whole universe, a deliberate practice of delight that echoes through every part of the created world. . . . All created reality, extending each moment from the hand of God, is shot through with longing."[4] In a first session with a person, I listen for that desire, that longing.

Many who write about our relationship with God—the focus of spiritual direction—mention hearts and desires. There we find images taken from music: attunement, harmony, resonance, amplification, reverberation, and more. The image that comes to my mind in spiritual direction is often that of dancing to music.

Many years ago I danced with my husband's uncle at an anniversary celebration. He was such a fine dancer that with him I became a good dancer. He led firmly and minimally, and I did all kinds of things I didn't know I was capable of. For the first time I experienced the music flowing through me as I danced. My attention wasn't anxiously fixed on my own movements, nor was I particularly attending to the man. The memory lives in me as a revelation of how my body can dance music. Now I know that such a capacity is in me, though I seldom experience it. At the end of that time of dancing, I was hungry for more. It evoked a desire in me to experience music with my whole self.

Fragility and impermanence lend intensity to the pleasure of pursuing desire. The dance came to an end. Jesus' parables of the lost sheep, coin, and son illustrate the pleasure that comes from desire fulfilled, a pleasure far greater than continual possession would have brought. The fragility and impermanence of mortality lend force to its preciousness.

Philosopher Emmanuel Levinas writes that "the relation to the Infinite is not a knowledge, but a Desire. . . . Desire itself cannot be satisfied. . . . Desire in some way nourishes itself in its own hungers and is augmented by its satisfaction."[5] Desire feeds desire. In dancing with that man my desire to dance was magnified rather than satisfied. As Levinas claims, that is true of relating to God, a situation of reciprocal desire. Stated in another way, Ann and Barry Ulanov write that "the answer to prayer is prayer—more prayer, fuller conversation, more listening, more straining to hear, more reflection on what is actually heard, on what has really happened."[6]

A spiritual director is like the man who helped me dance: a firm, gentle professional, familiar with tempo, patterns, variations, and steps. Spiritual directors know what it is like to learn to "dance." They have lots of experience "dancing" and know that there is no end to growing in the practice. Sometimes our partners, directees, hear more in the music than we do and move into steps we had never imagined. Sometimes we, the spiritual directors, are the ones who suggest steps.

When a person arrives in my office for the first time, I recognize the desire that has brought him or her to me, the perhaps not mentioned but inevitably present fears that surround that desire. It is more difficult in our culture to speak of prayer than it is to speak of sex. The Ulanovs write that "prayer is exposure."[7] To pray is to expose oneself to the One prayed to as well as to what is deepest within oneself. Reading the Psalms, the Bible's prayer book, shows that prayer opens the one praying to every variation of human feeling and experience. Ordinarily, we exert ourselves to contain powerful feelings, especially those that express unmet longing, as the feelings of prayer often do. How much easier it is to turn from those irresolvable feelings to a problem within our control. Yet in prayer we allow our whole selves to be held by something larger than we are, just as the music holds and flows through the dancer. That something will change us, placing our feet in unexpected places.

As I await the knock on the door, I turn to God and pray to be a trustworthy partner in the dance of prayer.

Notes

1. Howatch, *Glittering Images* (New York: Fawcett Crest, 1987), 205.
2. Gen 6:5–6.
3. *The Book of Common Prayer and Administration of the Sacraments and Other Rites and Ceremonies of the Church according to the Use of the Protestant Episcopal Church in the United States of America* (New York: Seabury, 1953), 6 (hereafter cited as the Book of Common Prayer).
4. Belden Lane, "Spirituality as the Performance of Desire: Calvin on the World as a Theatre of God's Glory," *Spiritus* I (2001): I.
5. Levinas, *Ethics and Infinity: Conversations with Philippe Nemo*, trans. Richard A. Cohen (Pittsburgh: Duquesne University Press, 1985), 92.
6. Ulanovs, *Primary Speech: A Psychology of Prayer* (Atlanta: John Knox, 1982), 107.
7. Ibid., 116.

2

Held in the
Current: Grant

H is name is Grant," Pastor John informed me, standing in his church's large parking lot. "He has a lot of questions about faith, and I thought you two might work well together."

That was this pastor's first "referral" to me, and I remember thinking, "John must be warming up to spiritual direction." I expressed my gratitude and gave John the private voicemail number people use to contact me about spiritual direction.

Days later, Grant called and left a message. He sounded quiet and formal. I returned the call to his office, and we set up an appointment to talk about what spiritual direction is, what he was looking for, and what I could offer. I often offer an initial one-time, no-fee, no-commitment hour of conversation. Some people never call back after that first hour together. Some ask for names and numbers of other spiritual directors or psychotherapists, and sometimes I think a person would be better off working with someone else, and I say so. Some want to see me again. Grant did.

Grant arrived in a gray suit that complemented his steel gray hair, looking every bit the corporate executive he is. He carefully folded his jacket, turned off his cell phone, and put them and his briefcase on my worn conference table, an action he repeats every time he visits.

He told me about his spiritual life: a long journey of faithful church attendance, Bible study, and prayer. He mentioned his desire for a more heartfelt experience of faith. Like many, he was experiencing his religious life as stale and rote. He went through the motions, but felt no emotion. He had hoped that theological study would amplify his spiritual experience, but it had not. He knew a lot about who theologians think God is, but that wasn't helping him know God. In fact, it was scaring him a bit. God's holiness seemed pretty incompatible with his own flawed humanity. The sense of God's holy otherness had become an impediment to prayer.

Grant had questions. Lots of questions. Questions about the Trinity, about the way Jesus' death and resurrection affected his own redemption, about the Person of the Holy Spirit and what Scripture meant in claiming that that Spirit lives in us. He had questions about Christian community, and what it means to grow in faith together. So much of the faith journey seemed solitary and unspoken. How could he even begin to talk with others about his intractable experience of spiritual alienation despite his steady striving in the faith?

I listened to him. Then he listened to me describe spiritual direction as I practice it. Having done all his speaking with eyes lowered, in listening he turned his gaze toward me. I spoke about my willingness to listen to him with an ear toward God in his life. I told him about my belief that God is present in all aspects of our lives, and about the way that belief helps me attune to hints of God in the world.

I also explained how spiritual direction is different from other listening professions. Spiritual direction is not psychotherapy, though it can look like it. I am not looking for pathology, diagnosing, or treating it, nor am I attempting to assist someone in problem-solving. All those activities are worthwhile, but are not ones I am trained in or am licensed to practice. I am very much in favor of psychotherapy when needed, have benefited from it myself, and know that some psychotherapists listen to their clients with spiritual attunement. A number of the people I work with are working concurrently with psychotherapists and tell me they find the two practices complementary. Those of my directees who are psychotherapists speak often about the differences in the two practices and make the distinction increasingly clear to me.

I told Grant about my experience with my spiritual director at the time. Knowing that I was going to talk with Sister Barbara kept me alert to what was going on with me spiritually. Her engagement with my life and her care for my spiritual health generated in me a kind of accountability. When I was with her, she helped me notice things I hadn't noticed on my own. Sometimes she challenged ways I was thinking about God and my experience. Even more than the time in her presence, though, I valued the time between our conversations for her work with me radiated far beyond the time we spent together. When I would have an experience of what I think of as grace, instead of just rushing past it into my to-do list for the day, I would pause and think, "Yes. This is grace. I'll remember to tell Sister Barbara."

Grant listened to what I said, nodding from time to time. His eyes drew me. At first glance they matched his suit and hair, another gray surface communicating reserve as he glanced up from his hands to my face. As he listened to me, I began to see his intense, shy longing for God. When I spoke of my faith in God's presence, I saw a flash of hope. When I told of my experiences with my spiritual director, I saw keen interest.

Shifting from my own story to the subject of our possible work together, I said, "All stories are appropriate for spiritual direction. Let me illustrate how I would orient myself as a spiritual director, in contrast to how many psychotherapists would work. For instance, you might say the following to me: 'One night when I was about ten, my mother yelled at me and I went to bed crying. Lying there in the dark I sensed a comforting presence that held me. I didn't see or hear or feel anything concrete, but I knew I was loved. That feeling was gone the next day when I encountered my mother's anger again.'

"If you told me that story, my first movement would be toward the feeling of being loved, not toward the turbulent relationship with your mother. Both parts of the story are important, and both hold spiritual significance, but my first move would be toward the comforting presence, helping you remember that experience, and holding you in it as much as possible. The experience of that comforting presence then will be there, remembered and real, as we turn to other subjects, including, perhaps, that of your mother's anger."

What looked like pain seared his face, as he dropped his head. I hoped I would get to work with him.

At times I wondered if Grant had had experience with psychoanalysis. In the beginning of our work together, he would come into my office without comment, silently perform the ritual of disposing of his professional luggage, sit down with barely a glance at me, look at the floor, and, after I lit the candle and he whispered a prayer, he would speak for about fifty minutes. After fifty minutes he would look up at me, and I would think, "Now I'll say something," but before I could, he would say resolutely, "I think I'm finished now."

I, then, would respond with my closing words, which are "Let's end our time with a moment of silent prayer." We bowed our heads and closed our eyes. After a few silent moments, I said "Amen," and blew out the candle. He would hand me a check, look at his handheld electronic calendar to confirm our next appointment, put on his jacket, reassume the weight of his briefcase and cell phone, and leave.

Working with Grant was challenging; however, over time, as we have become more comfortable with each other, it has become easier. At first I could not figure out what to do, though I had been doing this kind of work for years when I met him. Many questions presented themselves. What was my calling in relation to him? Ought I just to listen in silence? Should I interrupt him and say something? I prayed, looked at the candle and at him looking at his hands clasped in his lap. I regarded him, and wondered.

One of the great gifts of being a spiritual director is getting to imagine how God sees a person. I can imagine how God loves Grant. Grant is an earnest, hard-working man who strives to live a life of integrity. He uses his enormous intelligence and organizational skills for the sake of his work, which involves overseeing hundreds of people and programs, and for the sake of anything else he cares about, such as his family, church, and devotional life.

Sitting silently as Grant talked, I registered God's fondness for him, yet I also felt sad. Grant earnestly desired to be good and do right, and he seemed profoundly lonely. That touched me, and I felt as though God's compassion for Grant lodged in my heart. I also admired his courage and commitment to know God. Not many people with days as tightly scheduled

as his make the effort to climb the three floors to my office in the middle
of the workweek.

Every time I watched Grant fold his jacket and put it on my table I felt
the ache of sympathy in my throat. "Such a good man, and he seems so
alone," I thought. The ache would stay with me through those first mono-
logic sessions as he told me the story of his longing for God. I felt myself
straining to help him satisfy the thirst he felt for God. As it turned out, we
had to go into a place of darkness and pain before comfort was felt.

"Have I told you about my brother who died?" Grant asked, about a
year into our work.

Grant had alluded to sorrow in his family and to grief he had worked
on with a therapist. It was not clear to me that I would ever hear the story.
Mostly he explored theological questions and kept family history outside
the room. Yet the burden of suffering was evident in his hunkered posture
and lined face. I knew enough about human nature—my own and others'—
to recognize familiarity with suffering in his scrupulous attempt to figure out
how God works, and then to work within that system. Would that we could
figure that system out and deflect tragedy!

"He reached the end of his endurance and killed himself," Grant mur-
mured in hushed tones as he bent nearly double over his knees, his fists
pressed against his eyes.

Not sure I'd heard correctly, and praying not to blunder in this sacred
space, I softly echoed what I thought Grant had said: "Your brother killed
himself?"

"Yes," he whispered through clenched teeth. I breathed deeply, at first
relieved by not blundering, and then, arrested by Grant's pain, my breath
caught in my throat. Grant looked frozen. I waited for him to speak again.

Finally I broke the silence, saying, "I'm so sorry, Grant, so very sorry,"
leaning forward, aching to let him know I was with him. He nodded, still
clasping his hands to his face. He nodded again and, at last, took a shud-
dering breath. He shifted his position, sat back in the chair, arms down. I
knew he was not frozen anymore, and I, too, breathed more easily.

"I tried to help him, but I didn't do enough," he lamented and then
told me about his brother.

That was the first time Grant told me a story that he has talked about many times since. It is a focal story, central to who he is and how he understands and does not understand God, his family, and himself. It is part of a larger saga of family brokenness, fragile goodness, and his surprise at discovering the force of his own love and faith in a place of darkness. His brother's death threw him to his knees and broke open his theology. I felt the presence of unspoken questions, mine, and possibly his: "Why did it happen? How could You have allowed it, God? Why, God? . . . God?" Grant, however, did not give voice to questions carrying such accusatory freight, and I kept mine to myself.

Grant wept. Tears fell on his hands, clasped loosely in his lap. He sobbed. His shoulders shook with the force of his grief, and he moved more freely. I cried, too, my tears unseen by him as, head down, he wept.

During the course of our hour together, Grant told me about the memorial service for his brother. He had carried the responsibility for organizing it, by virtue of his skills, closeness to his brother, and his role as the "religious" member of the family. He gave the eulogy. When he stood in front of his brother's casket, he saw that it lay under the Cross. He spoke about that from his heart, to family and friends, some of whom seemed to have hardened their hearts.

Grant told his family about Jesus. He explained to me that what he knew that day was that Jesus meets us in the deepest, darkest, deadliest places of our lives. The only thing he trusted that could help him face his brother's death was that Jesus had experienced it all and understood everything his brother and he went through. No "why" questions were answered. But there was a Who. There still is the same Who. That day next to his brother's dead body, he felt the presence of God.

Shifting focus and looking sharply at me, Grant exclaimed, "I know that God is still there, but I don't want to re-enter the pain. I don't know if I can depend on God. He let my brother suffer and die. How can I open to One who would allow that?"

"Yes, how?" I agreed. Then, returning to the dropped thread of grace, I suggested, "Tell me what it was like to open to God that day in the chapel."

"It was like being caught by a current. I was falling, out of control, but all of a sudden I was in the grip of a stream that held and guided me. It was gentle, but I could rest in it. I ached all over, and I was cradled."

"Cradled." The word echoed in my mind. He was "guided" and "cradled." I encouraged him to say more about that experience.

"It was comforting. I didn't feel alone." He sighed and seemed to relax more. I wondered if he was re-experiencing that sense of being held and allowed to rest. If so, I wanted to offer time in which to savor it. We sat in silence for a few minutes.

The painful beauty of Grant's experience was piercing. I was grateful that God met and held Grant that way in the place of agony, and grateful that Grant allowed himself to be held.

I also was thankful for God's revelation to me through Grant. God is with us, indeed. I always appreciate being reminded of that. My theological understandings are fortified by what I see and hear as a spiritual director, though they also have been challenged and changed by this work.

My relationship with the Cross was informed and transformed by Grant's experience in the chapel. At times I have disliked the fact that an instrument of execution is the dominant symbol of my religion. I also have been leery of the symbol of the Cross because of how it has been used to persecute others in a stunning perversion of Jesus' sacrifice.

With Grant I saw, again and more clearly, how the Cross helps us bear the unbearable. Jesus, God incarnate, out of love for us chose to live a human life and bear the unbearable. Jesus suffered the terrible murder of his cousin John and the agonizing humiliation of his own death by crucifixion. The God who is with us in our pain has firsthand knowledge of suffering. The hand that holds ours is pierced.

The foot of the Cross met Grant's brother and also Grant as he stood beside the casket. I remembered that a year later when I stood beside the Cross and spoke at my young brother-in-law's memorial service. I cannot say I had the same experience of being met and carried by a current, but I remembered Grant's experience, and his faith through tragedy offered me some comfort.

"Thanks. I think I'm finished. . . . I'm exhausted."

Grant ended the time together. I checked to see how he felt about leaving, having entered into such wrenching and seldom-visited memories. He said he was okay, and that the silence had taken him into a space of encountering God, and the experience felt too raw to talk about. "Maybe next time."

The word "cradled" has stayed with me. It captures the message of a popular contemporary Christian parable on greeting cards and decorative objects that some consider sentimental and trite. The parable, "Footprints in the Sand," is a meditation on Psalm 77:19—"Your path led through the sea, your way through the mighty waters though your footprints were not seen"—and, for many, is more familiar than the Scripture. People tell me they hear the Gospel in its affirmation of God's abiding care for us, even if at times that caring presence is invisible. The narrator recounts a dream in which she walks the beach with the Lord, seeing scenes from her life flashing across the sky. In each scene she sees footprints in the sand, often two sets, representing herself accompanied by the Lord. Sometimes she sees only one set and is bothered because she realizes that in the low, difficult, suffering periods of her life there has been only one set of footprints in the sand of her journey. She asks the Lord why, having promised to be with her if she followed him, he abandoned her in the hard times. The Lord replies, "The times when you have seen only one set of footprints in the sand is when I carried you."[1] She was cradled.

This parable depicts spirituality, the lived experience of faith, the knowledge of acquaintance. I often heard Grant's theological questions, questions about how God is described in Scripture and understood by Christian scholars. That day when he told me about his experience beside his brother's casket, under the Cross, I heard about his spirituality of acquaintance. He was guided and cradled. There must have been just one set of footprints in the sand at that time.

As Grant told me about his brother's death, I kept returning to his experience of God and imagined I was making space for him to explore that experience. The issue of space is crucial in spiritual direction. A spiritual director holds space open. We offer a place set apart from the ordinary flow of life, in which a person can meditate on God without distraction or intrusion. Most people, myself included, are adept at filling space with work and entertainment. Even our time at church can become work (a duty, a place of service, a pause in which to make lists of things to do after church), or the passive reception of entertainment. Our minds like to busy themselves. Opening ourselves to God is a challenge and sometimes we need help.

Contemplation is possible when an open space is preserved. Then we can rest in attention to God. Our gaze goes deep into things that then can be encountered in their fullness. The word "contemplation" has to do with what it is like when we are in the temple with God's Spirit. In Christian Scriptures that place of meeting, that temple, is always at hand. We are told that our bodies are temples of God's Spirit. In his first letter to the Christians at Corinth, Paul wrote, "Do you not know that your body is a temple of the Holy Spirit within you, which you have from God?"[2] Apostles Paul and Peter claim that our community life is also a "temple" of the Holy Spirit, a "dwelling place for God," a "spiritual house" built of our selves that are its "living stones."[3] Therefore, we may enter the temple of God's Spirit individually and with others—at all times, in all places.

The temple, the place of encountering God, is with us, if we stop and notice. The hour with a spiritual director is such a temple. It is a protected, sheltered time and space, free of interruption and agenda, dedicated to contemplation. It perches on the threshold (the liminal space) between the solitary and the communal experience of God, as the directee's experience moves between private prayer and prayerful reflection in another's presence. It is a kind of inner sanctum for reflection, conversation, and silence before God.

In that sanctified space we encounter God and our own depths. Our bodies respond to the experience, and tears often come. When tears came for Grant as he told me about his brother's death, he whispered and choked on the words. His body expressed what he told me. An irony of my listening work is that part of what I have to deal with in terms of my own body is my hearing, which is less than perfect. Add to that the fact that people often drop their voices when they say significant, intimate things, and you can imagine how excruciating it is to find my own limitations impeding my attunement to someone who is trusting me to hear their suffering. Straining to understand, I wrestle with the options: Do I wait as the other continues to speak, hoping to grasp the gist of what's been said? Or do I ask the person to repeat what clearly has been painful to say even once? As Grant was telling me of his tragedy, I was burdened by my fear of hurting him by misunderstanding his words as he wept.

Tears accompany spiritual direction. They are a regular feature of the work, and the wastepaper basket in my office fills up not only with used matches and depleted candles, but also with damp tissues. Men cry no less than women. That was a surprise to me, because it has not been my experience in life outside spiritual direction. I seldom cry outside spiritual direction, but many sessions with directees and with my own director move me to tears. I understand this in several ways. Tears are a way the body expresses its openness to God. The rending or opening of our hearts can release tears, which biologists tell us is a way our bodies release toxins and heal themselves. Since Grant's grief about his brother's death resided in his heart, opening his heart to God released that grief, and the tears flowed. This, I believe, is part of God's healing work.

The Spirit prays in us with "sighs too deep for words," and sometimes God's work in us is expressed through tears.[4] When I was studying spiritual direction, we were instructed to "follow the tears." Tears signify the road to God. I once heard a classical psychoanalyst say, "All roads lead to Rome, and Rome is aggression." In spiritual direction, Rome is God, and one of the roads that leads there is tears. I look for tears in the eyes of directees, and I attend to their pressure in my own eyes. Grant's grief moved me to tears of compassion for his suffering. Tears, my own and others', guide my attention, and I direct the conversation toward what prompts tears, even if it goes against what seems like the logical flow of the conversation. I don't poke at wounds, but, rather, I follow the trail of tears that seems to lead to the heart's truth.

Tears often reflect an opening to God's grace. That opening evokes *penthos*, the Greek word for godly sorrow, compunction, repentance, the ability to see oneself clearly in the light of God's loving truth. It must be what the prodigal son experienced when his father welcomed him home. It's what we see over and over again in the Psalms. King David prayed to God: "You have kept count of my tossings; put my tears in your bottle. Are they not in your record?"[5] Tears are indicative of the condition of the heart and, we assume, are noted by God. They signal cleansing and make space for the fruits of the Spirit. "May those who sow in tears reap with shouts of joy," sings the psalmist.[6]

People might be surprised by how frequently tears are shed in my office, but colleagues have told me they are startled to hear so much laughter coming through my closed door. Tears and laughter are emotionally related, and when we open ourselves to God, our emotional core is touched. After the sobbing, there is often a sense of relaxation, deep sighing, maybe some shrugging surrender to reality coupled with gratitude for God's love. A weight is lifted from the heart, and laughter can follow.

Sometimes what is lifted is as heavy as a tombstone and has blocked life for years. At other times, the tears release something much smaller. There are times we stumble and trip over the same difficulty time and time again. One person hopes to pray for fifteen minutes every morning and repeatedly fails to do so after a few days into the practice. The failure becomes a source of shame and blocks her from praying at all. In an intense moment of confession, she tells me about it and cries. I picture a toddler careening to a plopping stop on the floor. Initially there's shock, frustration, and maybe tears. The mother sits and watches. The toddler looks up, and the mother sings, "Uh-oh." The toddler echoes "Uh-oh" and claps his hands. They both clap and laugh. And then the baby tries again. There was a time when my spiritual director's response to my painful confession was merely to say "Uh-oh" in a soft, but pointed way. It was a kind intervention that directed me toward making a better decision. I was grateful for her gentleness and smiled through my tears of contrition.

In addition to expressing grief, compassion, and contrition, tears arise in response to goodness ("God-ness"?) and beauty. Years ago a friend in his seventies told me that the older he gets, the more his tears are a response to goodness or joy rather than an expression of sadness. In his moving book about French villagers (primarily Protestant farmers) who saved thousands of Jewish children and adults from death at the hands of the Nazis, sociologist Philip Hallie recounts the first time he read about these villagers of Le Chambon. He had studied cruelty and torture for years and had come to do so "without a shudder." When reading about this village, however, "I was annoyed by a strange sensation on my cheeks. The story was so simple and so factual that I had found it easy to concentrate upon it, not upon my own feelings. And so, still following the story, and thinking about how neatly some of it fit into the old patterns of persecution, I reached up to my cheek to wipe away a bit of dust, and I felt tears upon my fingertips. Not one or two drops; my whole cheek was wet."[7] Hallie was responding to sacrificial goodness, which he claims, quoting Keats, goes through one "like a spear."[8]

We feel such tears when we stand at the foot of the Cross and bear witness to Christ's great love for us. I felt that piercing spear-thrust as I listened to Grant's story and experienced his goodness.

I have come to know Grant well and to view him as an anemone, opening and closing as the current of God's grace touches him. More and more he is open in our times together. He still comes in quietly and folds his jacket on the table, but he chats now before we light the candle and pray. He laughs. He looks me in the eye more often. He speaks and waits for me to respond. He still tells me when he is "finished," but he does it with a wry, self-reflective smile.

I think Grant trusts me and forgives my blunders. He tells me when something I say does not capture what he is talking about. He accepts my limited ability to answer his questions. He trusts me to do the really scary thing of inviting him to sit in speech and in silence, open to God.

Sometimes Grant will come to my office and say, "I feel as though God is absent. I even find myself wondering if I'm deluding myself with this immersion in theology."

"I understand that," I say. "You're not having much sense of God right now, and that makes you question your thoughts about God." After we spend time with his sense of God's absence, I might remember that I've seen his experience of God fluctuate. I might even remind him of one of his own experiences of God that he shared with me recently. For example, "I find myself remembering the night you told me about last time, the night you sensed God so close, almost breathing on you." Spiritual directors extend the gift of memory to the directee. The emotional life is topographical, and when we're in a valley, we remember previous valleys and anticipate future ones. It's helpful to have another person remember the ups and downs of the path we have walked, and continue to walk.

My directees entrust me with their experiences of knowing God, and I remember and guard them for future work. In our calendared, practical world it is difficult to notice God's presence and then to remember what we have noticed. This is true even of large, dramatic experiences of God. We have little language for spiritual experience, and most of us are used to compartmentalizing our spiritual lives into Sunday worship services, grace at meals, and whatever intentional spiritual disciplines we engage in daily, weekly, and seasonally. So a moment when our breath seems taken away—by, say, the sight of dew on a flower—is lost quickly. The experience is intense enough to stop us on the pavement for a second or two, but then we resume our pace and thoughts. It is often, however, in the contemplative space of my office that the memory of the dew surfaces, a memory that has been submerged for hours or days, like a seed held under the current of flowing water.

In the spiritual direction hour, the memory of that sacred moment floats to the side of the stream and rises to the surface where the water stills and pools. There in that sheltered estuary we look and marvel at it. Grant and I have done that many times, sometimes when I have reminded him of an experience he's had of God. We cease our forward motion across the surface of time and space, experience sensation and feeling, and notice what vibrates beneath words and concepts. We touch and examine the memory, breathe in its fragrance, sense its texture. Stopping to attend to it allows its reality to sift down into our experience, becoming more deeply sedimented in memory and flesh.

Eventually we rise from that deep place and together ponder the meaning of the experience in the directee's life with God. It has become part of the fabric of his or her life, taking its place among what has already been woven, and introducing a new thread that colors the whole. As Alyosha says at the end of Dostoevsky's *The Brothers Karamazov*, "You must know that there is nothing higher and stronger and more wholesome and good for life in the future than some good memory."[9] Memories, specifically those of goodness, which Alyosha calls "sacred," shape us morally and, by residing in our heart, contribute to our life with God. Spiritual directors help preserve such memories.

Early in our work together, Grant trusted me to listen as he reviewed what had been happening in his life, even when, for a period of time, he felt he had never experienced God. Telling me about the death of his brother was a breakthrough. He did not return to the story often, but it was something we shared and was present in our relationship.

During the second year of our work, Grant confessed that recently he had sensed God talking to him. It had happened a number of times over a period of several months, but he let it slip from consciousness, not really knowing what to make of it. He was embarrassed to tell me, and not sure it should receive much attention. It was intangible, the sort of experience not spoken of in his religious and professional circles. He did not want to get caught up in the pursuit of extraordinary experience. I respect that.

Eventually Grant told me: "I felt a sense of a Being near me, and God said, 'I love you. I'm the One you've been looking for.'" More than once he had heard God say this to him on specific occasions in specific places. When we talk about it, Grant lets me help him hold onto that message. Sometimes in holding onto it, he re-experiences it before my eyes.

Many of us say we "hear" God. If pressed, we readily admit it isn't an audible voice. No one else in the room would hear it. It is one of God's manifestations through our senses and imagination. It is one source of our knowledge of God, subject to the checks and balances of other sources (community, Scripture, tradition, and other experiences). Though there are other sources of knowledge, the experience of God's direct address is one that is precious and easily missed, dismissed, forgotten. In the open space of spiritual direction, there is the freedom to notice how God speaks to us, whether in the company of friends who don't see what we see, as was Saul's experience on the road to Damascus, or alone, like Elijah, who encountered God in the "sound of sheer silence" following the roaring of wind, earthquake, and fire.[10] I agree with authors in the field of spiritual direction who write that extraordinary prayer experiences are not to be sought, nor are they indicators of greater knowledge of God.[11] Many people, however, have unique or particular experiences of God and don't tell others about it. Many of these experiences involve hearing.[12]

Grant has heard God in vivid, riveting ways. Nevertheless, like all of us, he sometimes wishes he could control God's approach. Genuine concerns have propelled Grant to prayer, and God's response sometimes feels insufficient or frustratingly beside the point. Grant sometimes wonders what the point of faith is and whether he is deluding himself in prayer.

When we steer back toward the memory of God's presence and message, doubt and complaint fade before it. The causes of the day's anxiety do not evaporate, but shift out of the foreground. Over time we have seen together that rather than being drawn out of his life in order to chase ecstatic experience, Grant has been able to recall the times he has sensed God's personal love for him, and this has made him more open and loving in his day-to-day life. He talks about remembering God in the workplace, in his relationships with his wife and children, in his involvements at church. He does not feel drawn to tell people about his most private experiences, but he longs to let them know that there is a Ground to our existence that is trustworthy. I see change in Grant as he becomes more conscious of his relationship with the One who is the rock of salvation. Noticing his growing ease, humor, and care for those in his life, I see him standing on that rock.

When Grant lingers with the memory of God's closeness, I feel it too. I see it in his face, which loses its chiseled intensity and begins to soften, and I feel it viscerally. Some might see this as my empathic reception of his experience. I believe that it is also my direct registering of God's presence. Grant's awareness of God brings God more into my awareness, and I share Grant's experience as my own anxieties fade into the shadows cast by the light of grace.

Notes

1. Attributed to Mary Stevenson, 1936, http://www.footprints-inthe-sand.com.

2. I Cor 6:19.

3. Eph 2:19–22; I Pet 2:5.

4. Rom 8:26.

5. Ps 56:8.

6. Ps 126:5. I am indebted to Richard Foster for the versions of Psalms 56 and 126 he quotes and for his discussion of "The Prayer of Tears," in *Prayer: Finding the Heart's True Home* (San Francisco: HarperSanFrancisco, 1992), 37–46.

7. Hallie, *Lest Innocent Blood Be Shed: The Story of the Village of Le Chambon and How Goodness Happened There* (New York: Harper and Row, 1979), 2–3.

8. Ibid., 1.

9. Fyodor Dostoevsky [1880], *The Brothers Karamazov*, trans. Constance Garnett (New York: Barnes and Noble Classics, 2004), 700.

10. Acts 9:4; 1 Kgs 19:12.

11. See, for example, the writings of St. John of the Cross, Teresa of Avila, Denis Edwards, and Tilden Edwards.

12. See, for example, Andrew M. Greeley's *The Sociology of the Paranormal* (Beverly Hills, Calif.: Sage, 1975), which indicates that a high percentage of the United States population has had paranormal experiences. As a spiritual director, I've heard of many such experiences from mentally healthy people who hold such experiences lightly, as possibly exterior and possibly interior, meaningful, but no more meaningful than ordinary experience.

3

Remembering
the Pasture: Leah

Some people come to see me saying they have never experienced God and are not sure they believe in God. Of course, it is not lost on me that they are saying this to me in my capacity as spiritual director. So I listen. Something has brought this person to me. I trust that the Something is God.

This is a primary tenet of Christian faith: It is God who moves us to prayer and God's Spirit who propels our seeking for God. It is Jesus, the living Word of God, who abides in us as he invites us to abide in him. This is illustrated most vividly in the story of human genesis. God shaped the first people out of the God-created earth, in God's own image, and enlivened by God's breath. Image, form, and spirit all derived from God, yielding new life—free in thought, will, choice, and action. This is what I see in each person who sits across from me: God has created and continues to inspire this person, even if he or she does not see it that way.

Leah came to see me when she was in the midst of a demanding graduate program. She immediately launched into a denunciation of the judgmental, harsh Christianity in which she had been raised. She had traveled the world fleeing it and its manifestation in her family. Though young, she had the weariness of a soldier. Dark circles shadowed her eyes, and her golden hair was disheveled. The gray-yellow tint of fatigue suffused her skin, which, I came to know, was ordinarily the color of sunshine on peaches. Emotion played on her face like weather as she recounted child-hood injustices.

"I don't believe that God exists. I've never experienced God, but the God I've heard about is hateful. All I've known is the brutality of so-called Christians," she nearly spat out.

The more time I spent listening to Leah, the more I realized how much brutality she had suffered. A good deal of it had been done in the name of Jesus. Sometimes sadness for her swept over me, and I felt like crying. Sometimes I did cry with her. At other times I just seethed with anger toward people who had hurt her. I felt offended as I heard of people using the church of Jesus Christ as the pretext for cruelty.

Jesus said that "true worshipers will worship the Father in spirit and truth,"[1] and I listened to Leah's sad truth. I also knew she was coming to me because of some experience of or hope in the Spirit. I try to make sure that the space I invite people into is wide enough for them to discover and reveal their truth, and deep enough to explore their inkling of God. I think of Jesus standing on the shore while Peter and his friends labored through the night to catch some fish. These men were immersed in the grime and sweat of daily subsistence. That was their truth. Jesus encouraged them to throw their nets more broadly, and in doing so the men caught an abundance of fish.[2] They did not go to the mountain or travel to a shrine. God entered the reality of their lives and helped them explore its possibilities.

I bear witness to the grime and sweat, struggle and disappointment of everyday life. Yet I hold hope that there is more than hardship and that a larger view will allow a glimpse of Spirit. I am reaching for a glimmer of the holy. I bank on the probability that a person showing up in my office is doing the same.

For Leah, an experience of the holy had taken place in a pasture. On a high plain in midwestern farmland, a young girl had spent hours tending her wounded heart in a pasture. The oldest in a family of five, she cared for her brothers and sisters while her parents were preoccupied with the work of the farm and the slow death of her oldest brother. Every morning Leah rose before dawn to milk cows, gather eggs, and send her siblings fed and groomed to school. At the end of the day, she returned home on the old school bus and resumed her chores. Every so often she found a free moment and headed for the pasture.

"Tell me more about that experience of peace in the pasture," I urged during our first meeting, sensing the pulse of what I was listening for.

"I was alone. But I didn't feel at all lonely—in fact, the opposite. I felt like myself there, alone, in a way I didn't around my family or even at school. It was as though in the pasture it was okay to be who I am. Everywhere else I didn't fit in, I was wrong."

"It sounds as though it was almost like your real home."

"It was. I felt I'd come home when I was in the pasture. I could move freely there, even sing. I could lie on the ground and absorb the heat from the day. I was happy." She shrugged her shoulders, hugged herself, and, eyes closed, slowly twisted from side to side, enacting the bliss she had felt. To me it looked a lot like an enactment of being held by a loving other.

"It sounds, too, like the one place where you weren't expected to care for others."

"Yes. There was a lightness, a freedom there. It was probably the only place I could be a child. Everywhere else, I had to be like an adult. But with *none* of the privileges of adulthood." She glared at me as she said the last sentence, and I nodded, acknowledging what she'd suffered.

As I directed her attention back to the light and freedom, Leah relaxed and looked at the ceiling as though a movie was showing up there. "It wasn't like floating out of who I was. It was like becoming more who I was. If that makes any sense." I nodded, and she continued.

"You know, and that's the part about church that really fried me. Everything at church told me I wasn't okay as I am. Being female was especially wrong in that church and to that patriarchal farming culture. Women had no voice and were either insignificant or dangerous in that male world. It was as bad, or worse, in church. But I couldn't see why anyone would seek out the God preached from the pulpit. All that was talked about in church was hell, fire, and damnation. I hated that." Her eyes flashed.

Leah had a prophet's conviction about what was true and what wasn't. I responded, "It sounds as though you didn't believe what you were told by the church."

"No. I didn't—don't! I just don't think it's right. I think what's more true and right is that way I felt in the pasture." She looked at me questioningly. "So," she asked, "are you saying God was in the pasture?"

"Is that what *you're* saying?" I returned the question, not liking to evade direct questions, but knowing she needed to answer this one herself.

"I'd like to think so. I'd like to think that being with God is like that: free, light, real, accepting of me."

"And is that what you sensed there?"

"You know, when I go back to it in my mind, it did feel as though there was someone there with me. I didn't just feel okay about myself to myself. It felt as though I was okay as myself in the eyes of another. As I said, I didn't feel alone."

"So . . . the eyes of another," I repeated.

"Yes. Maybe you could say 'God.' It wasn't the God I'd learned about though. It wasn't the God my church and my parents talked about." Again, the flash of anger. Then, relaxing, she admitted, "There was, though, in the pasture, the sense that I wasn't alone. That I was loved. That I was okay as I was, and was made to be as I was." She paused. "Yes, I felt loved."

We sat with that, and she cried. Then she would look at me and shake her head, as though trying to clear it. She laughed, too, in the midst of her tears. She pouted and frowned, wrinkling her brow with concentration, then sighed, relaxed, laughed again, shifted position, crossing her legs first one way, then the other. Sometimes she wrapped her arms around herself and twisted back and forth, in that comforting gesture that looked as though an imagined other was holding her. It was an emotional kaleidoscope. Leah was allowing me to see a lot in our first hour together.

"Wow," she finally exclaimed. "That was really interesting. I'd forgotten about the pasture. I guess I did have some experience of God on my own. So," she said, tapping her chin with her index finger, and smirking mischievously, "maybe I would like to see you for spiritual direction." We both laughed.

"'Wow' is right," I thought. How absolutely right that God would meet that oppressed young girl in a pasture and let her know she was loved. I was glad to see how God and she were able to reach each other, despite the religious teachings that had been erected between them.

As a spiritual director I have listened to many people tell me they have had no experience of God. After sitting with me and looking for traces of God in their lives, most people discover them, and those traces, on close inspection, radiate the sense of God's presence in the past and in the present. Because of what I have witnessed, I believe that those imprints of God, when found, change lives. Spiritual direction, in effect, equips people with spiritual Geiger-counters.

As a person who believes in the presence of God in the world and assists others in detecting that presence, I relate to the experience of the Samaritan woman who met Jesus at the well, a story told in chapter four of John's Gospel. Jesus told her about her life, and she marveled. She discovered that he knew not only her sins, but was also aware of her longing to know God. Suddenly she knew what others did not: Jesus represented God, and God will be steadfast in love, no matter how imperfect we are.

The Samaritan woman was so excited by Jesus' revelation that she forgot why she was at the well. She left her water jar and visited her neighbors saying, "Come and see the man who told me everything I've ever done!" Her Samaritan neighbors set off to find Jesus and spend time with him, on their own, without her. Finally, they told her, "It is no longer because of what you said that we believe. We've heard for ourselves, and we know that this is truly the Savior of the world." They persuaded Jesus to stay with them for two days.[3]

Like that Samaritan woman, my sense of being known and loved by God became so strong that at some point during my thirties, I put down my water jar (my work outside contexts of faith) and moved more and more into work that matched my deepening sense of God's call in my life. I wanted to help other people get to know God. One way or another— through teaching, writing, creating educational programs, and spiritual direction—I have been inviting others to "come and see."

Through the years, I have met many people who want to see. They do not necessarily want to know what I personally have seen. They want me to help them see for themselves. They learn about and cultivate relationships with God that are, not infrequently, very different from mine and often more lively, like Leah's.

Several metaphors have been used to describe spiritual direction, and an especially robust one is that of midwifery.[4] Spiritual directors are present, striving to be helpful, as new life stirs in another. We have been trained to know some of the stages, potential complications, and appropriate emergency procedures, but each birth is a miracle to which we bear witness. We come alongside the person who is laboring, taking risks, and putting a former life on the line for the promise of a new one.

Our relationship with the person giving birth is inordinately intimate, but it is contained by the context, by time, and by focus on the other. She or he has a private, growing relationship with the Spirit of God, attended to by the director, but in no way dependent on or referential to the director's faith. Many times, as in my experience with Leah, contact with Jesus is more extended and colorful than what I have known myself. As midwives must do, I stand in awe.

Notes

1. John 4:23.

2. John 21.

3. I have benefited from Sandra M. Schneiders' analysis of this narrative in her book *Written That You May Believe: Encountering Jesus in the Fourth Gospel*, rev. ed. (New York: Crossroad Publishing, 2003). See her work for a thorough, biblically contextualized examination of this passage.

4. Margaret Guenther writes beautifully about this metaphor for spiritual direction in *Holy Listening: The Art of Spiritual Direction* (Cambridge: Cowley, 1992).

4

A Face in the
Mirror: David

When I received a voicemail message from David, I felt as though in some unconscious way I had been anticipating his call for a long time. I had never met him, but regularly heard about him. A few years earlier he had moved to the San Francisco Bay Area to assume the senior pastoral position at one of the large Protestant churches here. He had an established ministry record and was a popular Christian speaker and writer. What made him especially interesting to me was his keen interest in Christian spirituality. Our areas of interest seemed similar, and our meeting inevitable.

I had, however, expected it to take place in a context in which we were both speaking or teaching or some day when I happened to attend a service at his church. I had never thought he would call about seeing me for spiritual direction. I was impressed that, with his full life, he sought spiritual direction, and I wondered what I would be able to offer him.

In my experience, pastors are among the most burned-out caregivers. Until the past decade or so, most pastors were men. Men are less apt than women to seek help from professional caregivers and may lack the strong friendship networks that women often have. And with the ethical restrictions about dual relationships with parishioners, pastors are often emotionally isolated. That isolation, coupled with the demands on pastors to be exemplary leaders, managers, caregivers, and saints, makes them ripe for burnout.

Serving as spiritual director for several pastors and knowing others as friends, I see how demanding and public their lives are. In a small pond, they are big fish. They suffer the burden of fame: They are watched, talked about, and evaluated. There is power in the role, but also expectations of near perfection. The pastors I have known who handle this burden most gracefully are in small congregations where they are seen with all their strengths and flaws, virtues and sins. Some pastors of small churches are able to honor their need for privacy and communicate their need for members of the congregations to serve as their partners in ministry. The larger the congregation, the more difficult it is to be known in any other way than through large public events and intimate episodes of crisis caregiving (such as hospitalizations and deaths). These encounters can serve to elevate and distance the pastor from others. And the first time the pastor errs, he or she takes a precipitous downward step off the pedestal. Elevation is precarious.

David and I had one telephone conversation about spiritual direction before he came for an appointment the following week. Just getting through to him by phone, past the people who manage the church's phones and his schedule, was a challenge. I wondered how he'd be able to extricate himself from that system in order to drive to Berkeley and see me.

Once David was settled in my office, his first request was "I want you to be directive with me."

I explained to David that spiritual direction *is* directive, but primarily through the direction of attention—not through teaching or admonition, though both those directions are possible.[1]

"I need someone I can tell anything to and have a solid, honest response in return. I don't want you to toss pillows to cushion the impact when I fall or bump into hard realizations, and I don't want you to hold back when you disagree with me. What I most fear is self-delusion; I can't have you colluding in that," he declared.

"Okay. I'll do my best. And I want you to tell me honestly when you think I'm holding back. Check it out. Feel free to ask what I'm thinking or feeling in the conversation. Let me know your reactions to what I say. We'll keep our cards on the table, as best we can. This can be a safe place for you, David." I went on to tell him, as I always do in a first session with a directee, "Nothing you say will leave the room, and no one will know we're working together. If I hear indications of elder abuse, child abuse, homicide, or suicide, then I need to help you in ways that would move the conversation out of the room and include other helpers, but other than those unlikely instances, everything you say is just between you and me. And God, of course." He answered my smile and sighed.

"Yes, 'God, of course.' That's what I want. I want a place where I can pray, and it really is just between me and God. A place where I can wrestle with what I think about issues of faith and do so without anyone depending on me to have the answer. A place where I'm just David, not Pastor David." His eyes filled with tears, and I felt the burden of how public and scrutinized his life must be.

All leaders are scrutinized. Many feel recognized without being known. A spiritual leader is particularly exposed, because he or she speaks from personal knowledge of and about God and is looked to as someone whose life ought to reflect seasoned spirituality.

Listening to David, I realized that though I am not a pastor, I have some of the experiences he has. Initially I saw how we each are prone to similar temptations: the temptation to feign peace, wisdom, and charity when, at times, we're feeling nasty, brutish, and short; the temptation to puff up with pride because we're recognized, sought out, and listened to; and the temptation to "coast" spiritually as long as we do our job and no one discovers that we're not doing our work.

As I sat with David, it began to dawn on me what God might be doing in my life through this relationship. It was not just a matter of whether I could help David; it was also about God changing me. I was forced to look at his self-delusions and know many to be my own, and I was challenged to love aspects of myself as I learned to see and love those qualities in him.

A variety of experiences has taught me that often what I react to most negatively in another person is a quality I later, with disgust, recognize in myself. As a child, this was brought home to me very concretely when I recoiled from a keloid scar on a classmate's elbow. I had never before seen that kind of raised, red, gelatinous scar, and I was simultaneously revolted and mesmerized by it. Sitting behind her at my desk, I would glance at the scar and shrink from it, over and over again held in the grip of a horrible fascination.

Weeks later, I felt something on my own elbow, in a location I could not see. An examination in the bathroom mirror revealed a scar like my classmate's. The source of horror was, inescapably, on my own body. Realization reverberated through me, sinking from sheer physical awareness and surprise to the eerie sense that there was a message in this discovery. Such a literal and moral object lesson seemed sent from on High. As the discovery of my elbow scar released me from the spell cast by what I found hideous in another, compassion for my classmate flowed through me. My childhood experience still rings strong in my conscience whenever I start to abhor something in another, reminding me to pause, examine myself, and proceed with caution. This has happened time and again. I have come to expect it. The first tug of terrible fascination sends me searching for a mirror.

The word "keloid" derives from a Greek word meaning stain. All human beings carry stains of one kind or another, and in spiritual direction I have come face to face with the darkness marking my soul. Unlike Peter Pan, we have shadows that are so firmly attached that we do not see them. Noticing another's stain or shadow is an opportunity to remember our own. My directee David unintentionally held a mirror before me, and in that mirror I saw what I had not wanted to see: my own busyness, and more.

Even before meeting David, I reacted against his busyness in terms of the inconvenience it posed for me as I tried to set up our initial meeting. I regarded his busyness with some judgment, just seconds before I was slapped on the back by the awareness that I, too, might be described as "busy." As I sat with him that first hour, however, and listened to him speak of his desire to pray, my disdain melted in the warm swell of compassion. After he left, that compassion for this busy, sincere man lingered in me, softening, by association, my regard toward the reflection I saw in the mirror.

Sometimes the interior recoil from a directee is the first sign I have that I am becoming engaged by the other. This engagement signals openness to the unknown in the other, myself, and God. It can feel threatening; something in me that I do not fully acknowledge or understand is responding to something I see dimly in the other. I pray that God will help me love the other and that I won't become blocked by what I react against, will reveal what is causing my strong reaction, and, above all, will enable me to trust as I move forward in the relationship. Wendell Berry captures this experience in a poem about how sometimes in the woods what he is afraid of approaches and lingers until what he fears in it leaves, and his fear of it also departs. Then "it sings, and I hear its song."[2] Some of the relationships that initially intimidated me have, in the end, brought lovely melodies into my life. Those melodies pervade the dance of spiritual direction.

In that first session with David, when I invited him to tell me about himself, he replied, "I've already had several years of therapy, so there are some stories I'm just not going to repeat. What I want to talk about is the way in which I feel blocked from God." When I nodded in consent, he began to tell me about the responsibility he feels toward his family and his congregation.

"The crushing sense of solo responsibility comes mostly around the issue of money. I'm the sole support of my family, and sometimes what I bring in doesn't feel like enough. So I take on extra work, like speaking at conferences and retreats, to augment my salary. I worry about what would happen if I couldn't do that, and I sometimes resent carrying the whole load, though I absolutely support my wife in staying home with the kids. No question about that. I think there's no more important work in the world than raising kids, truly. It's sacrificial, sacred work. And my wife's doing an excellent job of it. Our kids are lucky to have her for a mom, and I know they're going to really see and appreciate her when they're grown." It was a strong pitch.

David stopped himself in the midst of his impassioned speech. "You know, that's all true. But as I say it I feel myself moving into my public self, my pastor-teacher self. I want to say simply, quietly, and not for publication that while I affirm my wife's choice to be an at-home mother, I feel the weight of financial responsibility it puts on my shoulders. And that responsibility, added to the similar responsibility of being, essentially, the 'chief executive officer' of my church, makes me feel alone. It feeds my perfectionism. I have to do everything right in order for the finances to flow properly. Does that make sense?" he asked, tilting his head and looking softer than during the passionate speech.

"Yes, it sure does make sense. You feel the primary financial responsibility at home and at work. That feels kind of lonely. It sometimes feels oppressive. And you said it creates a block between you and God, you think," I mentioned, returning to his reference to God.

"Yes. That's right. I'm not sure why that's the case. Let's work on that one. . . ." He furrowed his forehead and looked at his shoes.

After a few moments he looked up, and I saw he was feeling great emotion. I was surprised. "Clearly, this cuts deeply. I never cry," he confided, looking embarrassed and contemplating his shoes.

As I offered the box of tissues, I encouraged David to "tell me what cuts so deeply."

He wiped his face and said, "Self-accusation. I feel guilty for complaining and, simultaneously, feel guilty for not turning to God with my problems. I teach this kind of stuff all the time and should know it."

"Guilt for complaining, and guilt for not?" I asked.

He smiled ruefully, and agreed, "Yes." He paused, took a bracing breath, and continued, "I guess my fundamental sense is that I should just get my act together and not feel resentful and burdened and isolated. I feel I'm overly self-involved. I want to tell God what's honestly on my heart, but I want what's honestly on my heart to be better stuff—like concern for others, personal gratitude, and love for God. It's embarrassing to have such petty, self-concerned clutter in my heart."

I agreed that it can be humbling to face what's going on in our hearts and minds.

"It is humbling," he sighed, making "is" into two syllables. "It stinks. I look at my life objectively and think, 'Fella, quit your belly-aching. You've got nothing to complain about.' And that whips me into shape for a while. But it doesn't last."

"You speak pretty sternly to yourself," I noted.

"Yes. Yes. . . ." David sat looking down for a while. He sighed again, saying, "I *do* talk roughly to myself. When you said that, I wanted to brush it away. I don't really want to think about how I talk to myself. I talk to myself that way to motivate myself, keep myself in line. Always have. I try to convince myself it's how God is talking to me. But I realize I'm creating a closed system. I put words into God's mouth instead of listening for God."

"So there's a rough-talking, closed system that keeps out your own feelings and keeps God out? Sounds stifling."

"It is. There's no freedom there. It's just me motivating me. Me flog-ging me to get things done. Me determining what needs doing. Me, me, me. . . . I do hear it. I hear that old familiar chorus, 'Mi, mi, mi, mi!'" he sang. He flashed a smile my way and blushed.

I asked David to tell me more about that place where the "Mi" chorus sings.

"When you say, 'place,' I think 'Where is God?'" He paused for a moment. "As I ask that, I see myself in the fog at the bottom of a moun-tain, slogging along, knowing I need to climb, but not even seeing the trail starting upward. I can hardly see or move. It feels as though I can hardly breathe. 'Stifling'—maybe your use of that word is conjuring some of this."

David paused and then continued to explore the image. "I keep push-ing on, driving myself to keep going. I don't see God. It feels as though God is up above, somewhere on top of the mountain."

I asked to hear more about the image of where God was. "As best I can tell, God's just sitting there. God's looking at me, but not coming down into the fog. God's distant, uninvolved, maybe uncaring. . . . Not a pleasant image," David said, looking dejected.

"I want God to come down the mountain, into the fog, and be with me. I want God to help me slog on, so I don't have to do all the work by myself," he asserted, hitting the arm of the chair with his hand.

"You seem angry."

"Correct. I'm angry. Why doesn't God get off his Olympian throne and help me? It seems wrong." He sat back in the chair, crossed his arms over his chest, and looked at me defiantly.

I felt caught by his energy and was reminded of how much I identify with him and the much maligned Martha of Bethany, who felt she was doing all the work while her sister Mary sat listening to Jesus.[3] Jesus just kept talking with idle Mary, not addressing the injustice of the situation. Pursuing the thought, I commented, "God is just sitting there in the sun-shine on top of the mountain while you struggle forward in the gloom. That seems unfair and lonely. God should come alongside you." I paused. "Is that right, David?"

David sat and thought for a bit. Releasing his crossed arms, he told me, "Okay, I can see where this is going. Maybe God's coming down the mountain is my idea, and that may not be the best idea. Maybe I just need to keep climbing and get to where God is waiting for me." He shook his head as though unwilling to hold that thought. "But I resent that. I'm tired of doing all the work. Why do I have to climb up to God? Why can't God come and help me out?"

David shifted in his chair, his posture becoming more open. He spoke slowly and quietly. "When I'm not feeling overwhelmed, I have a great time with God and don't feel burdened and resentful. But right now that's not where I am. I have sunk into the muddy, fog-soaked grass at the base of some mountain I can't even see. I don't want to be strong and resourceful. I don't want to rescue myself. I want God to come and help me, reach down, and pull me up."

Tears were streaming down David's cheeks. Again we were in that place of David's plaintive cry for God, a place of vulnerable honesty and the possibility of encounter. I could hear an earlier David crying, "Why, O LORD, do you stand far off? Why do you hide yourself in times of trouble?"[4] Would the David in front of me, like that ancient David, come to sense God's ear inclined toward his desire? Like Martha, would he sense an invitation to put down his burden and rest in the holy communion he longed for?

Captivated by the picture David had painted, I wanted him to stay with it and experience more of it before we moved on. I answered, "I'm moved by what you've said. I wonder how you would feel about us sitting with that image for a little bit." In response, he closed his eyes.

I had no idea where the image would move, but I felt he was opening his heart to God, unimpeded by the guilt feelings he had expressed earlier.

We waited as he breathed more and more slowly. I wondered if he was going to sleep. I looked at the candle. Eventually he shifted position and looked at me, amusement playing on his face.

"That was interesting," David remarked, his smile widening. I raised my eyebrows in anticipation.

"I stayed with that image of me slowly trudging through the tall, wet grass and the uneven, slick mud. God was distant and detached above me. I felt really sad for myself. I cried for myself stuck in that thick oppressive place. I felt compassion for myself as I slogged along, one foot in front of the next, in that horrible place. It was as though the compassion enervated me, and it was harder and harder to keep going. Finally I just sat down. I sat in the muddy grass. I let myself quit."

I pictured him a dark mound in the fog and remembered Rabindranath Tagore's words: "The hills are earth's gesture of despair for the unreachable."[5]

"As I sat there, I felt warm, kind of bathed from within, the way you feel when you drink a hot drink on a numbingly cold day. I started to feel some comfort in my own compassion for myself, if that makes any sense. I was able to accept it and not accuse myself of wallowing in self-pity. I just liked being with myself. I felt a kind of love for myself, misguided as I am." David laughed sheepishly. "I just stayed sitting there, enjoying the rest, feeling pretty happy." He modeled this by putting his hands, palms up on his knees and closing his eyes: a happy Buddha pose.

Continuing his story, David opened his eyes and sat up straight: "Then, suddenly, I felt some movement, like cool wind moving past me. The fog seemed thinner, and I could see more light around me. My view of things was translucent, not cumulus and dark. Through the swirling clouds I saw patches of light. And, then, in a patch, I saw God. God was on my level, standing at the base of the mountain, which was gradually coming into view, purple ridges above God. He was stirring the fog. Light was mingling with clouds, and the air seemed full of life. God was playful, laughing, and swirling."

"Lovely," I said, picturing the scene.

"Yes. I just sat there and watched. The cool light flowed over my aching body, and I felt its tingling touch reviving me. I still feel it as I talk. I feel light, refreshed . . . content."

We sat with that. I felt peace. I did not have to rescue David from the fog bank or construct some plan for reuniting him and God. I had felt the pull of the fog on me as I debated how to move in the conversation. I loved the way David let himself be overtaken by love for himself. It seemed right that compassion for himself preceded his awareness of God playing beside him. He had paid attention to himself in a loving way, and that did not block his experience of love with God.

Not for the first time John Calvin's words came to mind: "Knowledge of ourselves [is] a considerable assistance in finding [God]."[6] The Psalms show, time and again, that in being honest about ourselves—in joy, sorrow, gratitude, anger, sunshine, and mud—we discover God. There is no either/ or dichotomy between love of God and love of self. David faced his condition and relaxed. He accepted the fact that he was in the foggy flats at the base of the mountain and stopped flagellating himself for it. David's happy Buddha pose was not one of closed self-absorption. His upturned hands signified openness and a willingness to receive. And he did.

I often benefit from a transfer of God's grace from a directee to me. My knowledge of myself grows in the light of that grace. Transferred grace is like moonlight. It shimmers with the sunlight it reflects and casts a gentle light. This is true to some degree in all spiritual direction relationships, yet I knew that the light shed on my life would be intense in this relationship with David.

Notes

1. I have written about how I see spiritual direction as directive in Phillips, "Considering 'Direction' in Spiritual Direction," *Reflective Practice: Formation and Supervision in Ministry* 27 (2007): 105–99.

2. Berry, "I," *Sabbaths* (New York: North Point Press / Farrar, Straus and Giroux, 1987), 5.

3. Luke 10:38–42.

4. Ps 10:1.

5. Tagore, "Fireflies," http://oldpoetry.com/opoem/show/33282-Rabindra nath-Tagore-Fireflies.

6. Calvin [1536], *On the Christian Faith: Selections from the Institutes, Commentaries, and Tracts: I.1. Knowledge of God and Ourselves Inseparable*, ed. John T. McNeill (New York: Bobbs-Merrill, 1957), 4.

5

Forgetting to Ask
"Why?": Melissa

The voice on my answering machine was difficult for me to understand. The woman spoke slowly, carefully articulating every syllable. I thought I knew who it was, and I was scared.

A competent professional woman, Melissa was part of a church community I knew. When I had spoken with her at weddings and other events, I felt scrutinized—not in a harsh way, but by a perceptive, no-nonsense intelligence.

She uses a wheelchair as a result of a terrible injury suffered in childhood, which also affects her speech. Therein lay my fear. I was afraid I would insult her by not understanding what she said. I was also afraid of her suffering and pain. How would my faith stand up under such a heavy fate in her life? I felt certain I wouldn't be able to hide my fear from her.

My office is not wheelchair accessible. Young, fit people can be winded at the top of three flights of stairs, and the silent prayer time when the candle is first lighted allows an opportunity for catching breath as well as turning toward God. We could not meet there, so she kindly invited me to her home a few blocks from my office and across the street from the college where I had studied sign language to communicate with my deaf son. From the first time I visited Melissa, my son Andrew was on my mind. In her long-limbed, angular, blond, good looks, she reminds me of my son, and her affliction stirs the feelings of grief, love, and admiration I feel for him.

Parking in front of her place in my mini-van, I felt like a door-to-door spiritual director, candle and matches in hand. She buzzed me into the building, and I rode the elevator up to her floor. Her front door opened, and I heard her electric chair move in reverse as she gave me room to enter. We went into her main sitting area, I put the candle on her table, and we talked. I did not light the candle until after I explained why I like to use it and asked if she would like it, too.

Melissa told me about her experiences with spiritual direction, her relationship with her church, her marriage, her work, and the key places of pain in her life, places in which she would like to experience God. She told me about how important Christian faith has been to her and her commitment to Christian community, practices of Bible study, and prayer. She told me she struggles with God's being identified as male, but that she has a real affection for Jesus that is not diminished by his gender.

I finished explaining the basics of spiritual direction, told her how I got into it, and what I thought I could offer. Melissa put me at ease about understanding her by inviting me to tell her if I did not understand something she said.

We did not chat casually for long. Almost immediately we were talking about the intense pain she experiences in her back. She receives medical attention, but the problem continues. I strained to understand her better.

"So your back often hurts you?" I asked.

"Yes. It hurts much of the time."

"I'm sorry, Melissa. Pain can also be isolating."

"It is. I don't want to tell people about it, because I don't want sympathy. You can imagine that I've been the recipient of a lot of sympathy." I nodded. "Even strangers sometimes offer sympathy. Or they express admiration. People seem to think they understand my experience just by looking at me."

"So people think they understand you," I repeated. She nodded. "I can imagine. Even more isolating." That was the first of many times I have echoed what Melissa says to let her know what I think I am hearing. She corrects me when I get it wrong, and lets me know whether I am hearing her correctly.

"Of course, there are people who know and love me. My husband, friends. Great people. But even with them, I'm reluctant to talk about this pain. I don't want to be the focus of their concern. I'm already so dependent on them. I don't want to be pathetic." I was struck with the way integrity compounded loneliness.

"It sounds as if it can be uncomfortable for you when people who love you respond to your pain."

"It is. It really is. But then keeping the pain to myself feels like I'm not being honest with them, not trusting them."

"So then you feel the pain in your body and the pain in the relationship, too."

She laughed. "It's hard. It's hard to know how to be with it."

"My sense is that you'd like to find a way to be honest about the pain with those close to you and to be able to do so without feeling more dependent or, worse, pathetic."

"I think I'd like that. But part of it is that I feel responsible for the pain." She then told me a story, clearly wrestling with shame, about medical decisions she had made related to caring for her body, and questioning the motives behind some of her choices. "So I feel as though I'm paying the price for my sin."

That was wrenching for me to hear, and my heart rebelled against her judging her best efforts to make informed decisions. "You say 'sin.' That's a word I think of in relation to God. I wonder if you have any sense of God in this situation?"

"I think God would see some of my earlier decisions as wrong," she replied, looking at me with sadness in her eyes.

Remembering Melissa's affection for Jesus, I suggested that she imagine bringing her feelings about this situation to him.

Because God can seem impersonal and is hard for many to imagine, I often invite Christians to imagine themselves with Jesus. Jesus' gender can be a problem for some people, but usually his humanness and the stories we know from his life help people visualize the God with whom they seek to communicate. More often I ask directees if they would like to sit in silence with some feeling or image they are experiencing in our session, but with Melissa I wanted to see how she might imaginatively experience the Wounded Healer.

Melissa leaned over with her head nearly on her lap and was silent. I felt as though someone else was with us, regarding her with love. The brush of that loving gaze felt like static electricity on my skin.

Wiping her eyes with a handkerchief, Melissa looked at me and nodded. "That was good," she informed me. "I felt Jesus nearby. He didn't judge me. He just loved me. It reminded me of another time when a person had me look out the window at a group of children playing and imagine what Jesus felt for them. I felt the warmth of his affection. I felt my own shame shrink and disappear. It was really good."

We both just sat there. After a few minutes she exclaimed, "You know, I forgot to ask him why I have to go through this." We laughed.

Melissa's prayer experience with Jesus repeatedly comes to my mind. People sit in my office and ask, "Why is life so hard?" "Why does God let this suffering happen?" I wonder, too. I listen to a friend tell me about his young son agonizing through chemotherapy, lying in bed and moaning in pain. I want to be accusing and tell God how to run the universe. Yet I, like Melissa, have moments that feel suffused with God's presence and love, and I forget the accusations and questions. Light shines in the darkness. The darkness is not obliterated. It's pierced.

Melissa's very presence raises hard questions of my own. I learn that I don't have to fear them. Most of the questions are not for me to answer. Thank God, that is not my job. When I remember that, I feel peace. When I forget it, I see myself as God's advocate, God's defender and public relations representative, as though God needs my protection from scrutiny and challenge. When I remember that this work is about helping people come to God themselves, I relax into the spaciousness of God's Spirit and truth. There is room there for Melissa's questions as well as for my own.

In my work with Melissa, I have been moved by her ability to register and receive God's presence in ordinary life. Sometimes she cries out, "Why, O Lord?" David, Job, Jesus: all of us have cried the same. I am impressed that Melissa does not, on the whole, use the question "Why?" as a distancing mechanism that allocates blame. Nor is it a question that obscures the truth of her situation with an illusion of being able to figure it out and avert suffering. Rather, she keeps her eyes wide open to the truth of her situation and to the promise of God's love. I try to do the same.

6

Straining to Listen: Charles

T he work of spiritual direction forces me to pause and look for God's presence in the lives of people very different from me. Melissa was different from me, yet my emotional connection to her was strong, in part because of my closeness to other people with disabilities, but mostly because her ways of expressing feelings and faith are close to my own. From time to time someone who is a complete mystery to me crosses the threshold of my office. I lean toward the glimmers of grace as I glimpse them and still find the other's experience of the holy slipping from my grasp, my comprehension.

Yet the privilege of years of listening to people has helped me see some of the infinite variety of God's presence in human life, which we speak of in terms of our spirituality. Recently this was brought to mind in a concrete way. I was running with a small, ten-year-old dog that we had just adopted. My four-year-old hundred-pound Golden Retriever accompanied us, racing happily back and forth, looping the older dog and me time and time again. The older dog, leashed to me, grew tired and I was forced to wait for her to catch her breath. As I stood there, catching my breath, too, reluctantly stopped under the trees, I saw out of the corner of my eye the flutter of a Monarch butterfly. Its orange and black wings grazed my field of vision, and then disappeared from sight. I searched, but couldn't find the butterfly for a full drink with my eyes. But I knew what I'd seen. I am acquainted with Monarchs, though not intimately. I have read about them, and visited their migratory home in Pacific Grove. Had I not been familiar with the form, colors, and movement of that butterfly, I wouldn't have known what I saw. And had I been barreling down the trail with my youthful dog, I wouldn't have received even that glancing impression of the winged beauty. But I stopped, and, as a result, I caught a trace of the Monarch's fleeting appearance.

So it is with the directees whose experience of faith I strain to understand. The structure of our time together requires me to stop. The Christian faith is familiar to me, the Bible my daily bread, and I have witnessed diverse manifestations of God's grace in human life. With a directee, I lean toward the flutter of the numinous, and I am filled with wonder when I see it, however briefly and incompletely. Sometimes the search for what was glimpsed yields reward. One of the directees with whom I've had this experience is Charles.

When Charles first came to see me, I found him hard to read. He was a quiet, self-contained young man on the cusp of thirty. He was attractive with an athletic build, and his smooth and nicely featured face revealed no emotion that I could read. Scant eye contact with me, and little variation in tone of voice, rendered him impenetrable.

Charles was born in the United States to immigrants from Asia, who remain minimally conversant with American language and ways. His parents went through a nasty divorce when he was young, his mother worked several jobs, and the family struggled to make ends meet. He grew up knowing late-night hunger pangs, the embarrassment of wearing hand-me-down clothing, and the loneliness of never talking about his life. Yet faith had been a constant solace for him since a young age. He told me of carrying a Bible to school and reading it when he was on the playground. I could picture him, young and serious, Bible open on his lap while the rowdier boys ran around on the blacktop.

Our first hours together went by slowly, alternating between long periods of silence and a flurry of questions from me. Over time it became clear that Charles was seeing me to work on his longing for a "mate." An obedient Christian since elementary school, he had never had a girlfriend—

despite fervent, daily prayers for one. He sometimes prayed for hours at a time, petitioning God for a mate. Among his friends at church, he was known as the most disciplined man of God in the group.

Early on in our relationship, Charles told me he liked a woman attending his church. "I think she'd make a good mate for me." I expressed interest, and he elaborated, saying, "She's a strong Christian and wants to devote her life to inner-city work with the poor. I really respect her." As I listened to Charles, I found it hard to sense what he was feeling for her.

"It sounds as though you see goodness in her, and a similarity between what you both value. You've been looking a long time for someone like that."

"Yes. I don't know if God has sent her to me, though. I can't tell if she thinks he has," he said, in a flat sort of tone.

"So you're thinking there may be God's providence in meeting her, but it's hard to read. Sometimes our own hearts and minds tell us about such things, about what's right for us. I'm wondering what your heart is telling you now," I probed, not knowing what feelings lay under his placid countenance.

"I'm praying and reading the Bible and being faithful to God. God has to come first and, then, a mate."

In our first year of spiritual direction, I came to sense more of what Charles felt, though he seldom spoke of feelings. The feelings he was best able to express out loud were those of disappointment, as when this woman made it clear to him that she was not interested in pursuing a relationship with him and, moreover, was not sure she felt comfortable being in his presence, given how intensely focused he was on her. Over time, we together came to see that beneath Charles's disappointment lay anger—with God, the woman, the injustice of his frustrated desire—and, eventually, bitterness, as he began to realize that his strict obedience to God was not awarding him a mate.

As Charles faced his anger with God, I often felt like God's ambassador, guilty by association. God was not providing a mate . . . and working with me was not changing that. Charles already had wrestled with the possibility that he had been given the "gift of singleness," but was certain that that was not the case. So, what he was left with was unrealized longing, which, as Solomon the Wise declared, "makes the heart sick," sometimes translated as "bitter."[1]

We did, indeed, arrive at that place of his bitterness after more than a year of meeting. It was like being in a dry valley. Months went by with no evident life or movement. Charles began to face the fact that he could not move God's hand as he had hoped and tried to do. It was not fair. He had been sacrificial, faithful, diligent, and long-suffering. All who knew him saw him that way. He worked in a low-paying job he didn't like because he felt it fought injustice in the world. He lived almost literally in a garret in a poor neighborhood, with roommates who did not respect his need for privacy and quiet. He served his church in a variety of capacities that he did not enjoy, because he felt it was right to do so. But his heart was not joyful.

When Charles admitted his bitterness and faced it, his ability to continue a life of self-deprivation faltered. He was not able to spend hours each day going through the program of prayers and Bible study he had sustained for years. We spoke about prayer, especially the mystery of prayer as communication, not control, and therefore the importance of listening as well as speaking. We spoke of the need for honest expression in prayer, like that of King David and Jesus. And we spoke of the way prayer is affected by seasons in one's life, by emotions, understanding, imagination—just as any intimate relationship is responsive, variable, and dependent on honest expression.

Charles began trying different forms of contemplative prayer. He read about praying with Scripture in a *lectio divina* style, praying a short passage of Scripture slowly and meditatively, allowing and hoping for God's Word to speak to him. He was especially drawn to centering prayer, which involves letting go of verbalized petitions and customary expressions of devotion, clearing the mind of rational thought to make space for the indwelling presence of God. Charles listened for God, using ear plugs to block the sound of his roommates and sitting in his bed to pray. I imagined him in his small room, Bible on his lap, much like the child he'd been on the playground, seeking meaning and companionship in the Word of God. Picturing Charles's private prayer reminded me of Jesus' words: "Whenever you pray, go into your room and shut the door and pray to your Father who is in secret; and your Father who sees in secret will reward you."[2] Jesus encouraged private prayers of few words. That was how Charles prayed.

My sense was that, over time, more of Charles' emotional depths increasingly opened to himself, to me, and to God. When he spoke of his experiences of God in prayer, I felt emotion beginning to stir under his reserve, which was powerful to behold after so many months of hoping for a glimpse of his heart's movements.

Charles heard about a monastery from a friend and applied for a month-long visit to explore the longings for contemplative prayer he was experiencing. I wrote a letter of recommendation for him and prayed for him while he was there, hoping for more signs of life or color in his dry valley.

The life of faith is one of returning. Again and again we turn toward God. I have been impressed with the way Charles does that, despite disappointments that seem to signal God's inattention to his concerns. Even so, Charles turns back toward God. We are all called again and again to "hear" and to "set [our] hearts to seek God."[3] Sometimes we do so when the desires of our hearts are achingly unrequited.

Notes

1. Prov 13:12.
2. Matt 6:6.
3. 2 Chr 30:19.

7

Fully Alive:
Jim

Jim is a minister, part of a denomination that has expunged exclusively Christian language from its worship. The people in this denomination are seeking spiritual truth and life, community worship and service, with a minimum of traditional religious dogma. Although the church has Christian roots, its direction over the past several decades has been to widen its embrace and extend fellowship to people who have been alienated by orthodox Christian doctrine.

The people in this denomination are strong humanists, and demonstrate their love for others in a variety of tangible ways. I speak of my faith in language different from theirs, but I have great respect for their works of love and justice as well as sympathy with the view that Christians have not always been known for their love and kindness. When Jim came to see me for spiritual direction, we knew we were from different traditions, but wanted to work together and see if the work bore fruit. I believe it has—in both our lives.

Jim grew up in a conservative Christian family and left that church in his teens, finding its theology too judgmental and narrow. He worked in industry and raised a family. Not wanting his children to go without the experience of church, Jim took them to a nonexclusive church that he felt would cultivate their spirituality without indoctrinating them into religious prejudice and arrogance.

As he sat in the pew week after week worshiping the Spirit of love and life, Jim found himself often moved to tears. The symbol of the Spirit's flame in an earthen chalice was especially poignant for him, and his compassion for humanity deepened and expanded in the light of that flame. Jim's resonance with the symbol of the flame has opened my eyes to it more fully, and I often light the one in my office with a lovely matchbox he gave me.

While he and his wife raised their children in the church, Jim felt compelled to participate more and more in the life of that particular congregation as well as the denomination. Eventually Jim went to seminary while continuing his job. When the time came for him to make a choice between industry and ministry, he chose the latter, with his wife's blessings.

Jim first came to see me at the time he was making that decision toward full-time ministry, and since then has worked in several churches. He loves his work now, though from time to time he feels the church's careful restrictions on religious language constrain his preaching. He's drawn to use religious language and would like more freedom to read to the congregation from the Bible and use the name of God—the "G-word," as he sometimes calls it.

A few years ago, arriving at my office a bit late and looking harried, Jim started speaking as soon as I lit the candle. "I'm feeling overwhelmed. I have so much work to do, my father's sick and needs my attention, and every day I feel rushed and hassled."

I empathized with the stresses he was experiencing, and, relaxing into his chair, he elaborated, "I alternate between wanting to sleep all the time to escape the pressures and ramping up into a manic mode of workaholism. Both feel wrong." Jim shrugged his shoulders, expressing his sense of resignation.

I wondered out loud, "There isn't a place in between?"

Jim's pace slowed even more, and he responded, "Every so often. Sometimes I'm really focused and *in* what I'm doing. I forget what I'm worried about and am just in the present. Usually it's when I'm with someone."

That felt to me like a description of what was happening to him before my eyes. "Can you give me an example?" I asked.

"Well, you know, I've started volunteering a few hours a month as a chaplain at a hospital near my home. It scares me terribly. I can barely bring myself to walk into a patient's room. Sometimes I just walk around the halls and then go home, never getting up courage to walk into a room. I think I'm afraid of intruding on people's pain. . . . But, sometimes I do go into a room. And, you know, I'm even learning how to talk to people who are completely unresponsive. I ask the nurse about the person, learn a bit, and then just talk. . . . Sometimes I get the impression that this makes a difference. . . . Sometimes it feels as though we're in a holy place."

I could visualize him in his Birkenstocks, with his unpretentious manner, simply making himself available to others. Listening to Jim describe his experience in the hospital, I felt the galvanic skin response of awe tingling through my skin. The tingling awe was not vicarious. It felt as though he and I were in a holy place as he described making himself available to others in need. Our hopes and fears often meet as we follow God's Spirit, and I saw that in Jim. I listened to Jim tell me of his sanctifying work in the hospital, and told him I experienced it as such.

Taking my reflection in his usual humble way, Jim replied, "That's just it. It's an honor to be with people who are suffering. I'm in a sacred space when I'm with them. It's amazing."

"And when you're with a person like that, you're really there, in the moment, not tired, not frantic?"

"Yes. I feel fully alive. I feel I'm exactly where I'm supposed to be."

"Amazing," I echoed. Jim sat with his memory for a few moments. Looking at him and seeing the glow in his eyes, I thought of what the early church father Irenaeus of Lyons wrote in the second century: "The glory of God is the human person fully alive, and the life of the human person is the vision of God."[1]

"Yes, I'm glad I'm talking about this," Jim said after a while, "because I forget about it. It's so powerful when it happens, but then I get wrapped up with church work and problems, my family's needs and full lives. Then I just feel I'm never enough. There isn't enough of me to go around, so in trying to spread myself around, I'm never really present."

"That makes sense," I acknowledged, and, bringing it back to the experience, I continued, "But in the hospital you feel fully alive. Where you're supposed to be. Tell me about a time with a patient."

"Okay," he complied. "Well, last Thursday I was there and someone had requested a chaplain, but when I went to her room she had a visitor, and I didn't want to intrude. So, I thought maybe I'd go to the cafeteria and have an early lunch. On my way there I came to an intersection where two hallways meet. If I'd gone straight ahead, I'd have entered the cafeteria, and that's what I intended to do. But standing there at that intersection, I felt pulled toward intensive care and down a hallway away from the cafeteria.

"I walked, looking in rooms, feeling a rising sense of anticipation, but I had no idea what was up," Jim recounted energetically. "Then I came to a room with about twelve people in it, all standing around a bed. As I walked past the doorway, they turned and looked at me. A nurse grabbed my arm and said, 'We've been waiting for you. Mabel has just passed away, and her family would like a chaplain to pray with them.' They'd been waiting for me! And I'd almost gone to the cafeteria!"

I must have said "Wow."

"Wow, indeed. I asked the nurse a little about the woman who had died and was told she was a Baptist. A conservative Baptist! So I told the family I'd be with them in a few minutes and I ran up to the office, grabbed a Bible and the prayer book the Episcopal chaplain keeps there. I flipped through the prayer book to the service when someone has died, and I found the Twenty-Third Psalm in the Bible. She was a Baptist. I needed to use her language."

Captivated by Jim's beautiful engagement with Mabel's family and the person Mabel had been, I asked to hear more about "using her language."

"I felt I needed to use her language. And I wanted to," he answered, casting a sharp glance my way.

I encouraged him to tell me more about wanting to.

Jim took a deep breath and seemed to relax even more. "It felt like a relief. I get so tired of editing out all religious language for fear of offending people. It strips me of some words that are meaningful to me and, certainly, were meaningful to that family at the hospital."

"Tell me about those words," I invited, following the trail of his longing.

"Well, in the prayers I was able to pray to God. I was able to pray about Jesus understanding our suffering. In the Twenty-Third Psalm it says, 'He leads me in the right paths.' I felt God—and I don't like the 'he' part—had led me in the right path. God led me to that room. I should have been in the cafeteria, but God led me to where people were waiting for me." Jim's eyes were misty. My own sense of awe continued to deepen. Looking at me, Jim leaned forward and whispered, "God led me to where people were waiting for me."

We sat in silence as the candle burned.

"I felt God with me from the moment in the hallway when I decided to turn away from the cafeteria." He uttered the sentence as though it were a confession and, then, looked to me to respond.

I confessed, too. "I'm really very moved by this, Jim. I want to hear more about your feeling of God with you." Jim didn't often use the name "God" or speak so explicitly about sensing God with him. I felt like holding my breath so as not to extinguish the moment.

"It's hard to describe. It's the feeling that has prompted me all along to return to church, to go to seminary, to be a minister, and, now, to volunteer in the hospital. It feels like warmth and excitement. It feels like an intimate relationship. It feels like life. When I have that experience, even though I'm doing something scary like leading a service for Baptist strangers, I feel that I am fully who I am and where I ought to be. I feel I'm doing what I was made to do, and if I were to die right then, it would be fine. I'm not alone."

"You're fully with God, fully with yourself, and fully with those in the room," I said.

"Yes. All of it is one. We're all held together in it. I guess it's what people mean by grace. . . . I sense it here, now, in this room as I talk to you about it. That feeling of warmth and aliveness is in me now. I can feel my hair standing up and my heart beating faster." He described what I was feeling, too.

Jim sat in silence with his eyes closed. It felt as though my heart were moving toward him with admiration and poignant hope, for him, for humankind in general. There's something admirable about the way Jim has stripped himself of religious baggage and in that naked state offers himself to others as an instrument of love, a servant of God. He might not express it that way, but that's how I see it.

Much of the work of spiritual direction involves the gentle direction of attention. In this conversation about Jim's work in the hospital, I tried to hold him in the light and make sure I didn't cast my own shadows as I did so. He experienced grace when he turned toward the patient and the patient's family. Several times he tried to turn away from that experience and confer with me about issues in his life, including finding balance between work and family. I nudged him away from consulting conversations with me and back toward the focus, the hearth and heart of his experience of grace. That is really the direction in spiritual direction, as I understand it. As gently as possible, I try to say, "It seems as though the light is coming from over there," and I point to it, hoping that I don't point in such a way that I block the person's view.

A lot of trust is involved in spiritual direction. The person who comes to see me trusts me and trusts that God will work through our times together. I trust that God is in relationship with the other person and that good will come of that. I trust that the person I am working with is genuinely committed to relationship with God. This trust helps me let go of my own prejudices about how God works and with whom. Repeatedly in the Gospels we see the disciples flabbergasted by Jesus' choice of conversation partners. He talks to women, children, criminals, lepers, foreigners, heathen. Each of them has his or her own way of understanding and naming him. Jesus asks them about themselves, and he listens to them, as Jim did with Mabel's family. Jesus does not presume to know in advance what they'll say. He also eats with and receives from them. I felt nourished by the story Jim brought to my office.

With each person I encounter, I hear a tiny bit of his or her experience. My assumption is that God is present in each of those tiny bits. I try to listen for that sense of presence and offer what I notice. It isn't always easy. Jim uses religious language different from mine, and may find mine offensive. I respect that. But I trust that God is in his life and try to learn the language he uses to signal God's presence, just as he, in turn, does the same for the people for whom he cares.

In his careful, selective, and honest appropriation of biblical language as he works in the hospital, Jim is responding to God's integration in his life. He tells me of experiences of grace that are unfamiliar to me, and I need to be careful not only to orient toward what is familiar and comfortable to me, but also to intuit what is life-giving and healing to him. I rely on God's nudging to help me do this, just as Jim relied on it in the hallway outside the hospital cafeteria.

When I listened to Jim describe his grace-filled experience in the hospital and experienced God's presence, my mind returned to the story of the woman at the well. She raced back to town to tell people about Jesus and how he had known everything about her and might, in fact, be the Messiah. They followed her to the well to meet him, struck by what they saw in her. Transformation? Newfound hope? Radiance from encounter with the divine? Like those townspeople, I followed Jim to the place of his encounter, moved by the radiance of his joy. Like the Samaritans, I had my own encounter with God.

Note

I. Irenaeus [180 CE], *Adversus Haereses*, bk. 4, chap. 20:7 (see http://www.new advent.org/fathers/0103420.htm).

8

God's Embrace:
Carl

Melissa, the intelligent, intuitive woman who uses a wheelchair, is not the only directee by whom I have felt intimidated during our initial encounter. First encounters are momentous. They hook your own projections, fantasies, stereotypes, and desires. These meetings have been a school of self-knowledge, often showing me that issues I thought had been resolved in prayer, therapy, and life experience were, in fact, lurking in my psyche, ready to appear in the new relationship.

Carl and I first met when a project I was working on took me to a top-ranked university where he had a scientific research appointment. He was aloof, and I imagined him my intellectual superior. We both had gotten our degrees from fine universities, and he had stayed in that tenure-track, mainstream academic, competitive world, while I had gone onto the track of theological education and spiritual direction. Meeting in the university context made me self-consciously aware of being on a less rigorous academic track.

I met him a second time at a retreat where I taught and offered brief spiritual direction sessions to those who wanted them. For most it was their first exposure to the art of spiritual direction, and they were curious. Carl was one of only a few people there that weekend who did not choose to spend one-on-one time with me in spiritual direction. I wondered whether a negative impression of me kept him from availing himself of the opportunity.

Usually I discover that I've completely imagined that another person thinks poorly of me. Especially as a novice spiritual director, I was overly concerned with myself, getting things right, and being helpful. I sometimes thought the directee was scrutinizing my work and finding it wanting. In fact, most directees are working to tell their own truth and are not judging the listener. I was reminded of how inaccurate my imaginings can be when Carl called and asked for a spiritual direction appointment. In the several years we have worked together, I have never heard anything indicating that he holds me in low regard. In fact, I believe him when he says he finds our work helpful, and I feel his respect. He seems completely welcoming of God's work in him through spiritual direction with me.

When we first started working together, Carl told me he wanted to work on three issues: his job, his church, and his singleness. He was considering changing all three, but wanted to make sure he did so prayerfully. He is a careful man, wary of impulses that might lead him down the wrong path. In part, that wariness had motivated him to create a fellowship group in which he, and everyone in it, was held accountable to one another as they tried to discern how to follow God's way as they made major decisions.

All the people I work with are, I believe, sincere in their faith and demonstrate integrity in their lives. They teach me how to live. That is acutely true of Carl. It is also true of the close group of Christians with whom he is associated, the ones I met when I led their retreat. They form a community of worship, study, social action, and mutual commitment to discerning together how God is present and directive in their lives. They do not all go to the same church, but all are Christian churchgoers. They are highly educated and strive to follow Jesus in their daily lives. In coming to see me, Carl was taking some of his discernment work outside that group process. I wondered what that might mean for him, for his life with God, and for his participation in the community.

Recently, a group of spiritual directors and scholars of Christian spirituality asked me to respond to the question, "Is ecclesial community necessary for spiritual-seeking?" What an important question in our day of independent spirituality and the overall thinning of communal life! My answer to the question is "Yes." Within Christianity there is a call to community: for worship, fellowship, and discipleship—all aspects of our dynamic, growing spiritual lives. Many people, however, seek spiritual direction when they want to gain reflective distance from their ecclesial community or tradition. When the relationship between the spiritual director and directee is outside the community, it is possible to look at traditions, beliefs, social arrangements, and community practices, to see to what degree they do or do not resonate with one's own experience of God and the life of faith.

As a spiritual director, I pay attention to people's experience of community. Also, I hold open a space for exploration of the relationship with God freed from particular interpersonal and dogmatic expectations. With Carl, I have felt able to hold his community in high regard, valuing his part in it, and at the same time to listen as he has reflected on it with a certain detachment, sifting the spiritually helpful from its less helpful spiritual aspects. The community can be generous and caring in its support of its members, but at other times the care can deteriorate into control that discourages and confines.

As we worked together, Carl increasingly moved his discernment about the other two major issues in his life—work and marriage—out of the community process, into his prayers in solitude and with a small circle of friends, and into our work.

The more Carl and I talked, the more evident it became to me that he wanted to be a husband and father. As he discovered that desire, he also lost a relationship he thought was heading toward marriage. His heart was yearning for love, and wounded by it.

"So, it was at the beginning of your relationship with Sarah that you realized you wanted to be married?"

"Yes. Before that I'd never really been sure if that was what I wanted. I'd been in relationships with other women, really wonderful women, who were interested in marriage. But I wasn't. Then with Sarah I felt ready for marriage, so much so that I overlooked indications that marriage to her wouldn't be easy. Friends even tried to warn me about it. But it was as though I was suddenly committed to the state of marriage and just kept trying harder and harder to make it work. Sarah broke up with me quite brutally, but maybe I wasn't picking up on the earlier, more subtle signs of her reluctance."

"It sounds very painful. You lost her, and you lost the near possibility of marriage that you were longing for."

"That's right. I did. I lost both." He inhaled sharply. "The pain still kind of takes my breath away."

As we sat with these thoughts, it felt to me as though we were acknowledging the goodness of Carl's longing as well as the pain connected to it.

I asked Carl what it had been like to pray about this situation. I often ask people about prayer. One of my assumptions is that people in spiritual direction want to attend to their relationship with God, and communication in that relationship, experienced verbally and nonverbally, expressively and receptively, is what I mean by "prayer."

"I still feel that desiring marriage is a good thing. It feels as though it's okay with God that I want that. At this point I don't feel as though God is calling me to a single life."

"So that change in you, the change to wanting to be married, remains the same. And it was through this relationship with Sarah that awareness dawned?"

"It did. I had really thought it was about her, but it has stayed with me even as she has left. I guess that's good. It hurts, though." He winced.

"So the desire is 'okay with God,' and it causes you pain?" I asked.

"That has surprised me. At first I was praying for God to change Sarah's heart. I felt as though God had put the desire for marriage in my heart, so it must be right for Sarah and me to stay together. So I thought God would change her heart. But I didn't get a 'word' from God, as I had thought I might. Sarah didn't change her mind; in fact, she moved farther away from me and our relationship. So I didn't get what I wanted and was looking for from God. But the truth is that God did come to me in the pain."

Carl paused and looked at me in a pointed way before speaking again. "It's hard to talk about," he confided, looking shaken. Then he whispered, "I felt God holding me."

I strained toward his words. He continued, with effort, "I felt as though God were holding me. Hugging me. Supporting and comforting me. I could feel God's arms and warmth. I just cried in those arms. I cried, and God held me. It went on for a while. When it was over, I was spent."

I pictured him being held by those strong arms and felt grateful. Carl is quite self-reliant and responsible. I imagine he was that way as a child, too. It was reassuring to see he did not have to bear his pain alone.

Over time it has been important that I know of Carl's fundamental trust in God's love, so memorably experienced as being held by God. He has courageously moved forward in ways he feels are right for his life, and I often picture him held by God. This is a glowing ember of God's grace, which he shared with me. We turn toward it together, and I carry it in my awareness as I listen to him.

Carl's story of being held by God also told me that God works in him through his imagination, and that what he imagines he also experiences physically. I encouraged him to explore the contours and movement of the images that come to him. These images are like postcards from the edge of hope, reminding him that he is loved and regarded, even if it seems from a distance.

9

Crossing the Road: John

John, a lean man with lanky grace, quietly entered my office and placed his journal and Bible on the floor next to his chair. I lit the candle and said, "We light the candle to remind us that God is here with us." He closed his eyes, bowed his head, and prayed silently for a long time. He was wearing work boots and a wool plaid shirt over jeans and a t-shirt. His curly hair was still wet from showering. He clasped his hands firmly together and leaned over in prayer.

As I watched the flame glow, I heard him whispering. I couldn't make out all that he said, but listening to the repeated sibilance of Jesus' name, I could just make out that he was asking for his heart to be transformed. Saying "Amen," he looked up at me.

"I've been trying to talk with my parents about my ministry as I understand it now. I'm not sure they understand, and I'm not entirely sure I understand it either," he confided.

I nodded, engaged by the serious gaze of his gray eyes. He continued. "What I'm going to tell you has something to do with it, though. Monday I was called to the factory even though it was my day off. Over the weekend I'd heard that Billy had died in a car accident on Friday night. I didn't know him well because he worked another shift, but I'd overlapped with him a few times. I'd gone out socially with a group from work, and he was with us. He was a lot of fun."

Remembering Billy made John laugh. "He was kind of wild, too, and in his early twenties. He was gay and good-looking—the life of the party—and really could play the flamboyant gay role for our entertainment. He was one of those people who completely likes himself and others: confident, warm, generous. Fun! Talking about him now I just can't believe he's dead." John's eyes quickly filled with tears, which he roughly wiped from his cheeks with the flat palms of his hands.

John is a gentle soul in a workman's body. His hands are calloused from manual labor, and muscles show through his t-shirts. He is a pastor by training with a sense of God's call, and worked in a large, conservative, independent church for many years. Political currents at the church led to his resignation, and he has not yet found another church to serve. It has been a challenge for him because he is strongly identified—by himself and others—as a pastor. Moreover, he isn't fully comfortable with the fact that his wife has become the family's primary breadwinner. While he looks for another church to work at, he does contract work as a gardener and works part-time in a local factory. His body is angular and increasingly strong as the work shapes him.

I first met John when I was teaching a class on spiritual disciplines at an evangelical seminary. John audited the class, having finished his own seminary training years before. The class was a new one, both for me and the seminary. Often, I wasn't sure if I was reaching the students in my teaching. John sat in the back row of the class, his face resonating with understanding. Looking at him helped me register what material was helpful and which ways of expressing it were best. His responses directed me as I taught.

Also in the class was a man who had lost his voice. I really didn't understand the cause of his silence, but his muteness created a challenge when I paired up the students to engage in exercises and discuss their experiences with various spiritual disciplines. John gravitated toward the silent seminarian and encouraged him to express himself in writing. Watching them together, I felt the power of John's loving attention as he regarded the other student, and saw the man bloom under its warmth.

The class ended before I had much of a conversation with John. I knew he was working in a church and was more drawn to contemplative prayer than others in his particular kind of church. His face and the understanding in his eyes lingered in my memory. So it was with great pleasure that I heard his voice on the phone asking to begin spiritual direction with me. That's when he told me he was no longer a minister employed by a church and spoke of the deepening of his relationship with God through the extension of his ministry beyond his former role.

During our first spiritual direction meeting in my office, as I listened to him talk about Billy, I marveled at how far John had journeyed from his church's walls, walls within which Billy might not have felt welcome. John was now a "pastor at large," and I knew the world would benefit from his ministry.

In response to John's story about Billy and his tragic death, I said, "He sounds like a great guy and much too young to die. I'm not following why you were called to the factory on Monday, though."

"I was called in to do a little memorial service for Billy!" he exclaimed, rocking forward in his chair, slapping his thighs, then rifling his hands through his hair as his face expressed astonishment. "Isn't that wild? Wow. I mean, like, what was I supposed to do? None of the other workers go to church, but I have been having amazing conversations with them about the important things in life. When they go through hard times, they often talk with me. Even Billy had talked with me once about love and how he hoped to find someone to love with all his heart." He sighed. "So sad that he's gone."

I agreed, as John gazed at the carpet in silence. Then I prompted, "It sounds as though you have a special role at work. You're a kind of resident counselor or pastor."

"I think that's right," John said, cradling his chin reflectively in his hand. "It's so strange, too. I don't have a church, am not pastor of a church, but I feel more like a pastor than I did at the church. At church I felt like a teacher, an administrator, a preacher, and a leader—most of the time. At work I feel like a pastor. I listen to what's in people's hearts. They open their hearts to me."

"What's that like?"

"It's moving and confusing. I feel trusted with their feelings, questions, hopes, confessions, and all the stuff in their hearts. Yet it's confusing because there isn't much explicit God-talk or reference to religion. They know I'm a Christian and they respect that, but at first they weren't sure they could trust me."

"Because you're a Christian?" I asked.

"Yes. A Christian *and* a pastor. They tested me a lot at first." John elaborated, "Yeah, they would swear in front of me, tease me about it, like, 'Oh, excu-use me for swearing in front of you.' That kind of thing. When we'd go out after work they really noticed what I did or didn't drink, and I know they were watching what they said in front of me for a long time. They may do that still. But slowly we shared stories of our lives, difficulties and successes at work, and slowly we became more comfortable with one another."

"You became more comfortable, too?"

"Yes. Over time. At first I wasn't sure how I would react either." John laughed and seemed tickled at the thought. "I didn't know if I'd have a hard time getting to know people who live differently than I do, had been through a lot of relationships, some who were gay, people who had had much rougher lives than the one I've lived. I just didn't know how I'd react. But, you know, I came to trust and like them, too. Even love them, I'd say. They've touched my heart, the ones I've gotten close to. I really care for them, and I know they care for me. I feel relieved that that's happened."

"Relieved with how you reacted? It sounds as though the experience has revealed something to you about yourself," I ventured.

"Right. That's right. I didn't know what was in me, and I'm glad I'm more accepting than I thought I was. At first I wondered if I ought to be reacting the way I was, though."

John had wondered at first if he bore some responsibility for moral or evangelistic teaching when he began to work outside the church. It was not that he wanted to teach or felt led to do so, but he questioned whether as a pastor, even a pastor-at-large, he carried some mantle of religious authority that required that of him. Over time he has come to learn just what his mantle allows.

"I've wondered what sort of response I invite from people. Do I invite openness and trust? Or is my faith off-putting to others, making them feel judged? My church background always focused on what was missing. People who didn't have faith were lost souls. Those of us with faith faltered, strayed, and had to recommit ourselves to God.

"It makes me think of the attic at my parents' house," John said, settling in to telling a story. "When we were kids we used to like to explore it. It was big and musty. We often found dead critters up there: squirrels, birds, mice. Dead leaves came through the cracks in the roof, too. So, when we went up there and turned on the lights, some of what we found was dead things. But there were also surprises that brought delight: treasures from our childhoods—projects we'd forgotten about, an old sled and ice skates—and sometimes treasures we never knew existed, like my parents' old love letters." He radiated delight at that memory.

"The light did expose death and decay," he continued. "But it also revealed treasure. In my church we focused too much on the negative things that God's light exposes, and not enough on the good that is revealed. In my work now, I feel as though God is revealing the good in people. I don't see them as 'lost souls' and 'sinners.' I see them as God's beloved children, and seeing them that way is helping me see myself more that way, too. I don't have to try to look good for God. The light of God's gaze reveals me as beloved."

John's words transported me to a place where I felt that we were held in that revealing light of God's grace. "For the Lord God is a sun and a shield," the psalmist declared.[1] Moses huddled in the cleft of the mountain rock as God's glory was revealed to him. God shielded Moses from the scorch of that glory by placing a protective hand over him until God's back was turned.[2] Facing the light requires trust. Moses became bold in his desire to know God and see life fully illuminated. He had begun less boldly, afraid to look on the burning bush.[3] Intimate conversation with and reliance on God through life's toils and snares eroded Moses' reserve and unease with God. Less dramatically, John followed God's leading into the unknown and in the process gained confidence in God's omnipresent goodness. John trusted God's illumination of ordinary places: attics, factories, bars, and the fellow pilgrims encountered there. Listening to John widened the lens of my religious imagination, and my understanding of what it means to be a pastor.

John continued, "The light of God revealed Billy as beloved, too, and I'm glad I was able to see him in that light. He didn't find the love of his life, but he was—is!—beloved. You could say he's been found by the love of his life. I believe that."

"It sounds as if you saw him in that light of love."

"I did. And I think it is how Jesus sees him. Jesus said, 'The harvest is plentiful.' He didn't go around drawing attention to flaws. He offered abundance, and he helped others, like the fishermen and the crowd of five thousand, experience abundance. He saw treasures in the musty attics of people's lives."

We spent quite a while with those images. John spoke about how his "low station" in life was allowing him to flourish in certain ways. He has entered into places he never visited before and is seeing them in this revealing light.

"I've crossed the road. Like the Samaritan in the parable of the Good Samaritan. Others passed by the wounded man on the other side of the road, but the Samaritan crossed the road and responded to him. It's amazing what you see when you cross the road. I may have been afraid to cross before, or at any rate too busy with what was happening on my side of the road. But now I've crossed it and, like the Samaritan, have been moved by what I've discovered. I'm moved by Billy and his life. I'm glad I got to know him. If I hadn't crossed the road, I never would have heard of his longing for love, never would have gotten to enjoy his playfulness."

In my mind was the image of John leaning over the mute student in my class as the student wrote down his experiences. John has been a road-crosser for quite a while, though perhaps the roads are broader these days.

"Being out of my regular work is more rich and interesting than I would have ever thought it would be. It's not a desert. It's not a vacuum. The Samaritan got off his animal—and so did I."

Notes

1. Ps 84:11.
2. Exod 33:18–23.
3. Exod 3:6.

10

"Is This a Little Strange for You, Sweetie?": Ruth

Ruth was lying on a couch at my friend's house. I was there celebrating our mutual friend's birthday, a year following her near-fatal car accident in another country. I had not known Ruth at the time of the accident, but she was the one who flew to our friend's side and kept me informed of our friend's changing condition through surgery. What I knew about Ruth was that she was immensely loving and kind, and, like our mutual friend, a medically trained, analytically oriented psychotherapist.

She motioned me to sit near her on the couch. She said, "Hi, Susan. Nice to finally meet you. I'm taking it easy: I have cancer and am recovering from surgery. But I wouldn't have missed out on this celebration for anything." She laughed a tinkling laugh, and I marveled at the translucence of her skin. It was nearly white, but not unhealthy looking. Her eyes were the palest blue, and her short hair was like cornsilk. There was something ethereal about her.

I was shocked to hear she was sick. Cancer and the glow I saw in her just didn't seem to go together, and I was surprised I had not heard about her diagnosis. I expressed my shock and sadness. She assured me that the surgeons had caught it all, it was treatable, and she would be fine.

The conversation moved on. I thanked her for the many ways she had kept me informed about our friend's medical journey the previous year. She

86

responded, "Well, dear, now I'm having my own medical journey." She laughed her musical laugh again. "It really is quite a journey, too. Let me tell you how it began."

I settled into the pillows, and she began her tale: "About six months ago I was experiencing a lot of vaginal bleeding. We couldn't figure out what was causing it, so we scheduled an MRI. In the MRI bore—that's what they call the tube you're encased in—I underwent a miracle. A real miracle!" She grabbed my hand and leaned up on her elbow, looking fiercely into my eyes. "Jesus came to me." She flopped back to reclining, looking smug.

Ruth kept surprising me. I just repeated: "Jesus came to you? In the MRI bore?" The party sounds around me faded from awareness.

"Yes, dearie. I know it was Jesus because he had the holes in his hands. And he had the most pain-wracked, compassionate face I've ever seen. He didn't say anything. But I started to cry. Simultaneously I knew that Jesus was real—divine even!—and that the MRI was going to reveal something wrong in me." She laughed again. Stunned, I did not join her laughter.

"Is this a little strange for you, sweetie?" she asked.

"It's amazing," I managed to say. "It rings true." And it did: pain and love, truth and spirit. No zapping into a surreal place free of pain and cancer, but love in the muck, Jesus in the MRI.

I don't remember much more of that conversation. Ruth kept glowing and laughing as she talked about cancer and Jesus, and I was quiet. Eventually she said, "I hear you're a spiritual director."

She asked to meet me for an appointment. She didn't live nearby, but maintained an office in the county. She could see me during the weeks she was working there, and for the first meeting, she said she would appreciate it if I came to this house, our friend's house, where she, Ruth, would be recovering from another procedure the following month.

The day of our first scheduled appointment, I was in a stew. I didn't know much about Ruth and could not, for confidentiality's sake, ask my friend about her. I didn't know how to reach Ruth and wasn't sure how to prepare for our time together. We had not had the usual introductory conversation about the practice of spiritual direction. I hadn't said anything about my faith position or what I do in a session. Nor did I know anything about her faith commitments or practices. Would bringing a Bible with me be okay for her? Should I take a candle? How strange to be going to my friend's house with the tools of my trade.

On the day and hour of our appointment, I walked down the long driveway to the front gate and up the front steps to the porch. I knocked. I rang. I waited. No answer. So I opened the door and called "Ruth!" A faint voice floated down the stairwell. Up, up, up the spiral staircase I climbed to the second floor, following her hoarse words of encouragement.

White on white she was, lying in the bedsheets. For the second time since I had met her, I perched next to Ruth's reclining figure and she grasped my hand. She radiated joy in seeing me. I felt awed by her serenity and kindness. I asked how she was, and she laughed, "I'm sure I would be in a lot of pain if it weren't for the meds. I'm grateful for them."

I asked if she wanted me to tell her how I think about and practice spiritual direction. She said, "No, sweetheart. Why don't you just do it."

"Okay. I usually start by lighting the candle as a reminder that God is here with us, and then we take a few moments in silent prayer. Feel free to start talking whenever you like."

"Fine," she consented, and watched as I put my candle on the bedside table and lit it. She closed her eyes, blocking out the only source of color on the bed, and breathed deeply for such a long time that I began to wonder whether she was asleep. I waited. I wondered about saying something. I tried to be peaceful and prayerful myself.

After a few minutes Ruth opened her eyes, smiled, and whispered, "Amen."

She told me again about the appearance of Jesus in the MRI bore. Then she explained a little about her religious history. She had grown up as the only child in a family scarred by religious judgment. At some point before she was born, members of her family had been expelled from a church, and the pain of that experience lingered in their memory. Her parents did not go to church, but she, as a young girl, had had experiences of God that led her to seek God in church. For a few years in her childhood, her mother accepted her urging to attend services with her. Ruth loved it.

She loved the music, Bible stories, and prayers. It all confirmed experiences she had had encountering God in nature. She hadn't known about

Jesus, but on learning about him thought he was a lovely, godly man. Since her teenage years, she had stopped going to church. The pastor who confirmed her when she was in high school was "progressive" and had a theology of welcome and openness to people of all kinds. Since then, she hadn't been able to find another Christian religious leader whose theology she could affirm, a person she could rely on to be both truthful and loving. She told me she has no patience for Christians who generate negative energy judging people. She looked at me hard when she said it. I hoped I looked nonjudgmental and positively energized.

Then Ruth told me that as an adult she had explored a variety of religions, primarily Eastern ones, and had taken a keen interest in shamanism. I noted, to myself, that I needed to try to learn more about these faiths and practices so I could understand Ruth better. In particular she told me she had a relationship with a "power animal" that had been her spiritual guide for many years. I realized my ignorance about this and prayed I would be up to listening to Ruth.

It became clear to both of us that she was getting tired. So I asked her how she would like to spend the remaining minutes of our time together. She asked that I read her the First Corinthians passage about love. I told her I would be delighted to and that it seemed to me to describe how she is in the world.

Ruth lay back on the sheets, white on white, peace and breath, while I read Paul's words from First Corinthians, chapter thirteen:

> If I speak in the tongues of mortals and of angels, but do not have love, I am a noisy gong or a clanging cymbal. And if I have prophetic powers, and understand all mysteries and all knowledge, and if I have all faith, so as to remove mountains, but do not have love, I am nothing. If I give away all my possessions, and if I hand over my body so that I may boast, but do not have love, I gain nothing.

> Love is patient; love is kind; love is not envious or boastful or arrogant or rude. It does not insist on its own way; it is not irritable or resentful; it does not rejoice in wrongdoing, but rejoices in the truth. It bears all things, believes all things, hopes all things, endures all things.

> Love never ends. But as for prophecies, they will come to an end; as for tongues, they will cease; as for knowledge, it will come to an end. For we

know only in part, and we prophesy only in part; but when the complete comes, the partial will come to an end.

When I was a child, I spoke like a child, I thought like a child, I reasoned like a child; when I became an adult, I put an end to childish ways. For now we see in a mirror, dimly, but then we will see face to face. Now I know only in part; then I will know fully, even as I have been fully known. And now faith, hope, and love abide, these three; and the greatest of these is love.

Ruth breathed deeply, the breath seeming to buoy her higher in the bedding, and, for the second time, whispered "Amen." She looked at me, squeezed my hand, and added, "Well, sweetie, that's my religion." She laughed, thanked me, and I left. I had been there less than an hour, but it felt as if I were leaving on a different day than the one on which I had arrived. I was lighter. The world seemed wider, more full of hope. We had been in a temple where our hearts turned toward God. The Greeks have two words for time, and the distinction expresses the change I felt. *Chronos* (the time on a clock) seemed to have transmuted into *kairos* (time beyond measurement), etched on the heart. With Ruth I had stepped into eternal time.

As my work with Ruth progressed, I heard a lot about her relationships both with Jesus and her "power animal." I felt I was beyond my abilities as a spiritual director when it came to dealing with this ferocious, reptilian creature that loved her and spoke with her and had done so for years. She had many symbols of his force in her life and seemed to pray to him much as she prayed to God. The Spanish word *duende* came to my mind when she spoke of the animal. The word refers to a ghost, spirit, inspiration, magic, and fire. Poet Federico Garcia Lorca wrote about it as a dark and fertile force that holds life and death in creative tension.[1] It's a confusing concept, both lively and daemonic. Despite its frightening appearance, Ruth clearly experienced the animal as a friend, possibly even Aslan-like in his wildness and gentleness.[2] In addition to Ruth's relationship with her animal, I also was aware of the goodness of her relationship with God and her commitment to Jesus.

Confused, I sought supervision from a Catholic priest who had spent years in various countries working with people from many backgrounds. My hunch was that he might have some insight that would help me.

He listened. I told him about Ruth and her experience of Jesus. I told him about the fierce animal (to my mind, a beast) with whom she had a relationship and about my uncertainty in dealing with this unusual spiritual situation.

"I see," he said. "So, does this power animal scare you?"

"I guess so," I confessed. "I'm not sure if the animal himself scares me, or if my own lack of experience in dealing with such issues in spiritual direction is what scares me. I feel out of my depth."

He just looked at me. He nodded as I explained my feelings and what Ruth had told me. He did not satisfy my expectation that a Catholic priest with international experience would have ready-made tips for dealing with such supernatural challenges. (I, too, like my very first inquirer about spiritual direction, can make the mistake of expecting a spiritual director to be Yoda.)

Finally the priest suggested, "I think we should pray about this," and he closed his eyes and bowed his head.

I did the same. . . . Nothing. I waited. . . . Still nothing. Then after what seemed a long time, the image of a campfire in the middle of a circle of trees came into my mind. It was night and very dark. I was alone sitting before the fire, afraid and alert. Suddenly I sensed a pacing, menacing presence on the other side of the fire. I couldn't really see it whole, just occasional flashes of talons, a tail snaking upward, the glint of an eye. Back and forth the creature prowled, just outside the circle of firelight.

"Great," I thought with dismay. "Ruth's power animal." I had no idea what to do, and wondered about staying in this imagined scene. Then I received instruction from the fire.

I did not hear a voice, but I knew the fire was telling me to reach through it to the animal. I did not want to. I sat still, frozen. The fire became insistent, expressive, alive. Terrified on all counts, I started to reach around the fire toward the creature. I could smell the acrid burning of my clothes and feel the furnace heat. The fire had my full attention, never mind Ruth's animal! Destruction seemed imminent.

Then I knew: The fire is God.[3] As soon as I was supposed to approach the creature through God, my fear of it was eclipsed by my fear of the fire. God is more fearsome than any power animal. My encounter with the animal comes through God as I embrace Ruth, for whom the creature is real and precious.

I looked up, all fear gone. The priest was watching me. I told him what had happened and how I understood it. He nodded and got up to show me to the door. I never worried about the power animal again . . . but my illusions of priestly clairvoyance had been shattered. I realized what the priest had known: It is not about the beast, or the priest—it is about God and trusting my experience of God.

For me, the power animal never fit into any systematic theology or religious bestiary, but I was able to love Ruth and see her in the circle of God's gracious light.

Notes

1. For an extended treatment of the subject see *In Search of Duende* by Federico Garcia Lorca et al, ed. Christopher Maurer (New York: New Directions, 1998).

2. Aslan is the Christ-like lion in C.S. Lewis's *Chronicles of Narnia* (New York: HarperCollins, 1994).

3. There are well-known examples: God appeared to Moses in a burning bush (Exod 3:2). Of his experience of God on the night of November 23, 1654, Blaise Pascal wrote "Fire" in his essay "The Memorial," *Pensees*, trans. A. J. Krailsheimer (Harmondsworth, England: Penguin Books, 1966), 309.

PART TWO

Journeying

11

Encountering
Suffering and Love

The middle passage of spiritual direction is marked by a growing trust on the part of the directee in both the director and God. One of poet George Herbert's descriptions of prayer is "reversed thunder," and in my office I hear people thundering their honest frustration and disappointment at God, a favorable sign that the person trusts that such honesty is acceptable. The intimate work of spiritual direction also allows experiences of suffering to surface from (at times previously suppressed) memory into conversation with God, a process that is common in midlife when we have greater strength to face what is hard to face. In the candlelight, which represents God's love and truth, people reveal their love and truth.

Journeying and Rooted

Psalm One indicates that there is joy in walking on the right path and, at the same time, in sinking one's roots deep in streams of water. People seemingly are walking trees, on "the way of the righteous," "planted by streams of water."[1] Images of journeying and a rooted flourishing are intrinsic to a biblical understanding of spiritual development. In today's world we honor the pilgrims, pioneers, and frontiersmen and -women who preceded us in our homelands. We have been enthusiastic about exploring outer space, "the final frontier," as well as inner space through various therapies. Some hire personal trainers and coaches who help us meet goals, push through pain, and "go for the gold." We often equate thriving with striving.

Seeing life as a journey meshes with cultural focus on adventure and challenge, perhaps especially pronounced in the West. It fits the dominant values of the global economy: efficiency, consumption, innovation, expansion. Spiritual life can be reduced to acquiring techniques that propel the journey. Like any practice, spiritual direction takes on the coloration of the culture in which it appears. In the temple culture of Malta, the person offered spiritual direction on the temple grounds, and those seeking her attention probably had no choice of practitioner. In certain cultures, confession to a priest was and is a requirement for receiving sacraments, and priests had significant authority over parishioners. In some cultures, people are more rooted in their communities, bound and shaped by norms and expectations of life together, than we are in more mobile, cosmopolitan environments. In our fee-for-service culture, spiritual directors tend to practice in private offices, directees may "shop around" for the right director, move to a new director if so inclined, and take up the practice of spiritual direction when it seems desirable, letting it lapse when it seems less so.

The two images of growth, journey and rootedness, go in and out of vogue. Today we see a dominance of the journey image coupled with a longing for rootedness in a world more and more bereft of home and roots. The adage encouraging parents to give their children wings and roots has been fulfilled only in part. Geographic mobility, career insecurity, family dissolution, and multiple "future shock" forces have left us in perpetual peregrination.

Certainly the soul can bloom in transit. Not all our spiritual forbearers were desert fathers and mothers or cloistered monastics. Abraham, Joseph, Ruth, and Paul were peripatetic people of faith. But, as the wisdom of Psalm One reveals, each of us needs the experience of setting down roots as well as of walking on the right path.

As a spiritual director, I see myself as a companion to people on their journeys. As a companion, I accompany others who become more fully who they have been created to be, sinking their roots deep into the living waters of God's grace and bearing fruit in the world. On journeys and in gardens, nourishment is essential.

The word "companion" means one who shares bread with another, and I am a firm believer in shared meals or table fellowship as central to the spiritual health of any community. In spiritual direction we share the spiritual bread that feeds hungry souls.

In the story of the woman at the well, Jesus encountered a woman suffering from broken relationships. She'd had many husbands, and the man with whom she was living was not her husband—just as her people, the Samaritans, had followed other gods, but the one they revered was not the true God.[2] Jesus told her of the hope he represented—newness of life through faith in him—and she boldly chose life.

After the woman ran off to tell her neighbors about her conversation with this unusual wayfarer, Jesus' disciples returned from a food-gathering errand. When they urged him to eat, he told them he had eaten. The disciples were incredulous, not understanding what Jesus meant even when he explained it. It seems he felt nourished by the conversation with the woman. It was real, substantive, fortifying, and in those ways similar to the "living water" he had offered her. Without equating what they gave to each other, the encounter spiritually nourished them both. It fostered growth and flourishing at that point on their journeys through life. So, too, spiritual director and directee pause for an hour of contemplation and receive God's refreshment.

In spiritual direction we partake of spiritual food. Not every session feels nourishing, but, on the whole, we both honestly open ourselves to what we can receive from God. The process of opening can be painful, putting us in touch with wounds, unsettled feelings, and questions. In encountering our hunger, we feel its pangs; in opening our hearts, we experience our suffering.

Suffering and Its Questions

Much of the work of spiritual direction has to do with suffering, so suffering warrants extended attention in this book. Suffering is also central to the Christian faith, and much of it is unsought. Jesus suffered and died. Christians believe that the Hebrew prophet Isaiah's words about the suffering servant foreshadowed the story of Jesus' life and death.[3] In spiritual direction, people wrestle with the challenges that suffering presents to them in life, and do so in practical and often theological terms. Some of the suffering is that of transformation, by God's grace. The next section illustrates how the directees already introduced in this book have met such challenges. It is the responsibility of the spiritual director to maintain faith that the other's suffering is faced in relationship with a God of love who is acquainted with sorrow and suffering. The spiritual director's vocation is to represent that loving God.

The injustice of suffering poses the largest philosophical obstacle to trust in God. Many dismiss the possibility of a loving God because they find loving omnipotence incompatible with the state of the world. Those of us who hold a biblically informed faith struggle for understanding in the face of so much undeserved suffering. In our attempts to understand, we generate equations of control and blame, struggling to answer our heart's cry of "Why?"

Many answers to that question presume to judge either God or the suffering person. "If I had done the right thing, I wouldn't be in this mess," or "God must be cruel, because this suffering is unfair." In spiritual direction, attention is paid to the person and to her or his experience of suffering in the context of seeking to relate to God and, secondarily, to the question "Why?"

Today it is common to ask, "Why do good people suffer when God is all-powerful and all-loving?" We agonize *When Bad Things Happen to Good People* (the title of Rabbi Harold Kushner's bestselling book).[4] The tension lies in seeing God as all-powerful and all-good, capable of preventing injustice and suffering. Some resolve this tension by viewing God as not all-good, as we see in Greek mythology, and some theologies circumscribe God's power. In theology, the pursuit of such questions is referred to as theodicy, "a vindication of the divine attributes, particularly holiness and justice, in establishing or allowing the existence of physical and moral evil."[5]

Many philosophers claim that theodicy was not an issue for Christians until the seventeenth century, when the word was coined by the German philosopher and mathematician Leibniz, combining the Greek words for "God" and "justice."[6] God is placed on trial for human suffering, with the verdict usually blaming the sufferer and vindicating God. This way of thinking about suffering crops up frequently in spiritual direction. It is the kind of thinking I, too, am tempted to when I desperately seek to understand why God is allowing suffering, mine or that of someone else. If I figure out why, perhaps I can change circumstances and elicit God's goodwill.

With the Enlightenment came the view of human beings as rational and autonomous, finding understanding through universal principles and empiricism. People searched the world and human existence for evidence of God's character and justification for God's actions. But when we turn faith into an exercise in rationality, we can lose the relational dimension, and many did jettison faith as they embraced "enlightenment."

In this way of thinking, theodicy is a quest for logical reasons and chains of deductive inference, extracted from history and community. If we cannot attribute suffering to human error, we are tempted to put God on trial. We can buy insurance against all kinds of harm, but most policies specifically exclude coverage for "acts of God." The goal of theodicy is to evaluate the justice of God's performance of such an act, which, for people of faith, usually means creating justifications for God's action.

Our tendency is to demand legitimating explanations from God or on God's behalf, rather than viewing ourselves as people who listen to God and do so embedded in particular times, places, and communities of faith that shape our experiences of God. The Enlightenment move to make questions about suffering abstract and theoretical has been exacerbated by our continuing successes in technological solutions to all kinds of suffering.

We have developed tremendous capacities for understanding the world. We, especially in the "first" or "minority" world, trust the rational systems of government, commerce, and social life we have created. In many ways we have also harnessed nature for our own well-being. We are bothered by the inexplicable and uncontrollable, viewing disease, disaster, and death as crises that are, in large part, subject to our control. Conversely, we see success, health, and longevity as personal achievements, thus immuring ourselves against the threatening vagaries of fate.

For early Christians, suffering and evil did not have to be "explained." Much of life was mysterious and beyond human control, borne with faith and integrity in relationship to God and community. Good people in the Jewish Scriptures suffered unjustly (Naomi's loss of husband and sons comes to mind). There is no evidence in scriptural narrative that the faithful are spared suffering. Yet for many of us, that outlook is our visceral theology; that theology surfaces in spiritual direction where we share our unvarnished prayers.

The classical Hebrew reflection on suffering in the book of Job doesn't attempt to "explain," though Job asks "Why?" The book is not a rational, abstract exercise in theodicy. It is about probing the depths of faith in the midst of suffering. Job is a particular person undergoing particular suffering in a particular community, as we each are in our suffering. God responds to Job, not to a theoretical question. What Job receives is a relationship, not a systematic theological justification.

The "comforters," Job's friends, aim for such answers. They seek to comfort and console him, and so sit with him in silent mourning for seven days and nights. That is good—and more than most of us would do for a friend. They then, however, intensify his suffering by turning it into a problem for solving. Someone must be responsible for the suffering, and because their culture did not put God on trial for calamity, they turned an accusing eye on Job in allocating blame. Whatever the intentions of Job's friends, we see the cruelty of "neglecting the suffering while standing outside the realm of suffering and telling the victims how they could solve their problems."[7]

Who Shall Bear the Blame?

There are four classical types of Christian theodicy—theological explanations of why we suffer, seemingly unjustly, sometimes profoundly and, perhaps, unnecessarily.[8] Each of these ways of understanding suffering is current in Christian circles. I have encountered them in my own life when I have suffered and have witnessed them in my spiritual direction work. Each contains some biblical truth, yet each has been used to add insult to a sufferer's injury.

First, there is the view that we suffer because we sin and God punishes us. Especially in cases of unjust and extreme suffering, this view attributes cruelty to God. We can think of situations of suffering resulting from natural disasters, human genocide, and torturous illness. We struggle to see how guilt precipitated these events. This is the stance of ancient proverbial wisdom: Through moral living we can avoid suffering. If we behave immorally, God punishes us. This view lingers despite our knowledge of Jesus' teachings and stories. The father of the prodigal son is not punitive, sinful as his son has been; Jesus, post-Resurrection, cooks breakfast for Peter and commissions him despite Peter's recent denial of Jesus.

The temptation to attribute guilt of some kind (theological, societal, institutional, or personal) gives us the illusion of safety and control. For instance, we are horrified when thousands of people die in China from an earthquake, and may think, "Yes, but they built their houses out of mud." Genocide devastates Rwanda: "Yes, but they have a government unable to control historical ethnic hatred." Millions are infected with the HIV virus: "Yes, but they are engaging in unsafe sexual practices." The coordinating conjunction "but" indicates a heartless turn against those who are suffering. Actions yield consequences, and we can try to avert disaster. The Bible states that God punishes human sin. But we cannot say when and how that is so in particular cases, and, despite these truths, to do so is cruel.

The temptation in this theodicy is two-fold. First, it bears the unvoiced hope that by obeying the rules we can force God's hand to deliver what we want. If I pray correctly and am a good person, then God will have to reward me with life, liberty, and the acquisition of wealth. This is magical thinking. Second, this theodicy is tempting because it spares us emotional labor, for "yes, but" thinking quashes compassion. For instance, one might indulge a self-serving illusion of safety by thinking, "My friend had a heart attack, which could have been prevented if he'd lived a healthier life—like I do—with exercise, good nutrition, and better stress management."

Attempts to include all suffering in a paradigm of guilt and punishment offers, in Emmanuel Kant's words, "an apology in which the defense is worse than the charge . . . and may certainly be left to the detestation of everyone who has the least spark of morality."[9] German theologian Dorothy Soelle calls this view an attitude of contempt.[10] We blame—and scorn—the victim.

As a spiritual director, I hear directees express this theodicy of divine punishment, attributing their own losses and sufferings to personal sin and God's punishment. This presents an opportunity to be with the person in honestly examining conscience, experience, and image of God in the midst of real suffering.

A man I know persistently felt whenever he suffered that God was punishing him for sin. He thought God was, at best, indifferent to his pain. In looking back through his journals, however, he found that every actual experience he had of God was one of God's love and longing for intimacy with him. It was hard to hold that truth alongside the truth of pain, but doing so was transformative. His relinquishment of the controlling theodicy was difficult and slow, but it released him into a place of trust, where paradox existed and could be tolerated through faith. His prayer was transformed, in George Herbert's words, from the "sinners' tower" in which he imagined God had confined him, to the "exalted manna" of God's ever-flowing grace.[11] No longer estranged from God when he suffered, he was able to receive God's forgiveness and love.

Some of the people in this book, including me, have entertained a punitive theodicy for a time. A second traditional theodicy, which I've seen less frequently, is the view that evil and suffering do not significantly undermine the goodness of creation. In fact, the suffering of some may allow for greater good from an ultimate perspective, perhaps for some aesthetic harmony. Suffering is part of the created order, serving, we speculate, to illuminate the good and beautiful.

This view is also evident in thinking that is not religious. Without attributing responsibility for suffering, we can see how suffering sheds light on joy. V. S. Naipaul wrote: "Suffering is as elemental as night" and "makes more keen the appreciation of happiness."[12] Contrasts illuminate. That is the truth in this way of thinking. The theodicy of this form of thinking, however, posits an indifferent God who plays dice with the universe for aesthetic pleasure. With respect to this view, Fyodor Dostoevsky's characters in *The Brothers Karamazov* talk about the possibility of faith in God in the face of radical human suffering.

Ivan, reflecting on the tears that soak the earth, says: "Too high a price is asked for harmony; it's beyond our means to pay so much for admission."[13] This makes Ivan reject God. He respectfully rejects the ticket for admission to God's world of aesthetic harmony that seems to require the suffering of the innocent. His brother Alyosha also rejects a theological argument for innocent suffering. He turns his attention to the sufferers, giving up the attempt to explain suffering in terms of some kind of total solution and aesthetic harmony. He stands with Christ, attending to the afflicted, not gazing at a beautiful ideal or assuming the role of judge.

I have encountered this second kind of theodicy in several ways in spiritual direction. A person believes that God is in the beauty of nature, but God has no compassion for people. In fact, God is viewed as inflicting death and deterioration in order to render birth and vitality even more lovely. Seeing the beauty of contrasting light and darkness, for the Christian, involves believing that the One who is light cares and works against the darkness. A person who had long been hoping for blessings that never came told me she could see God's handiwork in nature and feel blessed by it. She felt sure, however, that God had no compassion for her and might even be enjoying her suffering. The image she used was that she was like a pair of shoes forgotten in a back closet of God's world. She was never noticed or used.

Without settling the question of whether God controls suffering and death, it is possible to stand with the God of compassion who responds with love to the person suffering, offering consolation and care, rather than exacerbating pain. It is the move into theoretical explanation in the face of misery that dooms theodicy. For as Annie Dillard wrote, "Every ingenious, God-fearing explanation of natural calamity [is] harsh all-around."[14]

A third classical Christian theodicy attributes our suffering to God's educational purpose in our lives. Some argue that suffering exists for our refining, maturing, strengthening, and betterment. In her book *Suffering*, Soelle quotes a contemporary religious tract by Brocks, Gremmels, and Preiss called "Readings for the Sick." It reads: "Affliction is a means of training used by God's salutary love."[15] Suffering, indeed, sometimes has a beneficial or strengthening effect. Yet radical suffering or affliction can destroy its victims.

The usefulness of the pedagogical argument for suffering is from the point of view of the sufferer, not the point of view of God. We can find sometimes that, by God's grace, good does come from suffering. Aeschylus, the Greek tragedian, wrote: "He who learns must suffer."[16] Contemporary sports psychology essentially affirms that point of view ("No pain, no gain"). But God is greatly diminished when viewed as an all-powerful schoolmaster prodding us toward greater understanding. It is my belief, and my reading of Scripture guides this belief, that God is love. God wants to know us and invites us into relationship.

For various reasons, many people of faith are, at times, inclined to adopt a Stoicism that is self-depriving and, perversely, self-aggrandizing. Dostoevsky wrote that "Maybe he [mankind] loves suffering just as much [as prosperity].... At times man is terribly fond of suffering, he loves it to the point of passion."[17] Sometimes people with a God-the-Schoolmaster theology can usurp that role and become taskmasters for themselves, seeing life as a school for virtue in which they intend to be teacher's pet. I have held this theodicy, and not always consciously. I have presumed to hold myself to standards higher than I felt God required, as I strived for perfection, hoping to preempt my own suffering. Unconsciously, I operated as though I were storing up credit or chits to claim on a rainy day—another form of magical thinking. While claiming to acknowledge God's sovereignty and righteousness, I thought I could be even more virtuous than expected, thus requiring God to protect and reward me. The challenge for me was to trust God and release my imagined ultimate control over potential suffering, a challenge I am at some times better able to meet than at others.

A fourth and final theodicy identified by theologians is one that is based on future hopes of an afterlife. This eschatological theodicy has given comfort to those who find no hope in history, no evidence on earth that evil and suffering are not the last words. This hope ought to be a grace that offers assurance, not a justification for suffering.[18]

Without denying the truth of this hope for the future as described in Scripture, it is important that hope for the future does not render us apathetic, passive, and indifferent in the face of suffering and injustice. We live and suffer. Present reality deserves our attention in spiritual direction, as in life. Hope must join with truth, not be used to silence it.

As a spiritual director, it is my intention to come alongside people in their suffering, hoping and acting with them for its alleviation. I strive to bear witness to the God who "will wipe every tear from their eyes," who promises that "death will be no more; mourning and crying and pain will be no more."[19] In order to do this authentically, I must stand with them in the truth of their lives. In the contemplative space of spiritual direction, by God's grace, a person can face suffering, encouraged by the listening, caring attention of the spiritual director.

It is not easy to look suffering in the face. A person I worked with spent a lot of time thinking about heaven and her eschatological future. Doing so helped her escape the pain of the present, made her feel she would eventually be vindicated, while successful people she knew would, ultimately, be damned. I believe that this kept her from realistically facing the realities of her life. At its worst, the focus on the afterlife has tempted her to suicide and the hope that others would be cursed. At its best, it preserves her sense of God's love for her, even though that love is not manifest in answered prayers in the here and now. In our work together we tried to face the present suffering honestly, neither eclipsing it with heaven's radiance, nor abandoning faith on its account. As she has experienced her suffering in all its harsh truth, she has become more receptive to the love that God offers.

Recognizing and Receiving God's Love

People have different experiences of suffering and, therefore, experience God's response in different ways. With time and familiarity, I grow to know what sorts of spiritual food are most satisfying to people I meet with, and I delight in seeing them expand their gustatory repertoire. My own experience reflects an expanding palate. I met with one spiritual director for many years. Initially in our work I was aware of how God met me in words. *Lectio divina*, the prayerful reflection on a few words of Scripture, was a satisfying practice. When I would sense a direct encounter with the holy, it was often in the form of a word or words filling my mind, as the words "Trust me" did during a particularly traumatic season in my life that involved a loved one's death and another's illness.

Over time, in part due to my director's gentle suggestions, I discovered that images could be a powerful channel of God's grace to me. I was surprised, never having thought of myself as very visual. But I spent time imagining myself floating on my back in calm water. That image constituted my experience of God. I went so far as to go to lakes and oceans and float on my back. No words could ever capture the spiritual truths embedded in the image. Resting in the image moved me beyond all attempts at explaining suffering with words, concepts, and theories. It changed me.

A person who met with me for spiritual direction in a time of tragic loss had a powerful experience of God that combined image and word. Previously steeped in Scripture, this person could not read it after tragedy struck. Gradually, however, this person sensed that God was hovering nearby. It seemed possible that they were sitting at opposite ends of a bench. My directee allowed this experience of God's nearness, as long as silence was maintained. Then, after months of sitting without speech, words from the Song of Songs began to be heard. God seemed to be calling for the "Beloved." Perhaps God was the Beloved. This experience of love reopened the door to God's Word.

The journey of faith is undertaken in our daily, ordinary, suffering-marked lives. My time spent floating in God's grace shaped how I encounter the world, just as time on the imagined bench with the Beloved was life-restoring for my directee.

Time spent with God is life-giving. Returning to tree imagery, each of us is a particular, rooted, growing being. We extend our roots into God's living waters, and it flows through us, strengthening and sustaining us, even in times of suffering. In the middle phase of spiritual direction, I see a soul, like a plant toward sunlight, orient toward grace. Grace begets healing, as the water of life flows through the person. It is not a closed system. With each person I have the joy of seeing how God's grace flows through him or her into the world, and more stories of those experiences will be described in the book's final section. Plants that have been scarred and starved in earlier seasons, will, when tended and nurtured, bear fruit, sprout blossoms, and offer shade and beauty. So, too, it is with people. The middle period of spiritual direction with people is about listening as they seek to stay on the right path, open their wounded hearts to healing waters, and mature in rooted growth.

A friend of mine lost her husband to a gradual death. She felt she would never feel joy again. At the time of his death, a tree near her house died. It became withered and dark, and the leaves curled in crisp fists. Several springs came and went. A few years after her husband's death, she passed the tree on a day in early spring. A few shoots of tender green were coming from a branch. That new, fragile life evoked hope in her. Spiritual directors bear witness to regeneration.

Notes

1. The blind man given sight by Jesus initially mistook people for walking trees (Mark 8:22–26). See Ps 1:3, 6.

2. John 4.

3. Isa 53.

4. Harold Kushner, *When Bad Things Happen to Good People* (New York: Avon, 1983).

5. *Webster's Unabridged Dictionary*, 2nd ed., s.v. "theodicy."

6. See Stanley Hauerwas, *Naming the Silences: God, Medicine, and the Problem of Suffering* (Grand Rapids, Mich.: William B. Eerdmans, 1990), 48.

7. Terry Tilley, "God and the Silencing of Job," *Modern Theology* 5 (April 1989): 268.

8. For an excellent account of these theodicies, see Wendy Farley, *Tragic Vision and Divine Compassion: A Contemporary Theodicy* (Louisville, Ky.: Westminster / John Knox Press, 1990), 21–22.

9. Kant [1819], *An Inquiry Critical and Metaphysical, Into the Grounds for Proof for the Existence of God and into Theodicy* (cited in Farley, *Tragic Vision, Divine Compassion*, 21). In this discussion of theodicy, I am indebted to the work of Wendy Farley and Stanley Hauerwas.

10. Dorothy Soelle, *Suffering*, trans. Everett R. Kalin (Philadelphia: Fortress Press, 1975), 114.

11. Herbert, "Prayer (I)," *The Temple: The Poetry of George Herbert*, ed. Henry L. Carrigan Jr. (Brewster, Mass.: Paraclete, 2001), 45.

12. V. S. Naipaul in a letter from Oxford to his older sister Kamla, quoted by Daphne Merkin in "Suffering, Elemental as Night," *New York Times Book Review*, September 1, 2002, 11.

13. Fyodor Dostoevsky [1880], *The Brothers Karamazov*, trans. Constance Garnett (New York: Barnes and Noble Classics, 2004), 227.

14. Annie Dillard, *For the Time Being* (New York: Vintage Books, 1999), 30.

15. Soelle, *Suffering*, 17.

16. Aeschylus [fourth century BCE], *Agammemnon*, l. 177.

17. Fyodor Dostoevsky [1864], *Notes from the Underground*, trans. Jane Kentish (Oxford: Oxford University Press, 2000), 34.

18. See Farley for greater reflection on this point.

19. Rev 21:3–4.

12

Commissioned:
Leah

Leah, who as a child had spent time in a pasture near her parents' farm, worked with me for several years as she continued her graduate studies. I am not a mystic, but I recognize one when I see one. Leah has vivid Technicolor experiences of God, waking and sleeping. What I see is how the experiences affect her and how the effect on her flows into the world, what Christians call the "fruit" of the encounter with God and the only way an outsider can evaluate mystical experience.

One of the great teachers of our faith and a renowned mystic was sixteenth-century Spanish nun Teresa of Avila, her rapture captured for all time by Bernini's sculpture in St. Peter's at the Vatican. She had no patience for navel-gazing inactivity that presumes to be love of God:

> When I see people earnestly trying to understand the kind of prayer that they are experiencing and being so self-preoccupied, not daring to divert their thoughts and so lose the slightest degree of the feelings of tenderness and devotion which they had been experiencing, I realize clearly how little they truly understand the way to attain that union with God. They think that the whole matter consists in such exercises.
>
> But no! Sisters, no! Our Lord desires *deeds*.[1]

Another praying, activist Teresa, Mother Teresa of Calcutta, said, "The more we receive in silent prayer, the more we can give in our active life."[2] In my work with Leah (who would humbly protest any comparison of herself with the Teresas), I had the opportunity to see, at close range as I had never seen before, the union of profound mystical prayer and engaged social action.

About a year into our work, Leah had to come up with a thesis topic for her master's degree. Given her field, the research would involve some foray into another culture. Being multilingual and well-traveled, she had many options. One of the possibilities that drew her would require the investigation of human rights violations, a dangerous undertaking. In the new chapter of her relationship with God, she understood that God was not calling her to a life of meaningless masochism, and she was wary of old rescuing patterns surfacing in her. Yet she continued to feel drawn to this particular project.

I invited her to pray about it, perhaps in image form. I suggested she might ask God to illuminate her thinking as she imagined herself embarking on the project, or she might see the whole project as a concrete image and hold that before God, waiting to see how it would move or change as she prayed.

It turned out that she and God came up with their own way of addressing the subject. One day she came into my office resolved that this project was the right one for her. I asked how she had come to that conclusion.

"I was praying and all of a sudden I saw myself in a throne room. I was at the far end away from the throne, and Jesus was seated on it, dressed in full royal regalia."

I expressed surprise.

"I was supposed to approach the throne, but I was scared. Then I noticed that Jesus was whispering in my ear, assuring me as I slowly walked forward. He was both on the throne *and* whispering in my ear."

All I could utter was "Wow," and she squirmed with delight at my speechless amazement.

"Yes. So, I just kept going."

"What was he saying?"

"He was telling me he loved me and that he would stay beside me and there was no reason to be afraid. I kept going. When I got in front of the throne, I knelt. Jesus got off the throne, and I bowed low as he approached me. Then he touched me on the shoulder with the flat side of a sword. As if he were knighting me, you know?"

"Yes." Not that I really knew, but I was following. "Knighting you?"

"Yeah, you know, like commissioning me. I knew it was for this project. I don't know what I'm supposed to do there, but I know I'm supposed to go and find out."

"So Jesus has commissioned you for that work."

"Yes. I'm sure of it. I don't necessarily think it's not going to be hard or scary. But I think that God's calling me to it, and Jesus is going to be beside me."

"As he was in the room as you approached the throne?"

"Yes. Exactly. I feel that. And somehow that's enough for me to go on in making this decision." She jutted her chin with determination.

"So you've been commissioned. What an amazing experience."

"Yes."

After several years of being in spiritual direction, Leah, who when we first met had claimed no experience of God, now felt commissioned by God. The sense of commission held. She did go on a perilous journey. You could say she traveled to the heart of darkness, but now she didn't go alone. The work she did shed light in that darkness, a light that served truth and justice, extending outward from the particular work she did into the history and politics of repression in a foreign country.

Before she left for that country, she and I kept returning to her sense of commissioning. We also thought practically about her safety. She consulted with government officials, scholars, and activists here and in the other country, and took what precautions she could to ensure her safety and that of those she encountered. In the end it seemed clear she had done what she could to minimize potential danger, and, still, she was certain God was calling her to take risks for the sake of this mission.

The light that suffused her international work also illuminated darkness in her own personal history. Through all the hard work and surprises of enlightenment, Leah retained her sense of commission. While in the foreign country, she sometimes felt God with her, and, when that feeling faltered, she reminded herself that even if she did not feel so in the moment, she was accompanied.

Leah returned to Berkeley and began writing. As her work progressed, the transcripts of interviews with political victims and their perpetrators formed a mountain of paper in her small apartment, and she placed a Cross on its top to meet the violence and agony contained in their thousands of words, and in the erupting images of suffering from her own childhood that were triggered. Just as Grant felt met by Jesus beside his brother's coffin under a Cross, so Leah felt comforted by Jesus in her work.

At the end of that year, Leah graduated with honors. Her thesis won praise from her professors and colleagues who were eager to see it published. In it, she quoted a survivor of political holocaust as saying that as long as justice remains elusive, she can still hear "the beast breathing." Leah's writing is helping to slay that beast of terror. Her work is also a vehicle for exterminating the beast that stalks her, the beast of cruelty within her early years on the family farm.

Shortly before she began writing her thesis, Leah drew a buffalo—for her, a good beast—and hung the picture over her desk. The buffalo is an animal she grew up seeing near the pasture. That buffalo watched over her writing while the writing took an emotional toll on her. The wooly creature was an imaginative foil to the victims' beast of terror and the haunting memories of her own childhood. That buffalo she had drawn was the only creature from the family homeland that was in town when she graduated.

Though no one from home came to applaud Leah as she crossed the stage and received her well-earned Master's hood, she immediately flew home after she graduated so she could see her brother graduate from high school. She braced herself for time spent with her parents. I wondered about self-inflicted pain, but she felt certain she needed to go and would be okay.

Before she left, we discussed survival strategies: Spend time in the pasture. Buffer herself with friends. Avoid the family church. Make room for herself and her relationship with God.

After meeting with Leah, but before she left town, I wrote a letter to her, congratulating her on her achievement and telling her I would be praying for her while she traveled. I wrote the wrong address on the envelope, so she received it after her return.

"Thanks for the note. I got it when I got back to the Bay Area, and I needed it then. I'm trying to decompress from the time at home," she expressed gratitude while her face reflected a brewing storm.

"I'm so sorry it got to you late. I'd wanted to give you one last 'hug' before you went there. So . . . you were on the family farm for eight days?"

"Yeah. Too long. My limit is five days, but for various reasons I had to stay longer. After five, I could feel myself losing ground. It was as though I was poisoned."

"Tell me what that felt like."

"I literally felt like throwing up. I was nauseous. It wasn't from anything I'd eaten. It was my experience of my family. My body wanted to expel them."

"Your body was trying to protect you, you think?" I ventured.

"That's right. It was acting as though I was being filled with toxins and it needed to get rid of them. It did feel like that. My mother really hates who I am. She asked to read my thesis, and after reading two pages said it made her tired. She gave it back to me. All she ever asks about my life is how I'm going to support myself now. I could feel the joy of graduation and the confidence my work had inspired all slipping away and being replaced by anxiety and self-doubt."

"That's what your body was trying to expel. Your body refused to accept all that toxicity."

"It did. My body knew. My mind was starting to slip into acceptance of her way of seeing me. I returned home here with that image of me in my mind. My friends said I was saying really weird things, and they kept countering all my negative self-talk."

"Your friends and your body hold another image of you that they want to love and preserve."

She started sobbing, holding her body with her arms as she did. She filled the wastepaper basket with tissues, as her body expelled toxins through her tears. I waited as Leah's sobs continued, then subsided. Suddenly she smiled, the sun coming from behind the cloud.

"Friends there helped me, too. They helped me see who I am, and they have done that for me for years. I scheduled my time so I had time with friends every few days. I scheduled other breaks, too. . . . I did go into the pasture. I remembered myself as a girl there. I loved that girl. I felt so sorry for all she'd been through. I cried for her. I also experienced again what it was like to be in the pasture and to be loved. God really was there for me when I was a girl. I just didn't have the right language. All God-stuff was the property of my parents and their church, so I didn't have any words to apply to the One who loved me in the pasture. But it was the same Jesus who commissioned me for my work. He was there with me in the pasture." She sighed, a peaceful sigh.

"So it's the same Jesus loving the same Leah."

"Yes. That's right. Even though my mother sees me as other than I am, I am the same Leah as the one who went to the pasture. I've been finding pastures ever since then. Sometimes I've chosen the racetrack instead of the pasture," she laughed, "but, at my best, I come back to the pasture."

"Is there a pasture where you live now, here?" I asked.

"I find it in different places. I find it with friends. I find it here," she answered, gesturing broadly to indicate my office. "I find it in my church's worship service. I find it at the beach. I find it when I walk from home to work."

"Tell me more about your pasture."

"I guess it's where I am my truest self and know that that self is loved. It's warm and calm. It's stable and comforting. Even when I'm alone there, I don't feel lonely." More deep sighs. We sat together a long time in what felt like that pasture.

I found myself wondering what happens to the beast when Leah's in the pasture, but, reluctant to leave the pasture, I just waited.

Finally Leah spoke again, saying, "Even though I did all those things for myself when I was home, I still was poisoned. I can't go back there. It's still too powerful for me, and I came close to losing myself."

"It sounds as though it was a fierce battle."

"It was. And maybe what I was battling is that 'beast' that breathes down on me. It's that power to make me hate who I am. It makes me hate God, too, because my mother's God is hateful. He requires appeasement. Everything is done in fear of God's wrath and judgment. Every tragedy is seen as booty he extracts. To that God and to my mother I'm a sinner not worthy of life. So being around them is life-threatening for me." She cast a quizzical glance my way. I waited.

She continued, "Maybe that's how my work helps fight the beast that persecutes others. The beast would annihilate the soul. I bring it into the light, and it can't bear that. That light—like the light in the pasture—illuminates the truth of those who've been persecuted, affirms and validates who they are and what their experience is. That strengthens them. It's like turning on the lights in a haunted house."

"Yes. I see that. I like that image. I can almost see the light washing over you as you lie in the pasture, and washing over the people you interviewed. The beast is banished or exposed. Is that right?" I asked.

"Uh-huh. It reverses things. It shifts the power to the person and to that person's truth, away from the persecutors. . . . Maybe that's what being in the pasture does for me. It's that Jesus is the light, and who I really am is visible in that light. The beast becomes invisible. Really, it feels as if the beast isn't there at all in the pasture. If I can just stay in that place of light, I'm safe . . . safe even when I go into dangerous places that I've been commissioned to go." Leah practically acted this out, her hands demarking the areas of light and shadow. Then she laughed and curled a foot under her leg on the chair. She seemed filled with delight.

The prologue of the Gospel of John claims that "the light shines in the darkness, and the darkness did not overcome it." "The light shines"—continuous present. Our experience of God is in the continuous present. We come to it again and again. There is never, in this life at any rate, a safe and final arrival. Faith is not a developmental stage we achieve or grow into. It is a continuous turning toward that light. We return again and again to the pasture that is always there for the finding. Then we leave that place, and whatever beast would destroy us can gain power. We are held in thrall by its demonic force, freezing, fleeing, or fighting as we react against it. Until we move again into the pasture.

Over time, we gain confidence that the pasture is within reach. As we come to know ourselves better, we learn how we can move into it. Leah's strategies for arming herself as she entered darkness involved placing pasture-times on her itinerary, marking out pasture-places she could retreat to when embattled, and setting dates with people who saw her pasture-self and held that image, even in the dark.

Recently Leah had a dream about a buffalo. Unlike the brown summer buffalo she had drawn and placed above the desk where she wrote her thesis, this was a white winter buffalo. As a child, Leah had been fascinated with buffalos' winter stillness. She saw their faint outlines in the pasture, barely visible against the white landscape as they stood unmoving while snow piled on and around them. That's what she saw "her" buffalo doing in the dream, and she told me, "In Native American culture, the white buffalo is a symbol of healing."

Notes

1. Teresa of Avila [1577] "The Interior Castle," part 2, *A Life of Prayer*, ed. James M. Houston (Portland, Ore.: Multnomah, 1983), 175.
2. Malcolm Muggeridge, *Something Beautiful for God: Mother Teresa of Calcutta* (San Francisco: Harper and Row, 1971), 66.

13

Stepping
Stones: Carl

Over time, Carl, by whom I was initially intimidated, has become increasingly relaxed with me and I with him. I know now that all my projections onto him of disdain for me were my misreadings of his shyness. He smiles and laughs, and is remarkably honest with himself and me, giving me fewer opportunities to imagine what he is thinking.

Carl is a professor and was seeking to move from one university to another. This was a point of contention with his fellowship group. It had been the practice in that group to subject life-changing decisions to the collective discernment and will of the group. Carl and I had many conversations about "call."

"Tell me what is going on now with your sense of calling in your work," I suggested.

"I'm feeling quite clearly called to move in a particular way, in a way that would give me more opportunity to work directly with students. But doing that probably means moving out of the area. That's hard because I'm committed to my community, too."

I asked him to tell me more of his thoughts about work.

"Well, when I'm with students I feel as though I'm really connecting with them as people, not just as a class full of students. I feel as though I see each one as a person, and I feel as though I've been given a way of seeing the person almost through God's eyes. I feel genuine affection and hope for each one. Sometimes it's expressed in different ways, like in a comment on a paper, or an encouraging word during office hours, and sometimes it really isn't expressed, but I still feel that my feelings of care make a difference in the student's life."

"It sounds as though you experience something of God's love for the other person."

"Yes. I think that's right. Each student seems unique and special. I can see the challenges the student brings to the situation, and sometimes I have practical suggestions that can help with that, but mostly I have hope for the student. That does feel like something from God. It also feels like I'm doing what I'm supposed to do. It's as if all my years of study and work have brought me to this particular relationship where I can hold hope for a student in a way that no one else can."

"That sounds like the ministry of your work."

"Ministry?" Carl asked.

"Yes. Where you are being the person God has made and prepared you to be in such a way that another life is touched, served . . . blessed."

"Maybe so. It does feel that way. In my community, though, we think of ministry as something we do through a church. So, for example, I'm part of a ministry our church has of taking food to the homeless in a park near where I live. I also serve on a leadership committee that makes decisions about the allocation of money in the church. Those are what I've thought of as my ministries."

"Tell me what it's like for you to serve in those ministries," I invited, interested in hearing about Carl's experience of ministry.

"Well, it does feel like ministry. It feels right and as though I'm doing what God would have me do, helping others, and participating in the life of my community. I really believe in what we have committed to."

I listened. And waited.

"There's something about the moments with my students, though, that feels even more powerful. It's as though all of me is being used. I'm not doing something predetermined that, really, almost anyone could do. I'm working on the edge of my knowledge, using all my capacities to try and meet the student in that encounter. It has a holy feeling to it."

We fell silent. In that moment I felt I was having just the kind of experience he describes having with students. I savored the vitality. It was as though the truth and goodness of his connection with students was present in the room. It felt like stepping onto that broader plane underlying everyday life, which Christians call the "Kingdom" or "Reign of God."

Finally Carl broke the silence, saying, "I like the idea that those experiences with students are ministry. I'll have to think about that."

I realized that it was a dangerous way of thinking within the context of his community. I had no interest in working against those good people who do so much in the world. I believe they engage in ministry through church, and do so better than many groups of Christians I know or am part of. Yet I also believe that what I heard from Carl was about genuine ministry occurring in his work at the university. It didn't carry that label, it didn't include religious language, yet he was helping to bring the light of God's grace into lives he had special access to through his work. I, like many people, remember teachers who were able to see something special and hopeful in me, and they shaped my life. Some of those encounters with people who were loving and hopeful in institutional settings helped me understand that God is everywhere, not just in nature and church where I most expect to experience the Spirit.

The holy will not be contained. We like to think we can capture, preserve, and cultivate it in buildings, liturgies, curricula, a holy land, people, language. All these, at best, are reminders that direct our attention to God. At worst, they become whited sepulchers, empty idols distracting us from what is always lively, surprising, awesome, infinite, and present—if we have eyes to see and ears to hear.

From that conversation on, Carl often spoke of the ministry of his teaching. He told me more stories of encounters with students that reverberated with grace for him. He continued to pursue jobs that would get him out of the lab and into more direct work with students. Each time he tried, the door was shut on him, but he held out hope for what he had tasted.

It was a year of disappointment. The three big issues he had hoped to resolve weren't budging. He wasn't dating; he still hadn't answered his questions about church; and no teaching job was coming through. He wasn't having more experiences of God's embrace, either.

But Carl worked hard to notice the inklings of God in his life. The temptation was to judge his life by the big issues and deem it stuck. Affirming moments with students continued, however, as did important moments with friends and family. His longing for marriage deepened, and he spent time searching himself for interior resistance to beginning a relationship.

"I think I have high standards," he admitted one day. "I wonder if I set the bar high with women in order to protect myself from getting involved."

"Do you think so?" I asked.

"I wonder about it. But I did have a dream about Sarah the other night." I raised my eyebrows at the mention of his ex-girlfriend's name—it had been a long time since he mentioned her, and I tend not to introduce her name because it might be jarring. Responding to my look of surprise, Carl continued, "Yes, I did. And it wasn't too painful. In fact, in the dream I felt okay about seeing her and letting her walk away."

"That sounds like change. What does it feel like when you think about her now?"

"It feels okay. I can tell there was once pain there. But I don't really feel it now. It feels like a relief." He sighed and then laughed.

"The pain relieved," I mused, thinking of God's amazing grace.

"Right. It doesn't change the desire to get married. That remains, and it aches. But it doesn't feel as if I have to go through the Sarah-pain in order to get in touch with the desire."

"So the desire stands more on its own now. As though it has been freed from something?" I strained to imagine this.

"It does. There's free space around it. It feels lighter, not so heavy."

"I'm glad," I said, marveling at the healing.

"It feels light and free, but it also feels a little more exposed, if you know what I mean."

"I'm not sure I do. Is it that the desire now has nothing keeping it from moving forward toward someone new?" I reached to comprehend.

"Something like that," he answered, recoiling a bit. "And I'm not sure I'm ready to move with it." We laughed.

I asked Carl what it would be like to bring the desire before God, and he closed his eyes. I sensed something happening, without knowing what. The image of spiritual direction as midwifery came to mind, as I sat beside Carl, trusting what would emerge from his prayer.

Eventually he looked at me. "I got the sense that it was okay to trust God with the desire. Almost as though God has nurtured it all this time that it was under the shadow of my grief about Sarah. I felt grateful. I feel less afraid now."

I expressed my experience of beauty in all that was going on with him and invited him into a closing moment of silent prayer. Carl nodded and bowed his head again.

You might be wondering about the invitations I extend to directees to bring thoughts and feelings to God in prayer, sometimes in silent prayer. This is certainly not what all spiritual directors do; in fact, mine seldom does. But there are times in sessions when it seems that the directee is sensing God's presence or is on the verge of doing so. It is then that I slow the conversation down and, at times, suspend it. In the silence I, too, listen for God. Time expands, and I am open to God's address to me.

I look at the candle and notice the light it sheds. I notice the liveliness of the flame's movement and its responsiveness to air currents. I notice its hardiness and think of the power it holds to illuminate, heat, melt, fuse, burn, and vaporize. I think about the courage of the person before me, as he or she trusts the proximity of the all-powerful God who is symbolized by the flame. Those times of silence with directees linger in my memory. As I write about them, they return to me, and I feel awe for what I have witnessed.

My work is influenced by the teaching and writing of spiritual directors who visualize the realm of human experience as a cone surrounded by the God in whom "we live and move and have our being."[1] On the cone's circular face lie the quadrants of human experience—intrapersonal, interpersonal, organizational, and environmental. All our experiences find their place here. We register many of these experiences at first with our perceiving faculties of sense and thought. For instance, with my spiritual director I once remembered how the ringing of a distant bell caught my attention in the middle of the workday. I remembered the sound and what I felt. It came from the environment into the organizational structure of my work-day, becoming an interior experience and memory.

An experience like hearing the bell may then sink to a deeper level below the initial experience (represented by the cone's surface), triggering feelings, inclinations, and responses. The sound of the bell made me stop working for a moment in order to relish its fading tone. As I remembered the experience with my spiritual director, I re-experienced it. As a person remembers such an experience, he or she may find that it feels as though it moves deeply within, sedimenting into the body and self in ways difficult to capture with words, much as one sinks fluidly into prayer. This place of wordless experience is represented by the narrow base of the cone where God's all-surrounding grace washes over experience, making distinctions between the deepest self and God nearly impossible.

In Celtic Christian spirituality, people speak of certain places, like the island of Iona in Scotland, as "thin" places where we feel God is extraordinarily close. In contemplative prayer, as we follow the pulse of God's grace into the depths of our hearts, we can feel ourselves arriving in a "thin" place where God's presence seems to surround and penetrate our being. When I remembered the sound of the bell entering my office and work-filled mind, I felt how it had reminded me of God's larger world, the finitude of human time and my time, and of God's resonant grace sounding through eternity. Suddenly, sitting at my desk in front of my computer, I brushed up against the holy.

That is an experience I often have as I sit in silence with a directee. I described it above as "awe," which Abraham Joshua Heschel memorably defined as feeling "in the rush of the passing the stillness of the eternal."[2] It seems as though I float in the holy with little sense of distinction between self and other. This may be akin to the "in the zone" or "flow" experiences described by athletes and artists, and the "unitive" experience of prayer described by mystics.

Catholic theologian Karl Rahner wrote, "Prayer can be itself only when it is understood as the last moment of speech before the silence, as the act of self-disposal just before the incomprehensibility of God disposes of one, as the reflexion immediately preceding the act of letting oneself fall after the last of one's own efforts and full of trust, into the infinite

Whole which reflexion can never grasp."[3] One falls, trustingly, beyond what can be expressed in speech. In Pascal's posthumously discovered memorial of his experience of God, he called this "sweet and total renunciation."[4] It is a submission to and immersion in grace, even when one's life circumstances are distracting or painful. I have seen people release themselves to God's grace though they were in periods of great suffering or doubt. It is a "quiet, shy, and faithful yes"[5] that enables a person to enter into this deep place where the Holy Spirit dwells, a "yes" that is, ultimately, a gift of that Holy Spirit.

This is the movement a person may experience with art. One enters the particulars of the painting, song, or poem, moving through thoughts and feelings until there is an encounter with what is both deepest in oneself *and* transcendent of self. In that encounter there is the experience of undergoing something, being touched and changed. The art pierces, cuts to one's core, like the spear thrust of goodness described by Keats. That pierced core is bathed in the truth, beauty, and goodness we recognize as God's grace. Self-consciousness fades.[6] Then, gradually, one resurfaces into the present circumstances, and life is perceived through the afterglow of the encounter. One's life is seen from an altered vantage through which it is enhanced, framed by a larger perspective.

These are the beliefs and hopes that inspire me to invite another to sit in silence before God. I sense that the experience is moving deeper and deeper in the person, to that place of inarticulate encounter with God. People tell me that that is their experience. When they move out of that silence into speech, they often are visibly moved and tender. The encounter with God suffuses their consciousness as they turn to look at other aspects of their lives. For this I have the image of an ember.

As the spiritual director, I am presented with and look for the faintly glowing ember. The directee reveals it through words that carry the gleam of the experience. The encounter with the holy has yielded this ember, which I shelter and fan as spiritual direction progresses. The ember sheds light, and its waxing and waning instructs our attention, as the directee and I strive to maintain its glow. Returning in memory to experiences of God, we blow on the embers that glow again. The flame of God's Spirit preceded the ember, and, conversely, "from one small spark can come a mighty blaze."[7] As Carl and I met for spiritual direction, we paid attention to the embers of God's grace in his life.

Throughout that year Carl continued to apply for jobs while ministering in his current position. He ventured out a bit socially. More and more his focus was on the job search, and months went by when I didn't hear about much else.

"It's so hard to keep putting myself out there looking for a new job. I feel so exposed and vulnerable to rejection."

"I can imagine. Each time you apply for a position you have to muster hope to see the application through all the interviews. It must be hard to be hopeful, again and again, and hard to do the self-promotion." We've talked a number of times about the distasteful art of self-promotion.

"It is! I hate it. To do that, plus my research and writing, and to be so invested in the job search while not letting on to my colleagues and the university that it's what I'm doing—it's too much. It's like living a hidden life, and it's not a pleasant hidden life. It makes me feel insecure and like a commodity for sale."

I empathized with the experience, imagined it must be lonely, and, with hope, asked, "What's your experience of God in it?"

"Let me think about that for a minute." Carl lowered his head into his hands. After a while he looked at me and said, "I get the sense that this is the way I'm supposed to be going. But I see myself as having hopped from stone to stone across a quickly flowing and fairly deep stream, and now I'm trying to balance with both feet on one stone. I can't see where the next stone is."

"What do you see?" I asked.

"I see the stream. I see my feet on the stone. I see that the stone is large enough for both my feet, and that I can balance on it if I don't scare myself. I see the last stone I was on and that it isn't as good a stone to stand on. But the way ahead is foggy. I can't see through the fog."

"Tell me more about the fog."

"It's thick. It's more white than dark. It moves. I almost get the sense it's obscuring something solid. I don't know what it is, but when I look at it I feel a tingle of excitement."

Offering back to him what he was telling me, I said, "So when you look ahead at the fog you feel excitement."

"I do. I don't know why. I guess there's a sense of anticipation. Almost promise."

"Promise." I repeated.

"That's right. Promise. What I really feel is that God is with me in the fog. And I feel as if God is promising something good for me. I feel newness in the promise, not just an old affirmation of God's having a plan for my life." He laughed, and exclaimed, "Who knew?! I feel confirmed in this call to keep moving forward in what feels like a ministry of teaching. I feel hopeful, even excited."

That spiritual direction session with Carl has lingered with me through the years. There he was stranded in the stream with nowhere to put his foot and only fog ahead. Yet when he paused in the fog and paid attention to it, he sensed promise. At times when I have felt stranded and fogged in, I remind myself of his experience. Being fogged in with no place to settle is a wilderness experience, which I think many of us enter time and again. I know I do. Looking toward what's ahead, even when we can't see it, is a move of faith.

Jewish and Christian Scriptures hold stories of the wilderness, an in-between, liminal place. We're beyond what was familiar and have not yet arrived at where we're going. We are prone to temptation and discouragement. We can feel disconnected from God and our own identity. There is opportunity in the wilderness, too. We can reflect on where we have been and how our identity has been held in place. Perhaps that identity no longer holds when we are away from the relationships and roles of the past. Clarification and change are possible; faith and hope, sustaining graces.

Carl allowed himself to imagine the transitional place he was in and stay in it. That isn't easy. He stayed in that place of not knowing, without imposing an action plan, retreating, or distracting himself from it. He also stayed in touch with his sense of call. It persisted through streams and fog, hard work, being on the job market, and through long periods of little movement. He made himself face exactly where he was. God kept meeting him there, just where he was. That's where God meets us, even though we can think we must scale mountains or walk through rivers in order to find God.

A year into the job search, Carl had news.

"They've made me an offer, and I intend to accept. I've checked it out with my family and close friends, and they all think it's right for me. I've pretty much accepted, but I want to listen to you if you tell me you think it's not right." I was touched that he paused before accepting, in order to reflect on the offer in spiritual direction.

Since Carl had first mentioned this college, among a number of others, I had had the feeling it was the place for him. But I didn't have a sense that my intuition was a message for him from God through me, so I'd kept it to myself. Now I felt like celebrating.

I told him, "It seems so right for you. Since you first mentioned it to me, I've had a very good feeling about it. In addition to that feeling, I also see how it's a place where your hopes of teaching as a ministry can be fulfilled. It's a place where you know people who share your faith and commitment to thoughtful, community-centered living." Words, words, words. I should have cried out, "I feel like celebrating!"

I knew that the realization of Carl's dream would most likely bring our work to an end. I would miss him and miss seeing how the other big issues of his life would be shaped by God's hand. His steady, honest faithfulness had been a gift to me. I was grateful to have seen him through this particular wilderness. It seemed that this time was preparation for a more settled life of mature, fruitful living.

"Going back to that stream image, I see through the fog now," he said. "What was there and gave me hope is the bank of the river. I'm setting foot on it now and beginning to explore the new land."

I pictured it as he said it. I could envision him on campus and in his home, creating a space of welcome for students and others. It was the fulfillment of years of steady preparation and prayerful growth. Silently, I prayed for his home to be blessed with the family he desired.

Notes

I. In understanding the flow of God's grace through the dimensions of human experience, I have benefited from the work of my teaching colleagues at San Francisco Theological Seminary's Diploma in the Art of Spiritual Direction program, including Elizabeth Liebert, Nancy Wiens, Mary Rose Bumpus, Rebecca Bradford

Langer, Kay Collette, and Sam Hamilton-Poore, and from those who influenced their teaching, especially Jack Mostyn and Andy Dreicter. Their work affirms Paul's words found in Acts 17:28.

2. Heschel, http://en.wikiquote.org/wiki/Abraham_Joshua_Heschel.

3. Quoted by Perry LeFevre, *Understandings of Prayer* (Philadelphia: Westminster Press, 1981), 151.

4. Ibid., 310.

5. Karl Rahner, *The Need and Blessing of Prayer*, trans. Bruce W. Gillette (Collegeville, Minn.: Liturgical Press, 1997), 21.

6. Margret Elson, a pianist, psychotherapist, and my friend, in private communication claimed this is "the performer's dream state."

7. Dante Alighieri [early fourteenth century], *The Divine Comedy: Paradise*, trans. Mark Muso (London: Penguin, 1984), canto I, st. 1:34, 2.

14

Bearing Witness to
What Faith Allows: Ruth

After that first bedside meeting, Ruth came to my office every few weeks for about a year. I learned that she spread light wherever she went, not just when she was lying on pale pillows. Upright, her laugh tinkled less and sank deeper in range. The peace she felt early on ebbed and flowed. She sought the wisdom of many as she faced her mortality. She searched her life and soul to understand her illness and its meaning. It became increasingly clear that the cancer was growing in her body.

Ruth came up with several theories to explain her suffering. One was that her mother's fear and revulsion of motherhood while pregnant had planted a seed of death in Ruth, the child she carried. Another theory was that Ruth's own perfectionism had spawned a life-threatening anxiety that could have led to this illness. Yet another theory she explored was that she had closed her heart to love's deepest reach, including the love extended toward her by God. In these and other theories someone, and usually she herself, was to blame for her illness.

Ruth confided to me, "I lie awake at night thinking of what I could have done to avoid the cancer. Could I have loved more openly? Could I have stressed myself out less? I also feel enraged with my mother for her rejection of me when I was first born, and even before that when I was an unwanted pregnancy. If she had welcomed me, would I be healthy today?"

"Those are searing questions, Ruth."

"Yes. They afflict me. At night it seems that answering them is imperative. In the morning they seem irrelevant. Whatever the answers might be, it's too late. I'm sick. Very sick. That will not be changed."

"I'm sorry you're so sick, Ruth," I said, the words sticking in my throat as tears welled up. I rebelled against her sickness. Sometimes the thought of the gravity of her situation made me sick to my stomach, as fear, anger, and grief churned together.

Wanting to hold the whole truth of what she was saying, I said, "I'm glad that the morning brings relief from the torturing questions."

"It does. It also brings vision, you know. In the light of day, I see my garden and my statue of Christ. I see my friends. I see color and movement and life." She smiled her radiant smile.

Sometimes Ruth ventured theories of blessing. Perhaps God had been with her from her earliest days as she watched shadows play on the wall beside her crib and felt comforted by a loving, though alien, presence. She often felt that God was using her current illness to draw her close and let her know Jesus' love for her. She wondered if through her illness she would become a messenger to others of God's unfailing love.

"It's only through this illness that I've come to know Christ, you know," she told me. "I wish I could have gotten to know him in a less dramatic way," she laughed, "but this will have to do. For years I felt that Christianity was oppressive, judgmental, mythological. I didn't really like Christians—no offense," she laughed again. "But now I'm not really thinking about Christianity as an organized, historical religion, or about Christians and the 'Religious Right,' I'm just aware of Christ. There he is, holes in his hands, love streaming from his wounded heart. I feel like St. Patrick who wrote that prayer about Christ being above, below, before, behind, under, and through him. I feel *that* enveloped in Christ. When I start thinking dark thoughts about the religion itself or its followers, Christ is there pretty much extinguishing all those ruminations with the sheer reality of his presence. My sincere hope is that people will look at me and see that reality of Christ."

Often Ruth became tired of the work of thinking about and managing her illness: tired of the theories, of having to be her own advocate and medical researcher, even of attending to her patients. She would look out her kitchen window at a statue of Jesus she had put there. The statue showed Jesus' heart exposed on his chest, with rays radiating outward from it. She loved thinking about Jesus' heart of love.

As Ruth looked at the statue, she felt Jesus regard her with love. She put a vase at the base of the statue and began a practice of starting the day by cutting a flower in her yard and placing it in the vase at Jesus' feet. The beauty suffused her and restored her sense that all would be well.

I visited her in the hospital after a major surgery, when it was clear that the cancer had spread to vital organs. She was holding her Bible, some color in that sea of white, and asked me about Second Corinthians, chapter four, verses seven through twelve. Ruth wanted to know what it meant that the life of Jesus "may also be made visible in our bodies . . . in our mortal flesh." I asked what drew her to the passage. She responded, "That's what I want. I want this suffering and dying of my body to bear witness to what faith allows."

"To bear witness to what faith allows." I never saw her or thought about her after that without remembering that phrase. Ruth indeed bore witness to what faith allows. Paul wrote about our bearing witness to the light of Jesus, and Ruth transmitted that light. After that hospital visit, most of our contact was over the phone. Sometimes she sent me beautiful cards, calling me "dearie" and "sweetie" and telling me of her love for me.

Once she asked me to take her to my church for Easter. I drove to pick her up. Her home overlooked a large body of water, the color of her eyes. I found her looking at the Jesus statue, a lily in the vase at his feet.

Ruth had created an Easter bonnet for herself, a straw hat with a scarf tying it to her chemo-wispy hair, and a white flower centered on the brim over her face. She beamed at me from under the brim. I couldn't speak, so touched was I by her and the hat she had made to celebrate Easter. I will never forget the sight of that emaciated woman celebrating.

She was weak, and moving left her out-of-breath, but she was game for the outing. In church I sat next to her through the hymns, surrounded by standing, rejoicing singers. One phrase from Handel's *Messiah* resounded for us both: "We shall be raised incorruptible!" We hugged. I felt grief—and hope. Yes, "we shall be raised incorruptible," but I didn't want to watch Ruth falling. Yet, I had every intention of being one of those near her, witnessing her as she bore witness to what faith allows.

15

Rainbows—Welcome and Unwelcome: Grant

As time passed after Grant told me about his brother's death, I saw his formality soften. But one day when I was anticipating seeing him the next day, I received a voicemail message from him saying he was not sure we were scheduled to get together. He said in a clipped manner, "I see on my calendar your name with a question mark after it. Since next week is our regular appointment, I'm assuming we're not getting together tomorrow and that my calendar simply reflects a possibility we had discussed but never confirmed. Would you please confirm that for me? Feel free to respond to my work number." He sounded pretty formal. I wondered whether his vacation had been restful. I had so hoped he would have rest from his demanding job.

I returned the call to a message tape and said that I had us on the calendar for the next day, too, and would be happy to meet with him if that is what he wished. I also said I hoped that his confusion about his calendar was a sign that he had really been able to forget about work and schedules while he was away.

His responding message was good to hear. He laughed, answering, "Yes, it was a great vacation. I look forward to telling you about something that happened on it." He sounded loose and at ease.

The next day Grant arrived in formal business attire, but with a smile. As always, I was struck by the contrast between his well-groomed appearance and my not-so-groomed office. It took years for me to learn to notice how my office and I might look to a directee. Some, I imagined, saw shabbiness while others, I imagined, saw privilege and affluence. Casting a disinterested eye on myself in this way has helped me bring appearances more in line with the reality of who I am. Looking through my directees' eyes at my office inspired me to remove books inherited from others that did not represent my interests. But my office remains full of books, and some people have been intimidated by them. One person on our first meeting sat down, looked around, and said, "Books! Books! Books! I guess that says something about you." Another told me the sight of the books made her feel uneducated. Perhaps it's the books that inspire people to ask me for reading suggestions and assignments, something I try to resist.

Sometimes reflection on what my office communicates leads me to add something. I had not had a Cross in my office when I began doing spiritual direction. A few years into the work, I decided I wanted that explicitly Christian symbol to be visible. It represents my faith, and any directee I see needs to know that.

When Grant arrived, he and I began our time by lighting the candle, watching to see whether the new wick would take the flame. After a wick is touched by a match flame, there is a tenuous phase when any breeze will extinguish it. The flame moves down the wick toward the wax and then falters as it lands on the wax surface. The flame diminishes, wavers, and occasionally is extinguished on the wax. Usually it takes hold and swells, rising tall, straight, and full across the whole length of the wick and beyond. It did so. Grant waited to see that it did and then bowed his head.

He began with a whispered prayer of thanks to God. Then he told me about an early morning experience in the middle of his vacation. He and his wife were staying in a lodge on a lovely, unpopulated stretch of the northwest coast. Each morning he ran south on the beach as the sun rose over the hills and began to shed light on the ocean. He ran around a point of land and, when the tide was high, picked his way carefully over rocks.

One day the tide wasn't so high and the running was smooth, almost unconscious. He was aware of the peace and beauty of it and the soft roar of the ocean. He was saying to God, "Help me trust You." He prayed it over and over again as his feet hit the sand. As he ran, his attention was drawn to an illuminated cloud in the eastern sky. He looked up, watching the cloud shift in the light. Then he felt he was drawn to look to the west. What he saw made him stop and catch his breath. Next to him over the sea was a vivid, arcing rainbow. He was stunned. All thoughts left him, and he just absorbed it. Then he started to sing. "I don't sing well," he told me, "and I didn't remember all the words, but I sang what I could of 'Great Is Thy Faithfulness.'"

When he said that, I felt reverence—"a salute of the soul"[1]—and couldn't speak. All that was in my mind was an image of him, a man in mid-life, alone on a beach, singing at a rainbow. I have no idea how long we sat there in silence: He, I assumed, remembering the rainbow, as I imagined him singing.

The silence ended with him chuckling: "You might think I made it up, but my wife saw it and took pictures of it." That made my state of mind even more acute, for then I saw him on the beach singing, her on the deck photographing the rainbow, the two of them, unknowingly, worshiping together.

I joined his laughter and wiped my eyes. Grant told me that on hearing his story, his wife had said that the rainbow was God's response to his prayer, "Help me trust You." He wrestled with a sense that her interpretation wasn't quite right. Seeming to grope toward expressing what he felt, he said, "I didn't feel that the rainbow was a particular word to me from God. I didn't feel that it appeared just because of my prayer. Yet I did feel it was for me. But not only for me. It wasn't as if I prayed, 'Help me trust You,' and God sent a rainbow. It was more that I turned to God, and God revealed a bit of himself. It's like I got a glimpse of God's majesty. God wanted me to have that glimpse, but it wasn't that my prayer created the rainbow."

Grant was not arguing against the possibility of God responding personally and dramatically; he has had experiences like that. In part he was speaking against any idea of people being able to force God's hand. He did accept the rainbow as part of his relationship with God. He had turned to God, and God had greeted him. It was neither a didactic encounter on God's part, nor a magical one on Grant's.

Tentatively, I probed, "Saying that God answered your prayer by creating a rainbow somehow diminishes God?"

"Yes. The feeling was that I was getting to see a little fraction of the God who says, 'I am who I am.' He is beyond human conversation, though he sometimes enters it. I was allowed to see God in an unfiltered, though microscopic, way. I was filled with awe. It just made me forget everything I'd been thinking about in my head-down, stream-of-consciousness thinking. There were no thoughts. What came up was a song. It came up out of me, out of my body more than out of my mind. It must have looked silly. But it was all I could do. It was what I had to do."

I thought about the passage from Isaiah that declares that "all the trees of the field shall clap their hands."[2] It seemed like that kind of spontaneous eruption of praise. I found myself reining in my impulse to express my joy with abandon—and maybe my restraint was a mistake. Unlike Grant on the beach, I was self-conscious. So now, belatedly: "Hallelujah!"

Although Grant had sung on the beach about God's faithfulness and knew he had been changed by the experience, he told me that once back from vacation he doubted whether his trust in God had been strengthened. Back at work only a day, he felt the temptation to drop all awareness of God during the workday. He took this thought in two directions: one was his desire to find a way of holding onto the experience on the beach; the other was a need to make it clear that he is not some kind of saint. We talked for a while about holding on to it. His wife's photographs are helpful in that.

Then I listened to him speak of his unworthiness of God's self-display and eventually observed, "You looked up."

When I said that, he looked up at me. He rolled it around in his mind for a few seconds, and then admitted, almost sheepishly, "Yes. I looked up." He smiled. Then, as always, he added, "I think I'm done."

I left the office that day remembering Grant and thinking about looking up. Woody Allen spoke about the importance of *showing up* (claiming it accounts for 80 percent of success), and now Grant had taught me the significance of *looking up*.[3]

Grant does show up and look up. He also looks down as he studies God's Word and what scholars have written about God and God's Word.

He illustrates what is true for me, too. My spirituality is rooted in my theology and nourished by it. Sometimes, however, focusing on the theology can interfere with my attention to the grace that rains down from above. That day on the beach, God caught Grant's attention.

Several months later, Grant came to see me and told me how disconnected from God he felt.

"It's just been weeks of hassles and problems. Work is a challenge, and I find myself frustrated with people and the system all the time. There's so much incompetence. I'm pretty good at analyzing situations. That's one of my skills. I'm able to separate my feelings from the objective analysis and point out to someone how he or she has made illogical leaps that doom the plan. I also can tell them about it unemotionally. I don't get angry, and I know that some of them consider me unfeeling. But they trust the accuracy and objectivity of my assessment. At the end of the day, I feel exhausted by the work and frustrated that others didn't catch errors themselves. . . . So that's work. No sense of God there."

"You carry a lot of responsibility for the work of a number of people," I said, empathizing with a situation he was well aware of.

"Yes, I do. That's management's function. It's a real weight, but I'm pretty good at it."

"You sound quite alone in bearing the weight," I suggested.

"Right. That's just the way it is." Grant looked as though he were smelling something unpleasant. "I ultimately feel that the weight of responsibility is on me. I suppose you're suggesting I look at that." He gave me a slightly resentful glance. "Okay. Well, it's true. I feel ultimately responsible in many spheres of life: I'm the breadwinner in the family; I'm the dutiful son. In many ways I don't mind it. I'm capable, and I know it. It's fine with me that others rely on me." Then he sat quietly for a few moments. "There are times, though, when I worry about my ability to be reliable, and that makes me anxious."

"There are times like that?" I prompted, marveling that he would ever question his own reliability. He strikes me as wholly reliable.

"Yeah. Not too often. Usually it's just fine. But . . . recently. . . ." He slowed to a stop. I watched as he contemplated his hands. He held one hand in the other and then switched to holding the other hand. Then he clasped his hands together, dropped them into his lap, took a deep breath, and looked at me squarely.

"Recently I had a health problem, or I thought I did. I noticed something and went to the doctor about it. It didn't look good for a while. He ordered some pretty substantial tests. Then I waited. The tests were for cancer, and I had time to think about dying while I waited for the results. I didn't do very well. I was angry. I was very, very angry."

Grant's glower at me seemed to contain a lot of that anger. His body, though, had a slouched, almost defeated look.

"I was angry when I was at work and angry at home. My wife asked me how I was praying about it, and that just irritated me. I wasn't praying. I was angry with God, too. As far as I was concerned, having a terminal illness was an outrage. It wasn't possible. If God had allowed that, then I had no time for God." In this calculation, God bore the blame and Grant, the suffering, seemingly in isolation from one another.

"So you carried it by yourself."

"Yes. I carried it by myself." Grant looked at me defiantly. "I was the one with the problem, and no one else could do anything about it. I started to make sure my paperwork was in order so that the impact wouldn't be so great on my family. It made me furious to have to do that. I kept calling the doctor's office to find out the results of the tests, but no one returned my calls."

"You were left hanging in that scary place not knowing."

"Yes, I was. You say 'scary,' and I suppose I was scared. But I wasn't letting myself feel that. I just felt furious. How could this be happening to me! I'm not that old. I've been living a clean life, following the rules, even trying to trust God." He looked as if he was about to cry.

"It wasn't fair," I commiserated.

"Correct! It was not fair. Absolutely. Not fair." Grant shifted his position and said quietly, "But I know life's not fair. The good suffer all the time. I think I was having a tantrum. I'm not proud of it. I shut God out."

"You were experiencing such strong feelings of threat, anger, fear. That seems pretty normal to me. But you didn't share them with God?"

"No," he confessed. "I shut God out. I didn't want a conversation with a God who would let me suffer like that."

"Tell me more about that experience of shutting God out."

Grant hesitated, shifting a bit in his chair. "Well, one day after waiting several days for the results and not getting answers, I left a message for the doctor saying I had to hear back from him, and if he didn't respond I would complain. I was in my office and really mad. I walked over to my window and opened the blinds. My office has a sweeping view." He stopped again, shifting his position a bit more. Then he said, "Outside the window was a rainbow." He did not look happy about it.

I was tempted to smile, but resisted the impulse. I echoed, "A rainbow?"

"Yes. There was a rainbow right outside the window. It was large and vivid. I've never seen one there before." He looked at me and then dropped his head. "I shut the blinds," he mumbled almost inaudibly.

I sat there in the silence with him.

Finally, clearing his throat, Grant continued: "Then, within a few minutes, my doctor called and told me that the tests had come back clear. I didn't have cancer. I was fine. No problem."

"I'm glad to hear that," I said with relief.

"Yes. It's good news." He still didn't look happy. "But, you see, I failed. I failed God. I failed myself." His eyes were full of tears.

"By shutting God out?" I asked.

"Yes," he whispered. "The first big test I've had since I've been getting to know God differently, and I failed it."

"So you're disappointed in yourself. Maybe ashamed." He nodded. "Tell me how you're orienting toward God now," I encouraged.

"I guess I'm on my knees. I'm turned toward God, but I'm bent over in my shame and regret." He didn't look at me and spoke hoarsely looking at his hands, which clasped each other tightly.

"What's that like?" I asked, imagining his praying posture.

"It feels right. It's emotional and uncomfortable, but it feels right. The more I stay with it the more right it feels. I feel warmer now." We sat in silence. "I feel home."

"You're not shutting God out. You're not alone," I confirmed.

"Yes. I'm not alone. I'm back with God. And I'm so very sorry I was so angry and rejecting. I don't feel God is that way toward me, though."

"God's not angry and rejecting? What do you feel from God?"

"I feel warmth. I feel that God knows me and accepts me. I feel home . . . I'm done." Grant brought our time together to a close.

Accepting closure, I said, "Let's end our time with a moment of silent prayer." He nodded without looking up. My heart ached for him. At my "Amen," he whispered "Amen" and prepared to leave, avoiding my eyes. At the door he met my eyes and gave a shy smile. Then he left. I closed my door and sat alone for a while. I cried. I felt struck by God's goodness and also by Grant's. I thought of how often I don't look up and notice God there, how often I shut God out and presume to carry my load by myself.

To see spiritual growth as linear and cumulative is a mistake. Stages of faith aren't building blocks that get stacked one on top of the other. I frequently encounter this achievement orientation toward faith in directees and in my own self-delusions. How comforting to think that each sin recognized and confessed forever fortifies us against the same sort of sin. What false comfort to think we have triumphed over earlier temptations, faults, and limits.

As a child in the Episcopal church, I grew up saying the prayer of General Confession from the Order for Daily Morning Prayer. Sunday after Sunday, I knelt between my parents in a crowded church as we all prayed, "We have erred, and strayed from thy ways like lost sheep. We have followed too much the devices and desires of our own hearts. We have offended against thy holy laws. We have left undone those things which we ought to have done; And we have done those things which we ought not to have done; And there is no health in us."[4] Continuing the prayer, we then asked for God's mercy and restoration. "Amen," we said: Let it be. Then we would pray the same words the following Sunday. Week after week, I heard people of all ages, at all stages of faith, confess sin and ask for mercy. Jesus taught his disciples to pray, "Forgive us our sins," and that is what Christians have prayed for two thousand years. The prayer never becomes obsolete.

Growth in faith is about turning toward, and returning to God. We hope to turn and turn again. In the turning, we learn. Then, when we find ourselves failing, as Grant did, we might become better at recognizing it and better at remembering we can turn again toward God. We find out that we will never be "beamed up" to a place of perfection, to some kind of Nirvana. Like Peter, the one chosen by Jesus to establish the Christian church, we turn away from Jesus, perhaps even deny him. And then we turn toward him, even swim toward Jesus through cold water as Peter did, confessing our love for him. Time after time. We discover that we are not alone.

Notes

1. Abraham Joshua Heschel [1942], "An Analysis of Piety," *Moral Grandeur and Spiritual Audacity: Essays*, ed. Susannah Heschel (New York: Farrar, Strauss, and Giroux, 1996), 312.

2. Is 55:12.

3. Allen, http://www.quotationspage.com/quote/1903.html.

4. "A General Confession," *Book of Common Prayer* (New York: Seabury, 1953), 6.

16

Open Hands:
Charles

When he arrived at my office door after his monastic retreat, Charles was visibly changed. He looked younger. His usually impassive face was animated, and he spoke eloquently about his time at the monastery. It was a relief to get a sense of his feelings, especially after the long months of our early work during which I had found him so inscrutable. He looked as though he had come down from the mountain, his countenance aglow.

"I spent a lot of time in the garden with Brother David. There was only farmland as far as I could see. The land was flat, so the sky was wide and low."

"It sounds expansive. As though you could move freely in such a large space."

"Yes. It was so different from my cubicle at work, and the small living space I share. It was light, open, fresh." He leaned back smiling and took a long, deep breath. The peace of the monastery garden emanated from him.

"We also had worship several times a day, nothing fancy or long. Just straightforward prayers, chants, and readings. The brothers helped me follow along at first, until I found my place. They were all matter-of-fact, practical men with work-worn hands. Not at all the mysterious monks I had imagined. Even in the spiritual direction sessions with the abbot, he was completely practical. He told me how he prayed, said he shared many of my questions, and gave me a real feeling of ease."

"It sounds as if it was a wide open and welcoming spiritual space. I imagine you, Charles, now being more free, physically and spiritually, here in Berkeley," I offered, with hope.

"I think so. I can move more easily. You know I'd always thought of monks as grand masters of prayer and knowledge of God, so to see them as so normal was a kind of relief. I got the feeling they really had found the way for themselves, and that freed me to find my way, too. I didn't need to be a monk to find my way. I need to find who I am supposed to be and how I am to live. The monks definitely gave me permission to do that," he told me, shrugging as though to demonstrate his freedom from shackles.

"Wonderful. So much freedom!"

"Yes. I have a feeling that something significant has changed in me." Then he looked at me, and, laughing, confessed, "Of course I still want a mate. That hasn't changed. But maybe I can change my life in other ways even if I can't make that happen." Psychoanalyst Heinz Kohut wrote that humor, in addition to wisdom and compassion, is a hallmark of psychological maturity, and I believe the same could be said of spiritual maturity.[1] It was striking to watch Charles expressing humor around the subject of his greatest unrequited hope.

Other possibilities and hopes seemed to be freed from the heavier hope for marriage under which they'd been lying like shoots of grass under a stone. I had tried to direct Charles toward other possibilities over the years, and it now seemed to be a direction he was turning to of his own volition, thanks to the sense of permission he had gained from his time in the monastery. Possibilities suddenly emerged, and he was expressing some reflective humor about his longing for a mate. The time at the monastery had granted a wide perspective, indeed.

"That sounds really big, Charles. You have been so focused on the issue of marriage," I remarked, marveling at what I was hearing.

"Yes. I think that I thought if I sought other things I want in life, it would be like settling for a consolation prize. It would let up the pressure on God to give me what I really want. Does that make sense?"

"It does," I acknowledged. "I know I've thought that way about things. As though it's best to continue lobbying for the large issue and ignore other issues until the large one is resolved. I find myself wondering whether this affects your sense of trusting God."

"The trust issue isn't clear to me. I do feel more freedom. I get the impression that my 'lobbying,' as you say, isn't the way to go. But I'm not sure I trust. I'd like to trust that God will give me the desire of my heart, but I don't. Not really, not fully. And I don't trust God to decide whether or not I get married! I don't want to grant the negative possibility. Being with the monks made me very sure that the celibate life isn't for me. I talked with the abbot about it, and he said he was called to his particular way of life, the monastic life, and not necessarily away from marriage. But marriage is incompatible with that way of life, and so he accepts that. He feels he's choosing *for* something rather than *away from* something. I enjoyed the retreat, but I don't have that call." He laughed, adamantly shaking his head against a monastic vocation.

Charles continued in this animated fashion. "My fear is that if I were to say, 'I trust you, God, with this issue about finding a mate, and I will leave it in your hands,' that that would really be just another effort to do the right thing in order to be rewarded. You see what I mean? It wouldn't be real trust. It would be an attempt to appear trusting."

"I think I'm understanding. That's an important insight: If you went through the motions of placing this issue in God's trust, you might just be engaging in another exercise of trying to persuade God to do what you want."

"It would be acting. I don't want to pretend trust. I want to trust God with my life and with my desires. But I'm not willing to relinquish my desires, if that makes sense," he clarified.

"That seems honest, Charles," I responded. "You're trusting that God can handle your honesty."

"I guess you could say that. I hadn't thought of it that way." He sat for a few minutes and then stated confidently, "Okay, I think I do trust God more. I trust that God is willing to let me be me."

In summarizing what I'd heard, I spoke of the freer space in which Charles now found himself, and, even with reservations about specific outcomes, he was trusting that it was okay with God for him to move in a freer and less self-scrutinizing way.

"I do feel more free. It's more as though I've put the issue down. Not that I've put it in God's hands. It's right there between my feet," and he pointed toward his feet, at which we both glanced, "but my hands are free."

"Your hands are free. They've held this issue for a long time, and now they're free," I summarized, absorbing what he was telling me.

"Yes, they are." Now we were both looking and smiling at his hands with admiration. By God's grace we contemplated Charles's emancipated hands. So often in spiritual direction, we work with images. Many are from the culture, often our shared Christian culture. Having an image develop, with such particularity as the one to which Charles had come, felt as though we forever would be imprinted with it.

After some time, Charles said quietly, "It's peaceful to feel this. In the monastery I started doing centering prayer every day. This is how I often was left feeling in that experience, especially as it neared its end. I felt peaceful, contented." He was still looking at his hands.

Lifting his hands up in front of his face, he began turning them slowly, examining them. Then he looked at me and wondered, "So, now, what will these hands do? They are free. They can do many things." As he spoke, he spread his hands out before him, wider and wider, like wings.

My heart cried "yes" to what I was hearing. After he left my office, I asked myself if I had ever been in the situation Charles was describing. My most profound experience of unrequited longing was caused by infertility. My husband and I wanted a child and were unable to conceive one for six years. My prayer life circled obsessively around the issue. Trapped by my desire's gravitational pull, unable to land in its satisfaction or extract myself from orbit, I simply made small corrections in how I thought about it, modifying my view and mood without changing the predicament. I wondered if I would have ever come to an image like Charles's of placing the desire securely between his feet, thus freeing his hands. His hope seemed to expand, extending into new areas without abandoning the primary hope for marriage. Somehow his recent experience of God's liberating grace had freed him from the cage in which he had suffered from unrequited hope. He and God were together, and no longer seemingly at loggerheads.

Sitting in my rocking chair after Charles's departure, the candle smoke dissipating, I prayed about his outstretched hands. Then my eyes moved to where his feet had been. On what ground did those feet rest? On what ground did his desire lie, sheltered between those feet? Like Moses, I felt I ought to remove my sandals.

Note

I. See, for example, Heinz Kohut's *Self Psychology and the Humanities: Reflections on a New Psychoanalytic Approach*, ed. Charles B. Strozier (New York: W. W. Norton, 1985).

17

The God You
Believe In: Jim

Jim continued to minister in his church as well as in the hospital. Life seemed good, but later in that year something happened. For a number of months, Jim seemed to fight depression. He had very little energy and spent a lot of time sleeping. He arrived late for our appointments and was visibly changed, though I couldn't put my finger on exactly how. There was an impression of growing depletion, and between our sessions together I worried about him. Part of his normal conversation is humorous self-criticism, and his inability to motivate himself to energetic action was fueling the self-criticism. He would call himself a "slug" and joke about putting himself in the position where he repeatedly had to pull all-nighters while working on sermon and project deadlines.

I suggested that Jim get a medical check-up, thinking he also might need to see a mental health professional to determine what was afflicting him and whether he was in need of therapy. He told me he was not very aware of God, felt little hope, and barely was able to continue his work. We had a few meetings like this, and as Jim told me about his sleep-filled days, my concern grew.

Then one day Jim came to see me, and his energy level seemed high. He walked briskly into my office and took his seat, beginning to talk as I lit the candle.

"I did see my doctor, and the news isn't good," he announced. "They think I have a degenerative bone-marrow disease. Not cancer, but cancer-like. Incurable and, eventually, deadly. I can't believe it."

He burst into tears. I was riveted to my chair, shocked by his news. He seemed angry, and an outraged protest welled up in me.

"So what on earth is going on, anyway?" he yelled. "Here I am going about my business, doing my work, trying to follow it as it progresses. I'm feeling more and more confident as a minister and as though I'm in tune with the Spirit and with how I'm made to be. I've been doing my best. How can it be that just as all this is coming together, I'm going to die? It doesn't make any sense. It makes me feel like giving up, turning my back on everything spiritual, and just spending what time I have left enjoying myself."

"I'm so sorry, Jim." He saw the tears in my eyes, and more tears came to his own.

"Yeah, me too." He became quiet. He confided almost inaudibly, "It's pretty weird, but this has made me pray in ways I don't believe in praying." He laughed, through his tears. "I don't believe in a personal God who answers prayers, but I've been praying as though I do. I guess I'm in a fox-hole." He laughed again.

I said something about how very real the foxhole was and asked him to tell me about the prayers. As I listened to him talk about praying, I was praying: "Let Jim thrive, Lord."

"I'm praying for healing. I bargain, threaten, plead. I'm willing to become God's indentured slave for the duration, provided there's a duration."

"What is it like to pray that way?" I asked.

"It's funny. I see the irony in it, given that I don't really think of God as doling out good and bad health. I kind of get the feeling God sees the irony in it, too, and is a bit amused. But not in a mean way. I also feel compassion from God. But in my book, compassion is not enough. I want to be healed! I don't want to die. I want to be able to keep on in this journey I'm feeling excited about."

"Sure, of course you do. So much has been happening in your life and ministry, Jim. Such a sense of movement and future. And this diagnosis, it seems, has made all that even clearer to you," I suggested.

"That's true. I was feeling kind of discouraged and as if I was flailing around. I'd lost that sense of purpose I had several months ago. But this threat has brought it back in full force." Jim laughed, shaking his head. "More irony, I guess."

"It sounds as though when you're praying, you're praying with that clear sense of purpose and desire to live, and also praying with anger about the illness, begging God for healing."

"It's as if when something you have is taken away, or someone threatens to take it away, you suddenly are aware of how much it means to you. It's all of that. And you said it was more 'clear' to me. There is this funny way in which the experience *is* clarifying. If it weren't for the fact that I've been told I'm going to die, I'd be grateful for the clarity." Another rueful chuckle.

I asked Jim to tell me more about this God who shares the ironic view with him. It was one of the rare times when he spoke the name "God" freely. Jim uses religious language differently from the way that I use it, so I stretch to catch the nuances. I'm sure I don't always get it right, but he's patient with me in the process.

"There's a feeling of God with me, understanding and helping me to see. To see myself, even. Even a sense that God is sad I'm going through this. It's mind-boggling really. Ordinarily, I'd say that's as good as it gets and wouldn't think it could get that good. But in this situation, I want more. I want to live. I want God to be the kind of God so many people believe in, someone who intervenes and heals. Someone who listens to prayers and answers them." He finished the sentence forcefully.

Jim furrowed his brow and appeared to wrestle with his thoughts.

"Okay. I'm not sure I want that. I want that now, at this moment. But I don't really want a God who responds to the most eloquent request and rewards pious behavior. That gets me back to all that theology I rejected. If I go down that road, I'm right back with judgment, favoritism, fearful living. A God who killed his own son so he can look on us and not see our sin! That's a cruel God, and not the God I believe in." He seemed to have found some kind of traction in his thinking.

"Tell me about the God you do believe in," I encouraged.

"Huh. . . . That's harder," Jim said. "I believe that God is love and that the way we experience God's love is indirectly, through people, nature, beauty. I don't believe in God-the-harsh-schoolmaster, meting out rewards and punishments, making the sinner die a painful death and granting prosperity to the faithful. The part of me that feels threatened with disease wants to believe that and try to play the right game. But it's not what I ultimately believe. It would be too cruel."

I found myself moved by his altruism. He was willing to forfeit his chance of persuading God to heal him because he thought that such a belief rendered God cruel to sinners. In his way of thinking, to retain his belief in God as loving, he had to abandon hope of bargaining with God to grant him longevity.

What I said to Jim was, "You trust God's love."

"I guess I do," he admitted. "Trust is the problem at the moment. But, I guess, when it comes right down to it, I do believe that God is loving. . . . Ahhh," he sighed.

We sat in silence for quite a while, then, finally I broke it, saying, "Tell me what's going on now, Jim."

"I let myself back into that experience of God's compassion. This time I didn't fight it. I just relaxed into it, as though God were embracing me. . . . It felt like resignation. It also felt comforting, in a light way. I don't sense that I'm healed or that there's any promise that I will be. I just sense that God loves me and will be with me. It feels very sad, but also okay."

To tell the truth, I don't remember much of what was said after this. We both cried. I think I asked if I could hug him as he left, and I invited him to call me if he wanted to talk on the phone before our next session. I hoped I would have faith like Jim's when I found myself in a foxhole.

18

Praying over
Jerusalem: John

In part through fatherhood, as well as through his work in the factory, John was experiencing his world as larger than it had been. He had left the church of his employment and found the church of his heart. But it was not always easy to hold that view. It ran counter to the way he had been socialized, both in Christian circles and in the larger culture of professionalism. His parents, wife, and others who love him did listen to his experience, and their love for him was so solid that they responded to his sense of fulfillment, even though he was not living out his call to ministry in a conventionally demonstrable fashion. The struggle for legitimacy is as much an interior one for John as a social one—true for us all—and John's circumstances brought challenge to the fore for him as well as for those who love him and longed to see him serving as a minister in a church.

John's world expanded, but his living quarters remained small. Living in a one-bedroom apartment with his wife and children, he felt cramped. He didn't like how irritable he became in confinement, and we spent time talking about his experience of it. Eventually, I asked about any places of spaciousness.

"I go up on the roof in the early morning, if it's not raining or too cold. I take my coffee and sit there, my hands warming and the steam rising to my face." As John said this, he cradled a cup of coffee in his lap and smiled at it conspiratorially. "I also take a low-fat muffin, and the sparrows come a-calling. There's a sign on the roof that says 'Do Not Feed the Birds.' But, heck, if I don't feed them, who's going to?" He looked at me, laughing. "So I feed one, and that one sings. Then another arrives. So I know what the first one is singing, 'Come and see! There are muffins!'" He kind of acted it out, holding his coffee and casting quick downward looks at the remembered sparrows.

"So, you know what I think. I think that God has placed me in the company of sparrows. I've been invited by God to be a sparrow-feeder. It reminds me of what Jesus said about God's knowing each sparrow. As I watch each sparrow, I remember that God knows me, too. I'm a sparrow-feeder, and God's a John-feeder."

"Your morning sounds transformed by going to the roof."

"Absolutely. It helps me extend my antennae upward to God." His hands mimicked antennae growing up from behind his ears, and he made a kind of beeping, robotic noise as they did. Then he settled into a reflective pose and shut his eyes. He stayed that way for a few minutes, looking peaceful and smiling, as he held his warm cup of coffee. I didn't hear it, but I imagined him, Pooh-like, humming a little hum.

"I'm thinking about how many times during the day those antennae go up. It's not really under my control. I just suddenly am aware of God. That happens with the sparrows. It happened yesterday in the factory. A woman was there delivering something to the floor, and I was signing the order form for her. I was joking around and being friendly. Suddenly she said, 'My thirteen-year-old daughter wants to run away to Hollywood and become an actress.' Her daughter really sounded serious, she said."

John continued the story, "So I just said to her, 'It sounds like a story from a good book.' She immediately caught the reference: *The* Good Book. She said, 'Yeah, like the prodigal son.' She seemed kind of moved by the thought. I didn't say much more, but I told her I'd read a book by Michael J. Fox that told how very rough it can be for a young person to break into acting. Maybe her daughter would read something like that. But it was the connection with her, and the way we both were thinking about the story of the prodigal and his loving father—you know, without even saying it—that

really got to me and made me sense that God was watching us both. Knowing us both. Loving us. And her daughter."

"Right there on the factory floor," I observed.

"Right there. And it happens all the time. The other day a guy told me
how hard it is to sleep at night, so he drinks too much and then feels terrible at work in the morning. He felt really bad about it. Guilty. I listened.
I'm amazed he would tell me. . . ." John lapsed into a musing silence.

Eventually including me in his thoughts again, he recounted another
experience of God's ubiquity. "Even getting on the subway yesterday morning, I felt God. I was going to get in one door and decided to move three
down. I got on and there was a neighbor whose wedding I'd done, but he'd
moved away a year ago. It was great. And I wouldn't have seen him unless I'd
followed that nudge to go in another door," John said with great excitement.

"God seems to be everywhere," I commented. John nodded and then
sat again with his eyes closed for a while. He looked filled with bliss,
warmed by his coffee cup, and warmed by the sense of God's presence. I
watched the candle, enjoying the musing.

When he spoke again, John had moved onto another track. "I didn't
go to church on Sunday," he announced, looking squarely at me. "I didn't
feel like it. I argued with myself about why I should go, but, ultimately, I
didn't want to go, so I didn't. My wife was great about it, and she and my
kids went off to church together. I had the apartment to myself. I did laun-
dry and cleaned up. I wrote in my journal. I whistled. I thoroughly enjoyed
being alone and not going to church." He looked pleased with himself.

"Don't get me wrong," he warned. "It's not that I don't love my church.
I do. But I'm not known there. I might as well not be there. I don't make a
difference. The pastor knows my background. I've offered many times to do
various things at the church: teach, preach, help with the service. But I'm
never asked." John's voice, loud and staccato, conveyed indignation and anger.

"It's as though they don't see you," I commented.

"Maybe God is behind that," John suggested, slowly exhaling the words
and lowering the volume. When I looked questioning, he explained, "People see what they want to see, that's true. And they see what they can see.
But they also see what God allows them to see. So maybe God has not

allowed the people in my church to see me as a pastor. And their not see-ing has guided me. I went from closed door to closed door, until I found an open one. The open one is one I never would have come to if any of the other doors had been open. If I'd been able to find a church position, I never would have gone to work in the factory."

John continued to elaborate on how he understood his recent journey. "It's not that I heard from God. It would be great to be able to say, 'God spoke to me and told me to go to the factory,'" he said in a sonorous, mock-ing tone. "But God didn't. Or if he did, I didn't hear it. No. What hap-pened was he guided me. He guided me, in part through these people at church who didn't seize upon me as a pastor. God worked in my life through these other people who kept the doors closed. And so now I'm in a world with people I never would have known otherwise, hearing things I never would have heard. And—who knows?—maybe no one would be lis-tening to these people this way if I weren't there."

"The path becomes clear bit by bit, in part by doors being closed and people not responding to what you offer, and even in that—which has got to carry some disappointment—you have the sense of God's providence. A few minutes ago I thought you sounded angry. I don't hear that intensity now. You sound peaceful," I noted.

"I can't deny the anger. There's some anger with people, also with God for what feels like a red-herring call to church ministry. That's irritating, confusing. But underneath those feelings, there's a kind of peace. In that peace I see things come into view, new people and possibilities." John regarded his folded hands resting in his lap. I saw the play of feelings on his expressive face. "Most of the time I'm at peace with it," he told me. Then laughing, as though throwing a curve ball, he added, "Except when I'm irritated and cramped!" His face returning to seriousness, John assured me, "But, you know, God works with that, too."

"Really?"

"Yes. When I feel irritated and cramped, it's not as though I sense God wanting me to beat up on myself for it. Nor does God want me just to sup-press it. Does he want me to offer it to him? Does he want me to sit with it?" He looked at me inquiringly.

"Do you know?" I asked, thinking his question sounded rhetorical.

"I *do* know," John told me. "I sit with it. After a while I feel God with me in it. Then it doesn't really go away, but my view expands. I feel the irritation and crampedness of all the poor hard-working folks in the city. It's not that my feelings go away, but they are almost merged with the feelings of all the others like me. And I feel God holding us all, being with us all. It puts my life in perspective. Yes, I am cramped. *And* I'm not alone or unloved in it. It makes me feel love for the others who have the same experience. It's a rotten deal. Maybe?" He cast a questioning look my way before asserting, "But God cares about us."

John's transition to compassion from the experience of his own displeasure was moving to me, and I told him so. "It's as though your honest, unpleasant-to-sit-with prayer expands to include strangers," I observed.

"It does. Sometimes this happens when I'm walking home from the subway station in the middle of the night after the late shift. I'm exhausted. I feel sorry for myself. I think my life has become hard and not what I'd intended. Then I stand looking over the city, and I remember Jesus looking over Jerusalem. Remember? In Matthew twenty-three? Jesus looks over the city, laments the people's miserable condition, and says he wishes he could gather them under his wings like a hen does her brood. I think that as I stand there looking out at the lights." He paused.

Then looking at me, with damp eyes, John confided, "I know now what I didn't know before, about the suffering people endure and also bring on themselves. I know the sad stories. I know the hard work, the shattered dreams, the addictions and afflictions. I stand there feeling that my heart is going to swell out of my chest. I'm filled with God's love for the city. Sometimes I weep."

Listening to him and seeing his glistening eyes, I was filled with feeling for him and for the city he wept over. I thought about the door he had found, not an easy door to walk through. It took him to this lonely midnight commute between a crowded, noisy factory, and his family's tiny apartment. Yet, somehow by God's grace, through that door he had discovered the vastness of the world and the capacity of his own heart.

19

The Tree That
You Are: Melissa

Melissa, who in our shared prayer had forgotten to ask God why she suffers, is a consummate student. She has advanced degrees and approaches most subjects with earnest intellectual effort, as many of my clients and I do. As my director has done with me, I try to help people move out of their dominant mode of spiritual effort and notice God showing up in new and surprising ways. Because I know we often notice God through our less developed faculties, I don't always comply when cerebral directees ask me for "homework" or book suggestions.

"I'm wondering if you could give me a homework assignment I can work on before our next meeting," Melissa asked.

"I don't like to give homework assignments," I responded, hoping to discourage her from the request. "I want us both to be open to noticing how God shows up for you."

Melissa, cajoling, gave me a mischievous smile: "If you were to give me a homework assignment—just hypothetically, you understand—what would it be?" She leaned forward in her wheelchair, fully entertained by my quandary.

She won me over. "Okay," I surrendered. "Let's see. If I were to give you a homework assignment, it would be to imagine the tree that you are."

"Tree?" Melissa asked, sitting up sharply. "You want me to imagine the tree that I am?"

"Yes." I explained, "It's an exercise I do with groups in class or on retreats. I invite them into a time of prayer, asking God to show them the tree they are created to be and have become. Many make drawings. It's a way to play with God imaginatively, and it's often quite revealing."

"Okay," she agreed, enthusiastically. "I'll give it a try."

A few weeks went by before our next time together, and I found myself praying for her in tree imagery: for her roots to sink deep into God's grace, for her canopy to expand in the sunlight, for her to blossom and thrive.

When I went to see her, I had no plan to ask about the tree exercise. If it had been helpful for her, I expected that she'd mention it. We began in silent prayer as the candle flickered into high glow, and she spoke to me about a situation at her church. She was experimenting with different ways to enter into worship and was finding ways to experience God afresh in a familiar, unchanging setting.

When we were about halfway through our time together, Melissa said, "I thought about the tree." I was intrigued. "Yes. At first I thought it was going nowhere. I would enter into prayer and make a space for an image to emerge, but nothing came. It was blank. After a few days I wished you'd suggested a book to read." We laughed. "But I started thinking about the tree that I am, and then I remembered something. Years ago I went to a conference in another state. I had a free afternoon and explored the university campus. It was a beautiful, green campus, laid out in a completely accessible way. I could go everywhere."

The image formed in my mind of her zipping along past the lawns and gardens, sunshine filtering through leaves onto her golden hair.

"There was a tree there that was unlike the trees I'd grown up around in New England. It was the only one of its kind. I now think it was an oak, but I didn't know what it was at the time. It was enormous . . . and strong. It reached out broadly, and small plants grew in its shade. What really struck me was how twisted and gnarled it was. No branch reached out smoothly and straight. Every one twisted and turned and jutted out at a surprising angle. Yet it was green and alive. The predominant impression was one of strength and wisdom. Maybe even courage."

I could see the tree as she spoke.

"So, I found myself identifying with that tree. I, too, am not like the other trees. I am bent and not straight. Some people see me as warped, perhaps, like that tree was. But that tree was fully itself—alive, bold, unapologetic. Life pulsed through it creating leaves forming a canopy that sheltered other life. Birds and squirrels could rest and play in its branches. Its life was full, though different from the nearby evergreens." Melissa glowed as she described the tree.

I sat still, silenced by the poetry and glory of her story. I'm sure my feelings were visible, and she responded by going deeper into the experience.

"I spent quite a while with that tree. I saw in it a confirmation of me, a confirmation that felt as if it came from the One who had created the tree and me. Then I noticed a pine tree standing so close to the oak that their branches intertwined. I experienced that as a promise. For years I'd hoped and prayed that someday I would get married. I didn't view it as a strong possibility in my life, but it was the longing of my heart. Somehow I experienced that pine tree as a vision of my future husband. He wouldn't be just like me, but he would stand close and steady beside me, complementing me and joining my life.

"I hadn't thought about that for many years, but not that many years after that vision I did meet the man who became my husband. He is like that tall, straight, pine tree. I took a picture of the oak and the pine—I need to find it and show it to him." She settled more deeply in her chair, smiling dreamily and resting her head on her hand.

Tears pooled in my eyes and ran down the sides of my cheeks, feeling as though joy bled from my stretching heart. Scripture describes the experience of being "exalted" by God, which is similar to what some social scientists are studying today, using the term "elevation." I think that's what I was feeling with Melissa: "Elevation is elicited by acts of virtue or moral beauty; it causes warm, open feelings ('dilation?') in the chest; and it motivates people to behave more virtuously themselves."[1] I felt the dilation (and hope for the virtuous behavior).

"I'm almost speechless, Melissa," I whispered.

"It *is* beautiful, isn't it?" She beamed.

"It's amazing. Amazing grace. The grace confirming who you are as the oak, and the grace of the promise and its fulfillment. I'm overwhelmed," I managed to say.

"Yes, it is. It makes me feel completely at peace to remember it." It felt as though we were enveloped by that peace for quite a while.

At last Melissa spoke: "I feel just like that quote from Julian of Norwich: 'And all shall be well, and all shall be well, and all manner of things shall be well.' God is good. God is love. God knows me and cares for me. All I can do is breathe that in."

We both sat there breathing it in.

Eventually she broke the silence with a question, "So is that what you look for in this imagine-the-tree-that-you-are exercise? What else are you looking for?"

"Isn't that enough? You want more?" I asked, and we laughed. "I'm looking for the Spirit, really, and the surprise and truth that come with that. That's what I've experienced here with you. My impression is that in a totally surprising way you encountered truth, and that happened years ago beside the tree, and it's happening now as you're telling me about it."

"I like that: surprise and truth. It's both of those things. And it was the experience then, and is, again, the experience," she agreed. "The exercise makes my mind go to other aspects of the tree. I think about the life supported by the tree, the plants that grow in its shade and the wildlife that seeks refuge in its branches. When I think about that, I see another truth about my life. All my life I've been aware of the ways I rely on others to care for me and do things I can't do for myself. I've also worked hard to be independent and have entered a career where I care for others. As I think about the oak tree that I am, I see that I have nurtured my caregivers, sometimes. These days the people who come to help me get ready for the day are usually young women. Some of them are from other countries, and most of them are just starting their adult lives. They look to me as an older, more mature woman. They notice that I'm a Christian, and some of them are curious about that. I don't speak to them in an evangelistic way, but some of them have told me how they are aware that my faith affects my life, and they wish they could know more about it.

"With some of them, I've actually spoken about Christianity and what it means in my life. Some have gone so far as to read the Bible and go to church. They also watch my marriage, and some say they think it bears the mark of faith. . . . I think that some of those women are catching strength and life from my branches, like the creatures around the oak tree." Again she rested her chin on her hand and seemed to be looking at an image outside the room.

"That's a lovely image, Melissa. I really like that. These women see things in you that make them want to know more about what shapes you and sustains you. They see in you the things you said you saw in the oak: strength, courage, vitality, that unapologetic way of being yourself. They see that you are rooted and growing," I affirmed, aware that she was both looking at me and also at the oak she is.

With this tree exercise, my relationship with Melissa turned a corner. We had come to see an undergirding image of her that remained visible beneath all the physical pain and everyday trials. We referred back to it often. She found herself drawn to notice trees, much as I had been drawn, in a dark time, to float in water, imagining God's buoying grace around and beneath me.

Images hold more truth and surprise than can be expressed in words. So the oak tree, like the candle flame, became a reminder of God's faithfulness and love.

Note

I. Jonathan Haidt, "Elevation and the Positive Psychology of Morality," *Flourishing: Positive Psychology and the Well-Lived Life*, eds. Corey L. M. Keyes and Jonathan Haidt (Washington, D.C.: American Psychological Association, 2003), 276.

20

"It's Not about Me": David

One of the greatest challenges for David was to relinquish an agenda for spiritual direction. As the senior pastor of a large church, he was used to efficiency and organization. Spiritual direction struck him as self-indulgent if particular issues weren't being addressed and resolved, or an itinerary of spiritual tasks completed.

"Well, I don't know what I'm going to talk about today. I almost called and canceled, but then decided to come anyway," David began, easing into his chair.

"I'm glad you came," I responded. "It's good to see you."

"Thanks," he answered quietly. I could tell he was feeling uncomfortable with not knowing how to begin. Usually at such moments I feel the tug to offer a conversation starter, and sometimes do that if the awkwardness intensifies. I've learned, however, that it's usually good to wait because what eventually emerges almost always surprises me.

"I'm having a hard time at work again. People say things that drive me nuts. A man died at the church a month or so ago, and I can't believe what people said." He shook his head as though clearing out the baffling words.

"He died in an accident, an older man. He fell and died almost immediately. People said, 'I know he's in a better place now and wouldn't want to come back here.' They told another member of the staff, 'I see the power of your faith in the fact that you're not crying.' Wow. That one really bowled me over. That person's response was, 'Death doesn't bother me. I know this life is just the doorstep to real life.'" David shook his head even harder. "I believe in heaven—though I'm not sure what it will be like—but those responses seemed so cold. The man had died tragically. He left grieving loved ones who had had no warning that death was imminent. I liked the man. His name was Sam. I felt the grief myself, though I didn't know him well."

"It's so sad. Sam was someone you liked, and he died *at* the church?" I asked.

"Yes. I saw his body just after he died. It was awful. He'd been a warm, energetic person, one moment, and then, the next, he was a broken, empty shell." David's shoulders shook with grief.

"I haven't seen death happen often, but it always shocks me. I'm sorry, David. The change from life to death seems incomprehensible," I empathized. I felt I was talking too much, saying too little, wanting to communicate that I was with him.

Then he became angry. "Why do those jerks say the ridiculous things they say? How can they be so callous to the feelings of others? Why the platitudes and self-congratulation about faith in the hereafter? It drives me crazy!" David practically screamed. I was glad he could express such raw emotion with me. I experienced him trusting me with his feelings, trusting me not to say "ridiculous things."

Eventually, he explained, "This is why I sometimes feel least in touch with God at church. There's a way that some people conceive of God that's like a repellent force to me. I know that my job is to preach from and live out what I believe is true about God and what Scripture teaches. But especially in crises, this callous theology can be voiced. I'm left dumbfounded because I don't want to respond in a way that hurts the people saying these things. They're speaking from grief, somehow, even though it doesn't sound like grief to me." David sighed, stretching his long legs in front of him and crossing them at the ankles.

"So your care for them leaves you almost unable to speak. Tell me what your care for them is like."

"I do care for them," he confirmed. "I don't like their theology, but I know their stories. I see their lives. They try to be good and do what's right. They're sincere people of integrity. In this situation they were stumped. It was a very dramatic, traumatic experience for everyone who was at the church that day. They were threatened. So they moved into self-protective stances. What they said was really more about themselves than about the man who died. They believe that good Christians don't fear death but do trust in heaven. But death is scary. It's hard to stay with it without pushing back at it with life-after-death stories. I do see their fear. Under what seems like dispassion and platitude, fear is lurking."

"I can see why there would be fear. Sudden death is especially scary. It could have happened to anyone there. So close. One minute life, the next, death," I said, agreeing with him and wondering about his own feelings.

"Yes. That's right." He looked pensive and stopped speaking.

"And fear, David? Did you experience any fear?" I asked after some time had passed.

"I'm thinking about that. It occurs to me that my anger may have been my own distancing from fear. In my congregation I comfort the dying and bereft many times a year. Yet this time I had an unusually strong reaction. Maybe it's because death happened without warning and in my space, so to speak.

"But fear and reaction to Sam's death aren't the whole of my reaction. These kinds of theological statements bother me in nonfrightening situations, too, and increasingly so. That's an area of ongoing work for me."

David then shifted and moved back into the memory of the day Sam died. "I'm still wondering about my own fear. I know that the day after his death my sadness finally came out. At first I was in shock, trying to care for the people most closely affected and see that all was done that could be done for Sam and his family. But the next day I felt my sadness. Two women, secretaries at the church, talked to me about how they had been the first people to get to him. One held him and talked to him, comforting and holding him as he breathed his last breaths. The other got there a few minutes later and sat with his dead body, talking to him about her appreciation of him and her hopes for what would be next for him. They talked about what a privilege it was to be with him at that time. That really got to me. It was like the women at the Cross. So beautiful."

"Like the women with Jesus. Loving and faithful. You witnessed that," I said, noticing the circles of witnesses and thinking that I, too, was a witness.

"I saw their love and faith. And, you know, now that you say that, I see it. Yes, I witnessed it. They weren't pointing it out. They weren't saying, 'I have great faith. I have great theology.' They were just saying that it was a privilege to be with Sam as he died."

David sat in silence, looking at the wall behind me. Then, running his hands through his jet-black hair, flecked with gray around the temples, he softly confided, "The older I get, the more I'd like to be like those women at the Cross and not be the theologian, the one who talks about God. I'd like to *be with* Jesus, more than with theories of atonement and salvation."

"Tell me about being like the women at the Cross."

"You know I have trouble experiencing God sometimes. But more and more the way I'm most profoundly experiencing God is in other people. You said I witnessed the women's love for Sam. I did. I witness things in people all the time, things that don't get talked about but are essential to life. To faith. I witness the courage of people I visit when they're sick and dying. I see the people who come alongside them and care for them. I see people in great pain as they die, able to make jokes and take interest in other people. God is in that."

"You have the privilege of being there and seeing that. Of seeing God in that."

"Yes. It's a privilege. Like the women said about being with Sam. Even though Sam never regained consciousness, there was a great privilege in being with him as he died. God was in that. I have the same privilege and have been with people in my congregation when they died. When I'm at my best, I'm completely attuned to the person and whatever he or she is going through. I pray, and there is no effort in it. It's so natural that time seems to evaporate. I've sat with people for hours, with no awareness of time because I've been so engrossed with the person. Right then, there's no other place I'd rather be or other person I'd rather be with. I marvel at the person before me and how he or she is meeting what life is serving up. Sometimes it's someone talking to me about his or her life; sometimes it's being with a person as they undergo some undesired experience—illness, loss, death."

"Everything else falls away as you're with the other person," I said.

"Even I fall away, if you know what I mean. It's at times like that that I most experience God. It's as though I'm held by God. I rest in God. And God's strength and love move through me toward the other. Even when I'm just sitting there and not intentionally praying. It's as though I'm a channel for God's grace. At the time, I experience no exhaustion. It doesn't seem to be about me at all or about my resources, strength, wisdom, prayer power. It's not about me. Right?" David looked at me with some amusement.

"It's not about you?" I asked.

"No. It's not about me. It's through me. Maybe I'm necessary. Maybe I'm the one the other person wants to be there. But it could be someone else, too. It's about God's love being communicated. And that love is communicated to me through the other, too. Through the goodness, or faith, or endurance, or trembling honesty I have the privilege of witnessing." David spoke fervently.

"You don't feel alone."

"Right. I feel that God is there, and I am resting in God. It's as if God is the water buoying me so I can bear the impact of what is hitting me: the other's pain, death, grief. Because I'm floating in God, I can sustain the weight."

I thought, but didn't say, "Amen." Let it be. May David, and all of us, "float /into Creator Spirit's deep embrace, /knowing no effort earns /that all-surrounding grace."[1]

Note

1. Denise Levertov, "The Avowal," *The Stream and the Sapphire: Selected Poems on Religious Themes* (New York: New Directions Books, 1997), 6. Used by permission.

PART THREE

Fruition

21

Planted by
the Waters

In the later phases of spiritual direction with some people, I have the remarkable experience of seeing what a "long obedience in the same direction" yields.[1] I have seen the transformation of consciousness and lives as God is encountered, and faith is internalized, saturating every part of life.[2] The stories in this final narrative section show some of what I've been privileged to see.

In the professions concerned with the care of souls, the focus during the last century has been on helping people through difficulty rather than on cultivating well-being. Recently, some researchers have turned their attention to determining what makes for a good life. Two leading psychologists edited the millennial issue of the journal of the American Psychological Association, titled "Special Issue on Happiness, Excellence, and Optimal Human Functioning." Its introduction noted that "psychologists have scant knowledge of what makes life worth living. They have come to understand quite a bit about how people survive and endure under adversity. . . . However, psychologists know very little about how normal people flourish under more benign conditions."[3] That concern has led to the creation of a new and burgeoning field of "positive psychology." Classes in the subject now draw crowds of college students eager to study a subject that might make them happier.

Interest in the good life has been the subject of philosophical and theological inquiry for millennia. Psychology is now turning in the same direction, having spent much of its history employing a medical model concerned with diagnosis and treatment of illness. Words more common in the field of spirituality—such as "prospering," "thriving," and "flourishing"—have now entered the vocabulary of the social sciences.

Flourishing

Some social scientists have contrasted "flourishing" and "languishing" (a condition independent of mental illness). The former is characterized by psychological dimensions of well-being (self-acceptance, good relations with others, personal growth, purpose in life, environmental mastery, and autonomy) as well as by dimensions of social well-being (seeing society as meaningful, possessing potential for growth, on the whole acceptable and accepting, and themselves as able to contribute to it).[4] A Judeo-Christian view of flourishing might include those dimensions, yet they do not capture the spiritually relational core. Nor does the word "flourishing" adequately express the fruition that Scripture describes and that I see in my work with people of faith.

What fruition looks like in spiritual direction cannot be defined categorically, but it has to do with receiving grace and allowing it to work in oneself and through oneself into memory and into the world. It assumes various forms and expressions. Fruition is not a final achievement, a top rung on the ladder of ascent, or the final stage in successive accumulating stages of development. God seems no respecter of time and developmental expectations. As though due to spiritual tectonic shifts, grace from long ago can penetrate the present, and present grace sometimes shines into the past as we recognize God was present or, perhaps, that our hearts had been burning, beneath our consciousness, while registering God's presence.

The stories of our lives with God continue to unfold. What seems an ultimate summit over time becomes penultimate as more peaks come into view, often separated by steep, treacherous switchbacks that seem regressive. The journey image takes us quite a distance, yet it is complemented by the phenomenon of maturation; in my mind, as in Scripture, the images of journeying and growing complement each other. In a garden, a branch long embedded in the vine bears fruit more abundantly than a younger, greener limb. Seasons come and go with varying degrees of harshness that affect fruit-bearing. Yet the thicker branch weathers fluctuations more easily— may I claim more gracefully? I believe so. A kind of wisdom from experience lying deep in the wood provides resilience and grace, and in people manifests as trust. Trust is not blind certitude. Droughts will occur, and life will be hard. Trust is a willingness to enter the dance of life with eyes wide open. As one directee said to me in a time of great suffering, "I get tired of thinking about why or if God allows suffering. What helps me most is remembering God loves me. I remember his kindness." Faith, not certitude, is the stance that weathers drought.

Faithfulness begets maturity. Hadewijch of Brabant, a member of the Beguines, a thirteenth-century lay religious community of women, wrote about a vision in which she was transported to a tree-filled meadow. There she encountered a tree that represented human nature, its solid trunk symbolizing the soul.[5] As we grow in our relationship with God, our trunk thickens and strengthens. Rings form that hold our history: narrow ones from times of drought, wider ones from lush seasons. The accumulation of all these rings of various sizes thickens the trunk. Like many medieval women mystics, Hadewijch professed a soteriology (doctrine of salvation) that has to do with growing increasingly in love with God and with God's creation, and expressing it more and more fully. God's love flows through the person and into the world, as fruit-generating life courses through branches rooted in the vine of Christ.[6]

Fruition, in spiritual life, is not static. It is at times leaping, laboring, bearing, and persevering.[7] Sometimes it is merely, but attentively, waiting. Fruition is vital, and it is expected. We are meant to bear fruit. In our generativity, we are not alone. We don't create water, but as trees send their roots toward the stream, so we may stretch toward God, who sends the living water of grace to our roots. Trees are not passive, despite their subjection to the elements. In Scripture's garden imagery, we are planted, tended, and blessed with fruition. This is the prophet Jeremiah's vision:

> Blessed are those who trust in
>   the LORD,
>   whose trust is the LORD.
>
> They shall be like a tree planted
>   by water,
>   sending out its roots by the
>   stream.
> It shall not fear when heat
>   comes,
>   and its leaves shall stay green;
> in the year of drought it is not
>   anxious,
>   and it does not cease to bear
>   fruit.[8]

I bear witness to the truth of Jeremiah's vision. In a time of great grief, Grant was steadfast. In the face of unmet longing, Carl extended his roots to the stream and bore fruit. In a drought, Ruth was not anxious. Seared by heat, Melissa was courageous. Their trust was in the Lord. This stance of faith doesn't fall into an easy categorization as active or passive. It is what biblical scholars refer to as the "middle voice."

Abiding in Grace

Linguistically, we have lost the middle voice that lies between the active and passive voices. In using the active voice, one speaks of initiating an action. In the passive, one receives the action that another initiates. In general, the division between these voices is exacerbated in our culture: Lives are divided between long hours of workplace-striving, punctuated by vegetative reception of entertainment via television or the Internet. Even church services can divide people into performers and spectators.

An historic alternative to these familiar voices of activity and passivity is common in Scripture. In the middle voice, the person actively participates in the results of an action that another initiates. Eugene Peterson illustrates the three voices using the action of counseling: "I counsel my friend"; "I am counseled by my friend"; and, in the middle voice, "I take counsel."[9] A Christian worldview places us in God's world in such a way that we actively participate in the results of actions that another initiates. Our "trust is the Lord." I hear the growing timbre of the middle voice from those who sit across from me in the candlelight.

In John, chapter fifteen, Jesus' famous "I am the vine; you are the branches" speech, the branches that do not bear fruit are cut off by God, his father, the gardener. Those that do bear fruit are pruned. The life of faith is a life of voluntary formation as we accept Jesus' invitation to "remain in me." We "take counsel" and follow the one who invites us to do so. Spiritual directors confirm people in choosing God's direction and formation in their lives. This is different from a facile "I'm okay, you're okay" affirmation.[10] It is, rather, siding with the "better angels" of the person's nature, his or her middle-voice willingness to participate in God's grace.[11]

The stories that follow are works-in-progress, as each person represented here would tell you. Most of us would blanch were our spiritual directors to mention including us in a chapter about spiritual direction titled "Fruition." Our own stories are so close to us that we can't get the focal length necessary for a comprehensive view. Plus, we each know much more about ourselves than others, even our spiritual directors, do. We know what darkness lies in our hearts, leading to self-indulgence, neglect of the holy, failure of compassion. As Carl Jung wrote, "Even the enlightened person remains what he is, and is never more than his own limited ego before the One who dwells within him, whose form has no knowable boundaries, who encompasses him on all sides . . . as vast as the sky."[12]

We are finite and imperfect, *and* we live and move and have our being in God. Spiritual direction helps people hold onto those dual truths. My spiritual director often does so by extending both his hands palms up. We imagine that one palm holds my sense of despair or awareness of my flaws. In the other palm is my sense of God's immensity and love. My spiritual director then brings the first hand to rest in the second, and asks me what it's like to bring my desolation into the realm of God's grace. With his help, I remember my experience of God as loving, and I slip less frequently into theodicies. I also am better able to face my own errors, knowing that the

One to whom I confess them is forgiving. As the years have gone by, I have become more able, even on my own, to make that movement of bringing my personal reality to rest in the greater reality of God. More and more, I abide in God's grace. I have seen this same growth in the men and women who have come to see me for spiritual direction.

Fruit of the Spirit

A spiritual director sees growth, even, at times, when that growth is invisible to the directee. I have seen fruition in these nine lives described in this book. A spiritual director has a vantage that is precious. As one directee told me, "I run through the forest of my life, and you say, 'I see a tree.'"[13] I do, indeed, see trees. They are planted and rooted in God's grace, bearing fruit in the world. As they bear fruit, so I bear witness to them doing so.

Directors look on as hearts seek God, stretch, and grow. We are trained to notice and remember the "God stories" in another's life. When a directee is caught up in the stressful politics of church life and questioning how well she is doing as a pastor, the director remembers the resounding affirmation of that person's call to God's ministry. Connection with that call invigorates the pastor's love for those she is called to serve. When a directee is caught in the topography of emotional life, either in a valley and able to see only previous valleys, or on a mountaintop remembering only previous mountaintops, the director remembers the elevations that already have been traversed, anticipating continual altitude change as the journey progresses. That long view allows realistic hope and engagement with the life at hand.

Change takes place. Hearts learn to turn more reflexively toward God. What I call spiritual "immediacy" increases, as we more quickly recognize when we have turned from God and, therefore, are able to re-turn toward God. In psychotherapeutic work, many learn how to notice their "buttons," as in, "My family really knows how to push my buttons." Of course, all families do that, having had something to do with installation of the buttons. Therapy can help us learn what our buttons are and become more sensitive to them in order to extinguish old reflexive and unhelpful responses. With immediacy comes the possibility of conscious response before the gathering storm of resentment, depression, or retaliation breaks. It allows the possibility of seeing others as they really are instead of as extensions of ourselves or our family patterns. As a result, greater health infuses relationships.

This growth is also possible in our relationship with God. I have had the opportunity to see all nine of the people in this book (as well as many more) learn what tempts them away from God as well as what inclines them toward God. As we spend more time attuned to our lives with God, we learn which circumstances impel us away from God and what that feels and looks like. Talking to another who takes an interest in our spiritual experience allows us to narrate our lives, weaving coherence and meaning as we do. As we become familiar with our spiritual proclivities, we are more able to direct ourselves toward God and our better selves, even when we're in a slough of despond or a Siren-laden strait. This process is similar to training oneself to retain some lucidity even in a dream state, for the sake of steering the dream in the direction of hope, healing, or resolution.

For instance, a directee said to me: "I came home exhausted and couldn't do anything but drink wine and watch TV. But after an hour I caught myself. It was as though I saw myself through the window and felt pity on myself. I know that when I'm tired I'm most vulnerable to doing what I will regret later. That pity gave me the strength to pray that God would help me rest in him and would restore me. It helped. I was able to turn off the TV and go to bed early. As I lay in bed, I thanked God for helping me take the rest I needed. I felt cared for instead of like a used-up creature that needed to be anaesthetized out of my misery." Spiritual immediacy is a fruit cultivated by prayerful attention to one's self and to God, sometimes in the company of a spiritual companion.

Some fruition comes through the transformation of suffering. Without any presumption to understand the cause of suffering, mute resignation to it, or gratitude for having suffered, quite a few people claim to see that good has come from it. Some of these people have been my directees, and they have helped me witness that goodness with them. Some of the suffering has been wrenching and sharp, as with the sudden presentation of an incurable illness. Some has been slow and quiet, as with the gradual relinquishment of a long-held hope that had seemed essential for a happy life.

In the season of fruition, there may be the experience of enhanced night vision. Suffering may render the world dark, and certain forms of suffering include losing the sense of God's presence. As I have accompanied people through such times, I have seen some stand and wait for God. Just as on a very dark night turning off a flashlight allows one the gradual discovery of faint light from the stars above, so I have seen that kind of growing night vision in people with whom I've worked. Sometimes the light seems to come through the very places of suffering, as light shined through the resurrected Christ's hands onto the table where he broke bread with his grieving companions in Emmaus. So, too, in our lives, hope is extended to others as light shines through our wounds. One of my directees quotes Leonard Cohen's song *Anthem*:

> Ring the bells that still can ring.
> Forget your perfect offering.
> There is a crack in everything.
> That's how the light gets in.[14]

We learn to see the faint light that comes in through the cracks of our lives. This improved night vision helps us see others and attend to them, for the call in Scripture is not just to feeling better ourselves. We are to bear fruit by loving our neighbor, setting the captive free, giving food to the hungry, sheltering the homeless, loosing the bonds of injustice, clothing the naked. By doing so, we will be light in the darkness, well-watered gardens, and pilgrims guided by the Lord.[15]

I witness fruition in people with whom I continue to work and in some who have left our shared work and stay in touch with me. Even Ruth continues to shed light in the lives of those who loved her and were blessed as she bore witness to what faith allows. I carry in my heart the people I have known in spiritual direction. The relationship is eternal, the way any love relationship is. Sometimes one of their faces surfaces in my mind's eye and I feel as though the Holy Spirit is praying for that person through me.[16] Having been a recipient of spiritual direction, I know that the director lives on in the directee as well, as a person who shared a part of the road, a moment in the garden, and hope in things invisible to the eye.

Notes

1. Eugene Peterson borrowed a phrase from Friedrich Nietzsche for the title of his book *A Long Obedience in the Same Direction: Discipleship in an Instant Society* (Downers Grove, Ill.: InterVarsity Press, 1980).

2. See Alister McGrath's discussion of Christian spirituality in *The Journey: A Pilgrim in the Lands of the Spirit* (New York: Galilee, 2000), 10.

3. Martin E. P. Seligman and Mihaly Csikszentmihalyi, "Positive Psychology: An Introduction," *American Psychologist* 94, no. 1 (January 2000): 5.

4. For a review of this literature, see Corey L. M. Keyes, "The Mental Health Continuum: From Languishing to Flourishing in Life," *Journal of Health and Social Behavior* 43, no. 2 (June 2002): 207–22.

5. Described in Jane McAvoy, *The Satisfied Life: Medieval Women Mystics on Atonement* (Cleveland, Ohio: Pilgrim Press, 2000), 85, 94.

6. John 15.

7. Yes, I've mixed metaphors (or similes) freely here. Spiritual matters dwell in the domain of metaphysics so metaphors abound, each granting its own sightline.

8. Jer 17:7–8.

9. Peterson, *The Contemplative Pastor* (Grand Rapids, Mich.: Wm. B. Eerdmans, 1989), 103.

10. Philosopher Martin Buber and psychotherapist Carl R. Rogers once debated this distinction between confirmation and affirmation, Buber asserting that human nature is, at its core, in conflict. Encouraging the inclinations toward the good in another is what he called "confirmation." See Martin Buber, *The Knowledge of Man: A Philosophy*, ed. Maurice Friedman (New York: Harper Torchbooks, 1965), 166–84.

11. In Abraham Lincoln's first inaugural address as the Civil War loomed, he pleaded with Americans to heed the "better angels of our nature." Lincoln, *First Inaugural*, March 4, 1861.

12. Jung, "Answer to Job," vol. 11 of *The Collected Work of C. G. Jung*, trans. R. F. C. Hull (Princeton, N.J.: Princeton University Press, 1973), 108.

13. This directee has never heard my "arbor-anthropology."

14. Cohen, *Stranger Music: Selected Poems and Songs* (New York: Vintage Books, 1993), 373. Used by permission.

15. Isa 58.

16. Rom 8:26–27.

22

"To Whom Shall I Go?": Grant

In the maturing spiritual direction relationship with Grant, I was able to see the fruit of the Spirit's work in his life as well as the work of the Spirit in my growing understanding of spiritual direction. Grant's and my work shed light on how God's grace permeates the whole of life, and how grace is witnessed in the work of spiritual direction.

Some of the insights I've gained have been in the area referred to by psychotherapists as boundary maintenance. Psychotherapy and spiritual direction caution against "dual relationships," a form of boundary-crossing between caregiver and care-receiver. There are several rationales for caution. One has to do with power and authority. It's inappropriate to invite vulnerable self-disclosure from one over whom one wields power in another role or setting. So I tell my students I can't see them for spiritual direction while I'm still their professor. If I had a psychotherapist for a boss, I wouldn't seek therapy from him or her. It would be exceedingly painful to be fired by the person to whom I had told my most painful stories of rejection and my tenderest hopes of acceptance. I also would be loathe to reveal self-doubts to one responsible for evaluating my performance.

Another caution concerning dual roles has to do with dilution of the work. Continuing the example above, duality would compromise a boss's ability to be fully my boss or fully my therapist. My ability to receive therapy and directives from my psychotherapist-boss would be impeded by the confusing mix of relationships. The more the quality of the relationship is firmly delineated, the more pure, safe, and potent it can become.

A more common way in which roles can overlap in spiritual direction has to do with the personal and the professional. A spiritual director and directee may be part of the same congregation or have friends in common. With regard to that experience, there are no hard and fast rules, other than the clear absolutes against sexual contact, harm, and manipulation for personal gain.

As a practice, spiritual direction grew up in the context of communal living. Monks confessed to other monks with whom they lived, worshiped, ate, and worked. Martin Luther's spiritual director was a colleague and brother in the Augustinian order. Peter confessed to the one who had washed his feet. In many Christian communities today, a member of the community functions as a spiritual director by virtue of the community's acknowledgment of the *charism* (spiritual gift) that person bears. In some respects this informality in spiritual direction is refreshing in a world dominated by the strict professionalism and boundary-maintenance of the psychotherapeutic professions, at times accompanied by inflated pretensions to medical and scientific status.

In general, one proceeds with caution when the personal and professional lives of director and directee mix. It is usually advisable for the spiritual director to be sparingly self-disclosing at first, in order to allow the work to focus on the directee and give the directee as much room as possible for free expression without concern for the director's experiences or preferences. For instance, a directee may be able to speak more freely about his or her own health threat if he or she doesn't know that the director is a cancer survivor. The same is true about freedom to express political and other sorts of views. The time of spiritual direction should afford the directee the opportunity to speak openly without self-editing in deference or response to details of the director's life.

Too little self-disclosure, however, fans transference, the experience of curiosity about and projection onto the director. This can interfere with focus on the directee's relationship with God and the directee's experience of God as the true Director. As spiritual directors gain expertise, they become increasingly adept at modulating self-disclosure for the sake of the directee, occasionally sharing something that frees the directee to move deeply into self-reflection and honesty before God, and, at other times, not sharing something, thus allowing the directee more space for self-discovery.

In this age of information, few of us retain complete privacy, and we have less choice about self-disclosure. Many spiritual directors have public lives of teaching, lecturing, and writing. I've had directees "Google" me and come to a first session having read something I've written or knowing my upcoming speaking schedule and which lecture they plan to attend. We can, however, make some choices about boundaries.

In an inversion of the direction-in-community model of earlier times, some directors do not work with any member of their church. Others establish offices in cities away from the city in which they reside. Most of us navigate less boundaried waters, trusting grace, growing discernment, and sensitive conversations with directees about the significance to the direction work of outside-the-office interactions. My own spiritual director and the directees I work with all talk easily about these issues, and together we find ways of setting, changing, and evaluating boundaries. We aim for consciousness and dialogue in these matters, as in the whole of the direction relationship. My view is that this kind of realistic, thoughtful, and discreet mingling of lives is healthy for spiritual direction.

As with all ministries, those of us engaging in spiritual direction need to remember that we are watched by those who are aware of our work. What we write, say, and do affects others, especially those who are vulnerable to us. It is a sacred trust. The more honest we can be about our humanness, without necessarily revealing particular details of our lives, the less disappointed directees will be when they learn of our failings. Also, the more natural we are in this work, the less apt we are to suffer the roller-coaster ride from pedestal to pit when directees discover—as they inevitably will—that we are far from ideal human beings.

Grant and I learned to navigate our relationship as our lives began to intersect more and more frequently. He was asked to serve with an inner-city ministry to the homeless that I occasionally volunteered for. We discussed this and then worked together for a year, managing to keep our spiritual direction and ministry work separate and distinct. Occasionally, as part of the homeless ministry, we served Communion together. We didn't discuss this, but I experienced it with delight. I taught a course on contemplative prayer for New College Berkeley, and Grant attended. One of the disciplines I introduced was that of *lectio divina*, the ancient practice of praying with Scripture that has meant a great deal to me in my own prayer life.

Grant is an amateur biblical scholar, knowledgeable about primary and secondary texts, exegetical methods, and various interpretations. But praying with Scripture, allowing the Bible to open him to experiencing God, was new to him. He began experimenting with *lectio* before attending the retreat I led, and his experiences with it informed my teaching, just as my teaching informed his continuing praying with Scripture. He began to pray through the Gospel of John, word by word, verse by verse. The rule of thumb in *lectio divina* is to listen to a short passage slowly, multiple times, allowing one's mind and heart to be captured by a glimmer of the holy. That glimmer may be found in a word, a sentence, an image, a person, a feeling, a movement.[1]

Grant's immersion in the Gospel of John was a close encounter with Jesus. American Christians can have a sentimental understanding of Jesus—the Jesus holding children and lambs as pictured in Sunday school books. We sing songs about Jesus being our friend. We are moved by the Jesus who washes feet, comforts, restores life, and suffers out of love for us. Few dwell on the Jesus who curses a fig tree and excoriates religious officials (people a number of us may resemble more than we realize). Grant encountered this forceful, opinionated, uncompromising Jesus, and it wasn't comfortable. Face to face with Jesus, Grant saw his own hypocrisies and fears. He wondered whether he would have been a disciple or part of the crowd that was glad to eat the loaves and fishes but was reluctant to swallow the hard teachings. Would Grant have doubted a man who said, "I am the bread of life. . . . Those who eat my flesh and drink my blood have eternal life"?[2] Wouldn't a sane person think Jesus a megalomaniac, incomprehensibly suggesting cannibalism?

Grant fully experienced his doubts, honestly wrestling with them in our spiritual direction work. He mourned his loss of identification with the faithful disciples and demotion to the rank of common observer. What did he, a twenty-first-century American, think of a person who made such claims? Didn't they sound pagan and cultic? Grant withstood the temptation to move on to other more comfortable texts. With the courage of discipline, he remained with the sixth chapter of John as a vehicle for prayer, digesting what was put before him, and trusting that God was in the process. The work with him magnified my understanding of God, taking me where I had not previously accompanied another.[3]

"When Jesus feeds the five thousand, I feel comfortable sitting there and receiving from him. I feel a combination of contentment and awe. . . . I also am able to imagine myself as one of the disciples in the boat later on, experiencing the stormy night, being afraid as I watch the figure of a man approach across the water, feeling relieved to discover it was Jesus, and then, with him, arriving on land again."

"You've experienced quite a few feelings on this journey with Jesus," I observed.

Grant laughed. "Never a dull moment. Yes. Sometimes there's comfort, but there's always an edgy feeling."

"'Edgy'?" I asked.

"Edgy. Unpredictable. Even after receiving the bread and fish along with the other four thousand nine hundred and ninety-nine people and sitting there feeling content, when I stop to think about what just happened—I mean *how* it happened—I get agitated. Same with Jesus getting in the boat and all of us arriving safely on shore. It's great to know it's Jesus and to be on terra firma again, but when I pause to think about what has just happened, well, then . . . that's unsettling."

"I'd like to hear more about that agitated, unsettled feeling in Jesus' presence," I prompted.

"I've known for a long time that Jesus is fully man and fully God. I've accepted the resurrection and am not too ill-at-ease with the idea of a virgin birth. For years I've pretty matter-of-factly read and been preached to about the raising of Lazarus, the healing of lepers, and making Bartimaeus see. I won't say it's just been ho-hum stuff for me, but I don't stumble on it when I come across it."

"But now you're stumbling?"

"Hmm. 'Stumbling.' In a way. Because I'm taking the text so slowly, praying it, consciously digesting it with God, and imagining it, I have powerful emotional reactions that I don't usually have."

"And what do you make of that?"

"I think it's right. But it's not pleasant." Then, with emphasis, Grant continued: "Yes, it probably is right. Encountering the living God shouldn't be blasé. It *should* be provocative. Jesus shook up the status quo. There was a reason the religious authorities were outraged by him and he was executed." As I listened to Grant, I thought about how I, too, fall into a tame conception of Jesus that really has no Scriptural validity. "As I think about it," Grant decided, "I'm convinced it's right to be unsettled by this process of getting to know Jesus better. But it's not what I expected."

"No?"

"No, it's not. I thought I'd have an experience of greater intimacy with God. . . . Okay, I'm listening to what I'm saying here. Maybe this unsettled feeling *is* greater intimacy with God. Do you think?"

"Maybe. I find myself going back to your word 'edgy.' There's a coming together of things on this edge. Is that right?"

"Yes. There's the agitated, unsettled, sometimes even scared side of the edge. And there's also the contented side. Feeling happy after the meal, relieved to arrive on shore."

Having listened to him explore the unsettled edge, I invited Grant to get in touch with the contentment. He closed his eyes, and I thought about the kind of boundary psychologists call "ego boundaries." Grant has a firm grasp of his identity, coupled with a remarkable willingness to enter imaginatively into prayer that can be thought of as flexibility in his ego boundaries. He is able to take what is helpful from imaginative engagement and hold it in tension with other sources of knowledge (Scripture and doctrine, among others). His mind is a strong ally in prayer, allowing him to explore possibilities while at the same time maintaining the capacity to analyze what he experiences.

For some people, the boundary between reality and unreality is less clear and resilient. They can find themselves lost in imagination, unable to determine the difference between the two arenas of experience, and, in extreme situations, unable to exit the imaginative sphere easily. These imaginative exercises would not be helpful for people who suffer from weak, permeable ego boundaries.[4] They are also hard for people whose thinking is more concrete, who are not comfortable with imagination (for example, parables and metaphors might be challenging for people with more rigid ego boundaries). Most of us, however, know the experience of moving between the real and the imaginary and know that it is temporary and subject to our will. For instance, we've had the experience of waking from a dream and, for a period of time, having the dream images and feelings linger and mingle with our waking lives. At the same time, we maintain an awareness of what is real, and the lingering dream doesn't interfere with our functioning. We may even learn from the dream as it allows us to explore parts of ourselves not always accessible to consciousness. This is the kind of insight Grant received from praying with Scripture.

Grant opened his eyes, sat in silence, then, slowly raising his eyes to mine, told me about what he'd experienced: "Well, the edge is very real. I could move into the contentment, but then I would start to think about what Jesus had done or said, and I would feel the cutting edge of fear."

"What helped you move toward the contentment?"

"The contentment was strongest when I was looking right at Jesus, and especially when he was looking right at me. When he fed me, and when he was sitting next to me in the boat. Then I felt comforted by his presence. He was still a huge mystery, frighteningly so, but when I was close to him, his kindness and trustworthiness were what I registered most powerfully. But any time the distance grew between us, I felt fear and started to doubt."

"Important to notice."

"Yes. And I'm thinking about this with respect to a later part of chapter six, really the part that upset me a lot. The next day, after the trip across the lake, Jesus had a lot to say to the people of the area, the people of Capernaum." Grant took out his small Bible, the one he carries in his briefcase. "The people asked Jesus how he came across the lake, because they knew he hadn't gotten into the boat with his disciples. That's when Jesus started talking to them about him being the bread of life, and that they were supposed to eat him. They didn't get it."

"What's his first response?"

"He said, 'You seek me not because you saw the miracles, but because you ate the loaves and were filled,'" Grant read to me.

"That's interesting."

"Yes." Grant kind of squinted at me, seemingly wondering what I meant by that. "Then he went on about the meat that is everlasting versus the meat that perishes. He basically lost them. They didn't follow what he was saying, and they started to 'murmur.' They were losing faith in him, and he was not wooing them with miracles."

"What's it like for you when you're in this story?"

"I find myself moving away, too. Doubting, questioning, wondering. It feels cold. The contentment evaporates. I feel alone. I'm kind of disappointed and wish Jesus would reel me in. But he doesn't. He keeps on talking in this distancing, Sphinx-like way."

"Sphinx-like?"

"You know, in riddles. That's how it feels."

"You sound irritated by him," I suggested.

"I guess I am. I wish he'd be clearer, more pastoral, I guess." We laughed. "But there's more that I'm feeling, and I'm a bit afraid to mention it."

"Okay," I said and waited.

"I feel darkness. I don't know what to make of it. It scares me and makes me think I may be doing the *lectio* process incorrectly, or that it's not good for me somehow." He looked at me for help.

"Let's examine that," I proposed. "So, in the scene when Jesus is teaching, you start to feel separated from him, cold, estranged, even irritated and critical. That's in the scene. As you reflect on it, you feel some doubt about this form of prayer. Is there a sense of darkness in both positions, that of you in Capernaum, and you in Berkeley, both?"

"Yes. I feel it both places. 'Estranged' is a good word for it. It's not the whole of it, though. Some of the darkness is that of separation, estrangement. But it also feels as though the darkness itself is a force, not just an absence. I'm not sure what I think of that theologically. In opening myself to God, am I also opening myself to some evil force?"

"It's frightening to think so, isn't it?" I asked. Grant nodded. "There are many things I don't know the answer to, Grant. I'll tell you what I do know, though. I believe that Scripture takes evil seriously. Jesus went from the baptismal experience of the heavens opening and God blessing him, to the wilderness experience of being tempted by Satan, resisting, and then being comforted by angels. He seemed to experience these personal forces of good and evil that we aren't ordinarily aware of in our daily lives. So I wouldn't write off the possibility of your encountering some of these forces when you spend time in close proximity to Jesus. However, Jesus himself spends no time trying to become better acquainted with the evil forces, nor, for that matter, does he give much attention to angels. He invites us to get to know him, and his Father through him, and to invest our time in loving other people."

I prayed to be helpful as I spoke, and saw how closely Grant was following all I said. In those moments with Grant, I moved into more of a teaching role, and it felt right. I am a teacher, and I teach spirituality. Sometimes it feels that offering that part of who I am is helpful in direction. Not to offer it might be less than generous.

As Grant listened intently, his eyes meeting mine, I affirmed, "I believe that Jesus is the light, as John's Gospel claims in its opening verses. The light shines in the darkness. To seek God in the darkness, whether it's darkness we feel inside ourselves or darkness we experience as external, is an act of faith, hope, and love. The darkness is real, and so is the light." Wondering how Grant was doing, I drew him out: "I'm talking a lot here. What do you think about what I'm saying?"

"It sounds right. I do believe that good triumphs over evil. It's just acutely uncomfortable to feel the presence of evil and to feel it when I'm feeling estranged from Jesus," Grant acknowledged, holding his hands tightly and looking strained.

"I wonder if there might be a causal relationship between the two experiences, rather than just an incidental one."

He looked at me quizzically, and I pondered whether I, too, were sounding Sphinx-like. "Okay, let me see if I'm following you here. You're suggesting that I'm feeling the presence of evil because I'm feeling estranged from Jesus? I wonder. . . . It also seems as though being near Jesus is what brought on this experience of evil. Hmm. Let me move into the experience again." I nodded encouragement.

Grant closed his eyes and spoke: "Okay, I can imagine Jesus speaking these riddles to the crowd. I feel my own revulsion. In that I feel darkness inside me. That's interesting. The darkness is in myself. It feels cold and hard. A bit angry. But not as scary as the darkness I feel outside me. And that's a couple of kinds. There's that creepy, eerie kind of darkness. But I also feel the angry energy of the crowd. I find myself on guard, anticipating the crowd veering out of control and toward riot. That makes me worry about my own safety."

Grant sat silently for a minute or so, seeming to breathe more easily. . "Okay, I now am worrying about Jesus' safety, too, and, as I do that, my interior darkness lightens. I start to feel my affection for Jesus. I'm not really hearing the strange words he's saying, but I'm just looking at him and seeing the man I've come to love. I want to protect him."

We sat with that for a while. As Grant showed strong emotion, I offered a silent prayer of gratitude. Entering into an experience with evil intimidates me and triggers my desire to protect the directee, which usually takes the form of teaching. With time and experience, I am learning to trust this process. What I hope to do is rest in God, knowing there's nowhere we can go that is beyond God's presence. At the same time, I want to make myself attentive, available, and responsive to the directee, so he or she feels accompanied by God and by me. I learned about God's faithful presence in our lives and our imaginations as I witnessed God accompany Grant as he prayed in my office.

As Grant continued in silent prayer, I prayed, also silently, what I could remember of Psalm 139:

> O LORD, you have searched me and known me.
> You know when I sit down and when I rise up;
>   you discern my thoughts from far away.
> You search out my path and my lying down,
>   and are acquainted with all my ways.
> Even before a word is on my tongue
>   O LORD, you know it completely.
>
> You hem me in, behind and before,
>   and lay your hand upon me.
> Such knowledge is too wonderful for me;
>   it is so high that I cannot attain it.

Where can I go from your spirit?
    Or where can I flee from your presence?
If I ascend to heaven, you are there;
    if I make my bed in Sheol, you are there.
If I take the wings of the morning
    and settle at the farthest limits of the sea,
even there your hand shall lead me,
    and your right hand shall hold me fast.
If I say, "Surely the darkness shall cover me,
    and the light around me become night,"
even the darkness is not dark to you;
    the night is as bright as the day,
for darkness is as light to you.[5]

Interrupting my reverie, Grant asked, "Do you remember the next part of the story?" I shook my head.

Refreshing my memory, Grant said, "Jesus then spoke just to the disciples who expressed some criticism of him for saying such hard things to the crowd. Jesus seemed angry with them for this and said, I imagine with indignation, 'What? Does this offend you?' And some of the people who had been his disciples left him at that point. When I read this earlier and prayed it, I identified with those disciples, the ones who left. After spending time with it just now, here, I felt my love for Jesus and knew I'd stay, even if he was completely incomprehensible to me. When he asked, 'Will you go away, too?' I know now that I'd say, as Peter said, 'Lord, to whom shall we go?' It's not about the teachings per se; it's about the person. I can't leave him. Even when I feel angry at him, I love him."

Grant shrugged, indicating his powerlessness to do anything other than choose Jesus.

"So, in response to your comment about causality," he continued, "I do think that being near Jesus ups the spiritual ante, so to speak, and I become aware of forces of good and evil. But being turned toward him, watching him, making eye contact, leaning into him, moves me away from the darkness. From darknesses of all kinds: inside me, in the crowd, and whatever independent force of darkness might be present. It's good to know.

"But," he said forcefully, casting a sharp look in my direction, "it does mean that these *lectio* exercises are for real! It's not make-believe, not a Disneyland ride. It's only the strength of my longing for God that makes me willing to undergo this." He laughed. "I guess that's what Peter was saying, too." In an exasperated voice he quoted, "'Lord, to whom shall I go?'"

Then, shrugging again, he said, "There's simply no one else to be with." And with that, Grant let me know that our time together was at an end.

Grant and I sometimes talk about the experience of our work in the context of overlapping lives. I'm concerned about the temptation I experience to remain in a teacher role, a concern not limited to my relationship with Grant. He doesn't see it as a problem. I want to stay alert to difficulties, but my primary experience is one of positive transference between the forms of encounter we share.[6] When Grant walks into my office, I remember the joy I've had seeing him serve Communion. With most of my directees I hear about their love of others and their loving acts, but I don't get to see them in action. I feel blessed by seeing Grant's faith enacted in the world. The transference flows in the other direction, too; when I see him serving, I'm reminded of experiences of God that he's told me about, and the pleasure of the memory seeps into my worship. In addition, his *lectio divina* prayer experiences inform my own engagement with the practice, even whet my appetite for it, and help me in my teaching and spiritual direction work with others.

Shortly after the session I just recounted, I saw Grant serving others, and the sight of him evoked the sense of Jesus looking at me, asking if I wanted to leave or stay with him. In Grant's and my continuing relationship, I experience God's unfolding, surprising grace.

Notes

1. For example, another person with whom I work spent a year or more savoring the beginning of Genesis: "[T]here was darkness over the deep, and God's spirit hovered over the water" (Gen 1:2), *The Jerusalem Bible*, gen. ed. Alexander Jones (Garden City, N.Y.: Doubleday and Company, 1966). Each word was a window through which she saw God, herself, and the dance they shared. The Scripture forced certain recognitions that stung, but she received them in the context of hope and love. She saw that no matter how deeply she went in her self-examination, God's Spirit

was hovering there with her. For me, the words "deep" and "hovered" still reverberate from our hours together and come to mind every so often when I need them, a lingering gift from my year with that woman.

2. John 6:35, 54.

3. The sixth chapter of the Gospel of John contains the miracle of Jesus creating enough food to serve a meal to a crowd of more than five thousand people, followed that night by the miracle of Jesus walking on the Sea of Galilee to join the disciples as they rowed across the sea to Capernaum. Most of the chapter is dedicated to Jesus' teachings about who he is—the Bread of life, the Son of man, the One sent from heaven by the Father to give his life for the world. Many were willing to eat the bread he offered, but more and more turned away from Jesus as his teachings challenged and disturbed them. Ultimately, though also challenged by teachings, the twelve disciples remained with Jesus, Peter affirming Jesus' identity as the Christ, and Jesus predicted that even among these twelve one who was "of the devil" would betray him (v 70).

4. On rare occasions as another person has talked, I've noticed myself slipping into a warm, nearly somnolent state. Over years of working with people one-on-one, I have come to think of this as my response (countertransference) to another's permeable boundaries. Somehow the other's world reaches out to engulf me, and, therefore to resist the allure, I sound a warning to myself. I actively counsel myself to remain alert to what is happening, and direct my attention to God.

5. Vv 1–12.

6. In psychotherapeutic theory, the experience the client has of transferring understandings and feelings from relationships in his or her life onto the relationship with the therapist is referred to as "transference." The therapist's experience of feelings evoked by the therapeutic relationship and its transference is referred to as "countertransference." Here I'm using the word "transference" in a nonclinical way, as one would refer to any transfer of knowledge from one domain to another.

23

Deep Struggle,
Deep Calling: Jim

Several years have passed since Jim received his life-threatening medical diagnosis. The diagnosis stands, and he's pursued a number of difficult treatments. Sometimes his spirits flag, understandably, and his energy level fluctuates with the vicissitudes of the illness and its treatment. He's had times when he can barely walk because of treatment-induced neuropathy. At other times, he has the wherewithal to participate in bike-a-thons for cancer research.

Though not in a synchronized correlation with his physical state, Jim's mood also varies. There are times when he is so self-critical that he ridicules how he speaks in spiritual direction. "Well, there goes another thought irretrievably lost on a side rail," he might say. On such days he is often late to our appointment, his lateness then becoming another factor in his own poor opinion of himself. Surprisingly, his bad mood seldom turns toward others, including some seemingly callous medical personnel with whom he must associate regularly. He notices their lack of care, but is more apt to tell wryly funny stories about them than fault them outright. It strikes me that his pastor's heart is always present for others, though not necessarily warm toward himself.

As Jim's struggle for life has deepened, so has his calling. In multiple settings he is a minister, even if he's officially designated "patient" or "customer."

The resonance of his calling is even more evident, however, in settings where he is, indisputably, the minister. Then, the desire to speak what he understands to be the truth bubbles up through layers of physical exhaustion and emotional despair. Even when he's spent a sleepless night experiencing discomfort and anxiety, he assumes the pulpit with a word to speak.

"I want to tell people that if they disavow faith, I don't understand why they come to church. Frankly, I don't understand what helps them get up in the morning," Jim told me, on a day he had arrived late to my office, flagellating himself for the waste of much of the day. I wondered to what degree he was speaking about what gets him up.

"You talk about those who don't have faith. Are you saying that your faith helps you get up in the morning?" I asked.

Jim laughed a kind of snorting ironic laugh. "Yeah, right!" He slapped his hand on the arm of his chair. "Just think how much of the day I'd miss if I didn't have faith. As it is, I get to see the sun for, oh, maybe six hours a day."

"Even so," I pressed, "it sounds as though you feel that faith makes a difference there."

"Yes. It makes a difference. How would I get up at all if it weren't for that? Given this disease, how would I continue on at all if the sun didn't rise and there weren't the sense that what I do matters?"

I echoed, "The sun rises, and what you do matters."

"I think it does. It feels as though it does—not always in a big way. I can go on endlessly, you know, about how I don't do what I ought to do, but, yes, at the end of all my excuses, tangents, and qualifications, I do believe that what I do matters. That my life matters." As Jim said these words, it was clear he was getting in touch with feelings that lay underneath the anxieties and discouragement.

"Your life matters. That's a statement of faith," I claimed.

"It is. I feel in the deepest fiber of myself that it's true. It's not only true about me, it's true about every person. It's true about the homeless people I see in the parking lot near my office. It's true about the unconscious person in the intensive care unit. It's true about political leaders I can't stand. Each of us matters. Each of us makes the world a bit different because we exist. Each of us has something to contribute. I'm sure of that, and that's what I want to tell people," Jim made this avowal, nodding and looking at me with intense conviction.

"You light up and exude vitality when you say that, Jim," I observed, thinking, as I often did with Jim, of Irenaeus's affirmation that the life of the fully alive person is the glory and vision of God.[1] In Jim, I saw that fully alive vision of God, and I was thankful for the days, months, and years ahead of him, now that his disease had been, painfully, sent into remission.

"It's what keeps me alive. It gets me out of bed, *and* it keeps me alive. When I think I should throw in the towel on my work, call it quits, retire, and just enjoy my final years, I realize that there's no joy like the joy of my work," Jim asserted, again nodding firmly and accentuating his words.

We stayed with Jim's sense of joy. I had greeted a sheepish, self-critical man at the door and now saw one emanating confidence and enthusiasm. Jim has faith. I find that its pulse is deep and steady when I'm able to attune to its sound. The quiet of our time together enables us both to orient toward that pulse and register its constant throb.

"Your joy reminds me of Frederick Buechner's definition of calling: 'The place God calls you to is the place where your deep gladness and the world's deep hunger meet.'"[2]

Jim nodded. "I know that quote, and I do sense that calling. There's an extension of me toward the world's need, and in that stretch of my heart I feel joy. I feel anxiety, dread, resistance, and all the usual demons, too." He laughed. "But I also feel joy."

"You're connected to those who are in need, to your deepest longings, and to the One who calls," I ventured.

"There's a kind of intimacy in it, I realize, when you mention those different connections," Jim agreed, turning the idea over in his mind. "It also connects me with the faith of my childhood. I rediscover the boy I was, who loved to sing the hymns in church, even after I could no longer agree with the theology in the sermons. When I sang the hymns, I had that connection with God, with myself, with the communion of saints. It was joyful and peaceful. I felt whole."

There's a feel of Sabbath to spiritual direction. We enter into the rest God blessed and called "holy," a time of reflecting on the wholeness of creation and of union with God. In Hebrew, Shabbat means "stop," and it also connotes completion.[3] On the Sabbath, Jews say, *"Shabbat shalom."* Sabbath peace, wholeness, completion. When I hear it, I imagine God, old and grizzled like a Jewish patriarch, leaning down toward me, his forefinger held to his lips, saying, "Shhhhhh. Slow, stop, sit . . . savor the time."

In that moment with Jim, I felt that expansive Sabbath rest, a relishing rest in which I was grateful, aware of how fully grace imbues Jim's life. He lives with a serious physical illness and persistent self-doubt. Yet he is called by God and is assured that he matters. He is a herald of the good news that we all matter. That calling flows through him to the world.

Notes

1. Irenaeus [180 CE], *Adversus Haereses*, bk. 4, chap. 20:7 (see http://www.new advent.org/fathers/0103420.htm).

2. Buechner, *Wishful Thinking: A Theological ABC* (San Francisco: HarperSanFrancisco, 1973), 95.

3. I recommend Abraham Joshua Heschel's book *The Sabbath: Its Meaning for Modern Man* (Boston: Shambala, 2003).

24

The Greatest of
These Is Love: John

D o you know the children's book *Fortunately* by Remy Charlip?" John asked, settling his infant girl in her car seat next to his chair in my office.[1]

Transfixed by Lily's sweet presence at our feet, I had trouble focusing on John's words, slipped out of the stance of spiritual director, and forgot to begin our time in prayer. "What?" I mumbled, called out of my musings.

"The book is a long string of alternating events described with the refrain: 'fortunately' and 'unfortunately,'" John explained, and, referring to Lily's big brother, noted, "It's a book Christopher and I read together."

"I don't think so," I responded, trying to keep my eyes on John instead of wandering to the sleeping child. "I don't think I've seen that book."

"Well, it's great. Christopher and I love it. We've read it many times. Fortunately, I go up in an airplane. Unfortunately, I fall out of it. Fortunately, I'm wearing a parachute. Unfortunately, it doesn't work well. Fortunately, I land in a haystack. Unfortunately, there's a pitchfork in it . . . on and on. So much like life. And we've developed our own variations on it: Unfortunately, I have to wash my hands in the evening. Fortunately, I get to eat dinner!" he chortled with glee.

I could tell that John had much to say and was eager to do so. We chatted a bit and then I lit the candle, finally remembering, "We light the candle to remind us that God is here with us," and I added, "redundant as the reminder seems, with Lily at our feet." John smiled at his sleeping baby and moved into a long time of prayer. Expressions moved across his face, sometimes he whispered words of prayer. I was struck by the beauty of the father praying over the oblivious child. John had prayed over San Francisco as Jesus prayed over Jerusalem, and now he prayed over his child as God prays over us and all creation. That thought hit like a bolt, and I wondered how I would be able to listen when he spoke.

Lily was settled asleep on the floor, so John was free to follow his thoughts. He reverted to "fortunately" and "unfortunately" and told me about the changes having another child had necessitated. After several months of maternity leave, his wife had returned to her demanding job, which provided the bulk of income for their family. John's work life had to change to accommodate an infant in their home, which, he emphasized, was a *small* apartment.

"Fortunately, my work life is flexible. I can take some part-time jobs at night and on weekends when my wife is able to be home with the kids. That helps. Unfortunately, I've had to leave the factory work. I was able to squeeze in shifts before Lily's birth, but can't now. So, fortunately, I have friends who own a restaurant, and I've been working as a waiter there. Unfortunately, it means there's not much time for our family to be together. But, fortunately, I'm really enjoying the restaurant, now that I've got the hang of it." He looked at me pointedly and, gesturing like an orchestra conductor, said, "So, you're catching the rhythm? Fortunately, and . . . ," cutting an arc through the air with his hand, "unfortunately, and . . . ?"

"Fortunately," I chimed in.

"Right. Back and forth it goes. Each swing presents new possibilities. This season as a nearly full-time father has its fortunes and misfortunes. The evenings at the restaurant are among the fortunate-lys."

I invited John to tell me more about the restaurant, a job I'd heard about only briefly in the past. "I love the food. It's delicious. The chef owns the restaurant and has exquisite taste. The flavors and smells of the restaurant, as well as the food presentation and overall ambience, seep into people and into me. I love being able to serve people and see their growing contentment as they surrender to the experience. That's a big part of it for me, seeing people's joy as they eat and let themselves just *be* for a few hours.

"Last weekend a couple came in, and they seemed very happy together, even giddy. I was kidding around with them and everything seemed to glow. The woman said, 'You pick the food and wine for us,' and so I did. I ended up serving him the fish and her, the beef. It was kind of counterintuitive— you know?—since we think of men being more the red-meat eaters. They looked startled initially and then thrilled. It was right. I loved being able to play with them, read them, and then delight them." John spoke with rapture on his face.

John often quotes Scripture to me, and what came to my mind was the scene in the Gospel of John when Mary washed Jesus' feet with expensive ointment and "the house was filled with the fragrance of the perfume."[2] I mentioned that story, and we remembered it together as the candle flickered and Lily slept. There was something fragrant and filling in John's restaurant work. He was a caregiver, not merely a waiter. The couple saw that and saw him, having the eyes to see.

Soon Lily stirred and expressed her displeasure. I am familiar with this experience in my office. A number of people bring infants to spiritual direction, and a few brave souls have brought toddlers (usually not a second time). The parents arrive heavy-laden at my third floor office, and as I open the door I see my directee turn, stoop, lift, and ferry up a load of equipment from the landing below, all the while balancing a baby on the hip. Parenting requires a quartermaster's organizational skills, and John had them.

Most child-accompanied directees are nursing mothers. John has been one of the few men to bring a child to my office. I learned much from watching him. The inability to breastfeed offers challenges (unfortunately) and opportunities (fortunately). When Lily drank from the bottle John offered, it seemed a more conscious, interactive exchange than the rooting, dreamy experience of breastfeeding, which so easily flows into sleep. They maintained lively eye-contact throughout the feeding, and John alternated burbling words of inquiry and comfort to her while recounting his life to me. I felt I was navigating a hang-glider through various thermals, sometimes rising on a warm rush of air, speed slowing and feeling nearly weightless as I observed the father and child, only to enter a cooler patch and be thrust headlong into the invigorating onrush of air as John picked up the thread of his narrative. Fortunately and unfortunately, John's turning to feed Lily had ended the story of the restaurant meal. We moved on, to what I don't remember.

When John and Lily left my office, I sat back down in the chair I had been sitting in during our hour together. I closed my eyes. Smells mingled. There was the sharp scent of the extinguished candle. There was the pungent odor of Lily's soiled diaper and a trace of the milk that had preceded it. My nose registered activity while my ears felt the pulsing silence. As I breathed it all in, I felt that my house, my body, was filled with life's earthy fragrance.

John's life was full. Among other part-time involvements, he was training to be a spiritual director. He had begun the three-year training shortly after we began working together, and was in a fine program with requirements that fit into his multifaceted life. Surprisingly, I heard little about that aspect of his life during most of our years of work together, but toward the end of our spiritual direction relationship, I began to hear more.

With little Lily in their lives now and their apartment full to bursting, John and his wife thought increasingly about moving east, nearer to family. John searched the Internet for bed-and-breakfasts for sale, thinking they might start a retreat center, a place where his growing love of hospitality, culinary caregiving, and spiritual direction could be expressed. His wife circulated her resume, and together they prayed and weighed possibilities. It was clear to me that our season together was nearing an end. Fortunately and unfortunately, I faced the prospect—the move seemed so right for John, and I would miss him.

At family gatherings on the East Coast, John and his wife's families let them know they would love for them to move closer. They loved the children and wanted to watch them grow. John was the family pastor and had "married" his brothers. (Being nonclergy I never get over the humor of that use of the word "marry.") He had baptized cousins' children. He also had a more informal pastoral role in the family, listening to people's confidences and questions of faith. He was more and more a spiritual director. There was a sense that the transformation made possible by John's sojourn in San

Francisco was nearly completed. Fourteen years earlier he had arrived as a single pastor and moved into his one-bedroom apartment near the church, having driven cross-country without a hitch. Except that he ran out of gas a few blocks from the church before participating in his first service there. He remembered that as a foreshadowing of the difficult relationship he had with the church.

John's career path had changed from what he had thought it would be, but over the years he had married, had children, and his ministry expanded across the city into byways of ministry he had never dreamed of on the East Coast.

John brought Lily to his appointment with me throughout the first year of her life. One day he arrived with her wide-awake and clasping toys in her nearly one-year-old hands. No more the sleeping babe, she flirted with me, displayed her ability to elicit noises from various objects by banging them, and began to explore my office. John and I put small objects on high shelves, and the candle was moved to my desk. I assumed responsibility for watching Lily as John moved into prayer and our session began.

"Amen," he exhaled after a few minutes, causing Lily to look up at him from my shoe which she'd been examining.

"Well," John began, "we're moving east. This will probably be our last session because I'll be in the throes of moving for the next four weeks." While I was trying to absorb the sudden arrival of what I knew had been on the horizon, he handed me a gift. I opened it and discovered *Fortunately*, the perfect commemoration of our years together, communicating John's wisdom, humor, and season of young fatherhood.

As we talked about our years of sitting across from each other, attending to God's presence in his life, an odor began to waft from the direction of Lily's crawling explorations across my office floor. Our attention turned to her, and we saw her move from object to object, sniffing each one she encountered. John laughed and said, "No, you're not going to find the smell there. You can't see it. It's following you. You're the source of the stink!" He turned to me and twinkled, "A parable."

Laughter continued as I watched him lovingly change Lily's diaper, cradling her head with each turn he gave her body and talking to her soothingly, playfully, the whole time. I thought about what an excellent spiritual

director John was becoming. The years of ministry-in-the-world had rein-
forced his natural inclination to love people through their blunders and
stench. I could see him sitting beside another soiled person and saying, as
Jesus did with the Samaritan woman at the well, "What you say is right.
You've had several husbands and the man you call your husband is not your
husband. You're the source of the stink, and you're forgiven. I'm here to
offer you something from the One you're looking for. Here, receive some
living water."

St. Paul wrote about faith, hope, and love, calling love the greatest of
these.[3] This teaching comes in the middle of passages about spiritual gifts
and establishes the roots from which the variously gifted community of
faith grows. Time and again, the Bible returns to the foundation of love.
During Jesus' ministry, when a person's faith wavered or shame and guilt
threatened to extinguish hope, Jesus compelled the person to look at him.
Peter tried to walk on water, started to sink, and, at last, regained his foot-
ing when he cried out to Jesus, who grasped his outstretched hand. In the
garden of the empty tomb, Jesus asked Mary whom she was looking for
and, by saying her name, compelled her to look at him. Jesus restored his
relationship with Peter with a simple question, "Do you love me?" asked
over and over again.[4]

John has been willing to look at and reach for God through a long
series of fortunate unfortunate experiences, surprising life changes, and
what could be seen as a fairly brutal adjustment of vocation. "Do you love
me?. . . . Feed my sheep. . . . Do you love me?. . . . Do this for the least of
these. . . . Do you love me?. . . . I command you to love." I felt I'd been privy
to the calls God extended and to John's obedience. The words "obedience"
and "vocation" both, etymologically, have to do with our listening, and
John is a listener.

A story from before Lily's birth floated through my mind. John told
me about going to a park with Christopher and running in the sprinklers
with him. While they cavorted, a man watched them. John wandered over
to the bench where the man was sitting and struck up a conversation. The
man's name was José, and he was from Mexico.

John had said to me in a spiritual direction session years before, "José
told me that watching me in the sprinklers with Christopher reminded him

of his daughter's childhood. He asked about my work. I told him about being a pastor, but working in a factory and as a waiter. He said I reminded him of the Taylor Caldwell book *The Great Physician*. Wow. That really hit me. That book's about Jesus, and how Jesus tends to people. I was really touched by the way José paid attention to me. He saw in me what I long to be, beyond any particular job. I will carry that with me."

As John prepared to leave my office for the last time, he confided, "The call to San Francisco fourteen years ago felt like a call to spaciousness. I didn't understand it at the time, but these years have been an expansion into a larger space. My theology, my ministry, my understanding of myself, and mostly my experience of God have grown and grown, like Kingdom-yeast in the dough of life." And with a gleam in his eye, he added, "Even in a tiny apartment."

Notes

1. Charlip, *Fortunately* (New York: Aladdin Paperbacks, 1964).
2. John 12:3.
3. I Cor 13:13.
4. See Matt 14:28–31; John 20:15–16; and John 21:15–19.

25

Afloat in a
Coracle: David

David continued to see me for spiritual direction, through seasons that were arid and some that were awash with a sense of God's grace. His appointments were scheduled four to six weeks apart, and he often canceled a few days before coming. Ministers and at-home parents caring for young children are the two groups of people I see who have the least ability to control their schedules. Things come up. Parishioners need help immediately, and meetings are scheduled by other people, just as, for parents, children get sick, and child-care arrangements fall through. Both dynamics came into play when David faced a decision and wanted Julia to join him for a time or two of spiritual direction.

I seldom see couples for spiritual direction. I work with ongoing groups and have seen one couple regularly, though infrequently, who work side-by-side in ministry. On occasion I see a couple in the throes of discerning an important question that affects them both, and that is how I met Julia.

Before they arrived together on a sunny fall day, I prayed that I would be able to attend to Julia well, given how familiar I had grown with David. After praying, I arranged my office chairs so that they would be equally comfortable and each relatively near me and the candle. It took planning— and lifting.

As I answered the knock on the door, I glanced through the peep-hole. David was nearest the door, and Julia, petite and pretty, peeked around his shoulder, pointing at the door and stifling a laugh with her hand. I know what she saw. It's a sign that reads "After knocking on the door or ringing the bell, please step back from door as it opens." It is funny. Our New College Berkeley office manager put it there because the door swings toward the one ringing the bell, who could be standing on the top stair which is narrow. We've had a few close calls with people jumping quickly backwards to escape the door's backlash, and we wanted to prevent catastrophe on our stairs.

I already liked Julia from all I'd heard from David, and her conspiratorial laughter with David at my door made me like her even more.

She was a bit nervous about coming to see her husband's spiritual director, but she was mostly warm and amused. "So this is where David gets his spiritual adjustments," Julia said, sitting down and taking in everything in the office with her lively brown eyes. I'd never noticed David paying much attention to the office, but it was clear that Julia was soaking it in and on the drive home would probably tell him what she'd noticed, just as she'd pointed out the sign on the door.

I laughed with her and told her how our time together would be shaped. Her dark eyes twinkled with humor when I explained that, if it was okay with her, I would light the candle as a reminder that "God is here with us."

Together, the three of us decided we would listen to each of them in turn. Initially, David would talk and I would attend to him while Julia listened, and then David and I would turn our attention to her. She preferred that he go first because, as she put it, "He's seasoned." The final movement would be one in which they both could say what they wanted to about the experience of being listened to and of listening. Each of the movements, I told them, would be preceded by a time of silence.

The structure of this session was similar to the group spiritual direction model developed by Rose Mary Dougherty and her colleagues at the Shalem Institute, and I've found it helpful with groups and couples.[1] The five-minute-long times of silence and sequential attention to each person help maintain a contemplative space in which to pray. The normal back-and-forth pattern of casual conversation is broken, and attention is held on the one who has the floor, even when that person sits in silence. This approach allows that person to listen for God and what's deepest in him or herself, even in the company of others.

After lighting the candle, I said a short prayer aloud, asking God to help us listen to one another and to God during our time together. I offer these short spoken prayers when I am directing more than one person, because it helps us all move between the different kinds of listening times.

David began, saying, "Julia and I are thinking about making a big change in our lives. I've been offered a position directing an educational and retreat program at a center on the East Coast, and I'm drawn to it. I've grown tired of congregational ministry and would like a chance to minister in a different way. As you know, I've grown tired of hearing myself speak. I've also grown tired of a life with no margins, no time that isn't open to being hijacked by sudden work demands. And I've grown tired of certain doctrinal positions that, as a pastor in my denomination, I must affirm."

Glancing at Julia, David told me, "Julia knows all this. She's more comfortable with church life right now than I am, I think, and maybe she hasn't gotten tired of hearing me speak." They exchanged a smile, and he took her hand in his. "But Julia's being very kind in allowing me to figure out what's right for me. I'm grateful. I want to make sure, though, that we make a decision that's best for both of us and not just for me."

For the next twenty minutes or so, David shared his thoughts and feelings, many of which Julia and I had heard before. I found that in her presence he was less defiant about his growing dissatisfaction with work and seemed both exhausted and wistful. He used the word "tired" in every paragraph he spoke, and I commented on the wistfulness in his voice.

"Hmmm. . . . 'Wistful.' When I hear that word, I feel a bit of sadness and also a bit of hope. I guess I am sad that this time of church ministry is coming to an end." Julia's body straightened, and he registered it. "It does feel like an end, I think. I'm not feeling angry or revolted by my work, as I sit here talking to you about it," he confessed, directing his comment to his wife, "but I feel the sadness of loss." With a pained smile on his face, he said to her, "We've had such good years here, haven't we, hon'?" Julia's eyes filled with tears, as she nodded.

David spoke about the sadness he was feeling and then revealed that talking about it felt as though something was being lifted off him. "I feel lighter as I talk about the sadness. Something that was stuck and heavy seems gone."

As the time of focusing on David neared its end, I asked about the bit of hope he'd felt in hearing the word "wistful."

"Yes. There is hope. I don't really know what to say about it. It just feels like possibility. It's not necessarily connected to the job offer, either. I didn't really feel it before this time today. I felt tired. Angry. Finished, or wanting to be finished, with my position at the church."

David seemed to be moving back to that posture, so I asked, "But now there's a sense of hope beyond all of that?"

Julia glanced at me quickly, and I briefly met her eyes. In these situations it's the listener who is more attuned to what the director says. The one who is speaking, if all is going well, is listening more within, and the words of the director serve to improve the acoustics of his or her attention to the Holy Spirit, without shifting attention to the director. David and I had worked together long enough that I felt we easily moved into attention to God's movement in him and his life.

David didn't pay attention to what was going on between Julia and me. He appeared to be listening to the whispers of hope that were welling up within him. "I feel there will be good things ahead. That I will recover from the exhaustion and burnout I feel now. God is still calling me. I don't know that it is necessarily to the position I've been offered, but God has work for me. And I feel excited, not daunted, by that. I feel younger all of a sudden." At that he threw back his head and laughed. I saw joy splash across Julia's face. I felt the wave of David's delight wash over me, too. As the force subsided, we slipped into silent prayer, and for five minutes I just relished the experience of watching this couple who so clearly loved each other.

When it was Julia's turn to speak, she seemed shy. She'd come in warm and talkative, but David's openness to his own feelings and God's grace had moved her. She was without guile or shield. As she began to speak, she squeezed David's hand—they had been holding hands the whole time— and he nodded encouragement to her. She looked at him, occasionally glanced my way, and spoke to him.

"I want what's best for you, David. I want you happy and not tired all the time. You say you want me to pay attention to what's right for me, and what I think of is the preservation of our family. We're like a boat on a journey across the sea. We have a long distance to travel, and you and I are responsible for the children we have with us on board. You and I are rowing, though you are doing the lion's share of the heavy rowing. I, sitting in the bow, am keeping an eye out for what's ahead."

Julia suddenly looked at me and said with humor, "David tells me you like images, and that's my image." I smiled and nodded, and she turned back to David. "I sense that you're almost too tired to paddle. Sometimes we go in circles because one of your arms is more tired than the other, and you lose your rhythm and balance. I get tired of hearing myself try to correct you."

David looked surprised at first, and then he laughed and nodded, under his breath whispering, "Yes. Yes. That's right."

At that point I told Julia I did like the boat image and wanted to hear more about it. She answered that the family is in the boat, and only the family. "That's the precious cargo to me. David and the kids. I love other people very much and want to be in the marina with them, but there's a way in which the four of us exist as a separate, special unit, and our fates are interlocking."

"The four of you together constitute the boat?" I asked.

Julia played with the image: "I think the boat has existed as long as I have and will last my lifetime. I chose David to join me in the boat, and then we brought the children into it. Eventually, the kids will leave it. Some day I might be in it alone again, if I outlive David, heaven forbid." Both of them were tender and teary again. "When David talks about me and my life, I don't understand it the way he does. My life is about carrying this family from one port to the next, safely, happily, and with a modicum of adventure. And to do so while following God. Celestial navigation, to push the metaphor too far." She laughed.

"Tell me about celestial navigation."

"Okay," Julia agreed, sitting up straight and planting her feet firmly on the floor. "To get to land and safety, we need to look to God for guidance. When I think about the boat, I'm feeling I need to be able to rest and look to that guidance. To do that I need David to stop paddling in an erratic manner that requires my correction and attention. I need some time of floating and gazing upward."

That seemed like the heart of what Julia had to say on that day in my office. There was more conversation, but, in my mind, the movement of God's Spirit seemed to be toward stopping and listening. If both of them could pull in their oars for a time, perhaps they could feel sadness and hope, and look to God in an open, wondering way, rather than in an intense, deci-sion-driven way. Ancient Celtic Christians would set out from the British Isles in rudderless boats without sails, and pray for God to bring them to the shore of his choosing. The small boats were called "coracles." I longed for David and Julia to have some time to rock in the swells of grace.

I recommended keeping the Sabbath. David and Julia were seeing me at a time when I was newly converted to that discipline and full of zeal, which time has not diminished.[2] I wanted them simply to stop, rest from labor, cease striving. Float in the boat. Notice the stars. Breathe. Refresh.

That was the only time I saw Julia. David continued to see me for another year as he and Julia discerned the way ahead for their family. They picked a midweek day, without soccer practice or church meetings, as their Sabbath. They looked forward to it as totally free space, and they guarded it carefully. On that day each week, they both felt younger. They were able to appreciate the parts of their life they would be leaving and experience hope for what might lie ahead. David's decision to bring Julia to his spiri-tual direction appointment seemed to unite them as partners in the adven-ture. When they moved away, I had every confidence that their compass was set for true north.

Notes

1. See Rose Mary Dougherty, *Group Spiritual Direction: Community for Discernment* (Mahwah, N.J.: Paulist Press, 1995).

2. I've written on the subject of Sabbath in Phillips, "Sabbath Living," *Radix* 32, no. 3 (2006): 14–19.

26

A Broader
Gift: Leah

Following her completion of graduate school, Leah sought jobs nearby so she could continue in friendships and communities that were life-giving for her. Over time, she sank her roots deeper and deeper into God's work in her life. She trusted the healing that entailed examining and re-experiencing traumatic childhood events and family patterns. She was also able to see how she had been shaped by her past in ways that brought particular graces into her present life. It wasn't that she would have chosen the past pain, but it was her past and God was at work in it.

"I was born at milking time. My father didn't come to the hospital for my birth because he had work to do. Eventually, I had work to do on the farm, too," Leah began our time together, returning to a familiar story.

"Life on the farm was harsh. One of my jobs was to kill kittens by holding them under water, so that cats wouldn't take over the farm. I could feel them wiggling as I held them under until they stopped moving. I hard-ened myself against the experience. It was as though I was watching it from a long way off," she recalled, recoiling in her chair as though distancing her-self even now from the memory.

"There was a lot of death on the farm. Cows were being butchered next to where I was drowning kittens. Chickens were killed for meals. And peo-ple died. Sometimes in farm accidents."

Casting a squint-eyed look my way, Leah said, "I sometimes knew they were going to die. It was eerie. I would dream the night before of someone dying, or I'd wake up in the morning just knowing someone was going to die that day. I'd tell my mother, 'Someone is dying,' and she'd just frown at me. The most vivid example of this death premonition was when the boy next door died. I dreamt that he died on a tractor, in a ditch. He was ten, and so was I. I didn't really like him because he and my brothers and other boys would chase and tease me and the other girls." Then, she added with a sigh, "But he was part of my everyday life."

Continuing, she explained, "It was my father who told me he had died. In the field, the tractor he was on rolled over in a ditch, and he was crushed. The men tried to lift it off him, and they couldn't. They watched as he turned blue and died." Leah cried, and we didn't speak until the sobs subsided.

"Last night I prayed with my pastor and a few other people here in Berkeley. I told them about this, and I cried and cried. I told them that as a child I called these premonitions 'death vibes,' and saw them as a curse.

"The people last night at my church said the 'death vibes' were a gift God had given me and that I needed to find out why. They told me that gifts from God are to be used, and I need to find out how I'm supposed to use them."

Leah looked incredulous, shaking her head in anger as she cried. "Why would God give a little girl such a gruesome gift? Why? Why?" She yelled, hitting the chair's arm with her fist, demanding a response from me.

I felt myself reacting against the "death vibes" and the view of them as a special gift of some kind. I'd been working with Leah for several years and had heard of many experiences that seemed like glimpses of a larger world, glimpses that went beyond the objective evidence. I decided to approach it that way.

"I don't know the answer to that, Leah. But, having listened to experiences from your childhood, from the years you lived abroad, and from your recent research trip, I think what are being called 'death vibes' might be part of a broader gift or way of experiencing. You not only have had the sense that death is near, but also that danger is, and that sense has helped you make decisions to protect yourself. Sometimes you've also had the sense of God's calling you to different sorts of work and challenges, and you've felt that a particular path has been laid out for you to walk. You've also had the sense of whom to turn to in crisis, of who will be good and kind and reliable." As I spoke, I felt strongly how true this was and how important it was to see the gift whole. Long work with Leah allowed me to place the conversation in the context of many hours of stories about her life. I was glad the subject surfaced when we had such a rich relationship. Sometimes spiritual directors point out the forest as well as the trees.

"Yes. A broader gift," Leah mused, curling her feet up in the chair. "I *am* sensitive. Maybe it's part of that. I've often felt estranged from others because I'm so sensitive. But the sensitivity hasn't just brought me pain. It's also helped me discern safety and goodness. That's right. And I wouldn't want to give up that sensitivity. It really makes me who I am. It's like being able to see things in the world—and maybe beyond this world—that others don't see." She spoke with confidence, and laughed as she said "beyond this world."

After a few minutes, Leah looked at me soberly and said, "So maybe it's not a kind of curse from God. Maybe it's all part of a larger capacity."

"How does it seem when you view it that way?"

"Well, it makes me trust God more. It fits better with my understanding of God. And with my experience of God when I pray."

"Say more about that."

"When I pray, I know that God is comforting and kind. He knows my sensitivity, and he works to make me feel peaceful, even while I'm seeing a lot, taking in a lot. He's like God in the Twenty-Third Psalm—he leads me through the Valley of the Shadow of Death and helps me not be afraid. He anoints me with oil and feeds me. He cares for me."

"A lovely image."

"It is."

One of the blessings of being a spiritual director is seeing how God's Word is received by people. My mind often goes to a passage written by the prophet Isaiah:

> For as the rain and the snow
>   come down from heaven,
> and do not return there until
>   they have watered the earth,

> making it bring forth and sprout,
>> giving seed to the sower and bread to the eater,
> so shall my word be that goes
>> out from my mouth;
> it shall not return to me empty
>> but it shall accomplish
> that which I purpose,
>> and succeed in the thing for which I sent it.[1]

The Twenty-Third Psalm is one of those words from God that waters the earth, makes it grow and sprout, eventually becoming the bread of life sustaining those who receive it. Leah digested Scripture, and it informed her more mystical experiences of God. It has sustained her through many droughts and storms.

Leah is at the beginning of her professional journey. There are times when she lives from hand to mouth. Trusting God's provision is a challenge. In one especially thin time, she prayed day and night for a particular job. She felt that it was the right one for her, and she was in desperate need of it. Financial hardship confronted her daily, as her car deteriorated and she couldn't afford to repair it, clothes needed for interviews wore out, and her diet was sorely constricted by lack of funds. She came to see me on a rainy night after doing a day of temporary secretarial work.

"This is a miserable time for me," she moaned, dumping her umbrella and briefcase on the floor and tossing herself in the chair.

We began our time of spiritual direction with silent prayer. Taking a deep breath, Leah informed me about her work situation. "There is a job possibility. I don't want to get my hopes up, but it looks perfect. It would solve *all* my problems," she declared, with a sweeping arm gesture from one side, over her head, to the other side, elongating the "all."

"I spend a lot of time praying about it. I'm like the psalmist who prays day and night. My pillow is soaked with the tears of my pleading with God. It's on my mind all the time."

Resonating with her longing, I asked about her experience of God in the praying.

"Well, I wish God were clearer with me. I don't get an answer. So it's almost as if I'm making a case or begging for a favor. I can't tell if I'm making any headway with him." She smiled.

"It sounds as though you have no sense of God's response. Do you also have no sense of God listening?" I inquired.

"I'm not sure, now that you ask. Let me think." Leah sat with her chin in her hand, eyes wandering over the Chinese rug between us.

"It's interesting to think about. I had an experience two nights ago that comes to mind. I was arriving home late. It was a cold night, and I'd been delayed on public transportation and so was getting home much later than usual. I was hungry and tired. In general, I felt sorry for myself. And with reason!" she claimed defiantly. "Life isn't easy. I had no idea it was going to be this hard. It's exhausting, and I wonder if I can go on." With that, she folded her arms across her chest, bent her head over her body, and looked sad and distant.

Empathizing with the real hardship in her life, I asked if there was a story she had been about to tell me from that late night two evenings earlier.

"Oh. Yes," she responded, seeming to collect her thoughts. At this point Leah sat up and looked straight at me, her blue eyes round and clear. "As I walked to the front door of my apartment, it was very dark. Completely dark, except for the stars overhead. I stopped short of my door and looked up. One star seemed especially bright. Maybe it was a planet. It felt like God to me. As though God were there above me looking down on me, able to see the whole of the world in which I live and also able to see me, my circumstances, and my desire to publish my thesis and find a job to sustain me."

It was as though a clear light had entered our conversation, too. Leah continued, "And I prayed to God while looking at that star. It was a different prayer from the begging, pleading prayers I've been praying. I told God, 'I love you, and I'll love you whether or not I get this job.'" That said, she nodded for emphasis.

I could picture her in the dark standing under the star, hungry and tired, having driven home from the subway station in her rattling car. For a moment, I couldn't have spoken had I wanted to. I was overwhelmed with admiration for her courage and faith, the strength that made her nod her head as though to defy any who would try to break her resolve to love God despite the cost. She had come to a place of holy detachment from—or indifference to—the driving demands and worries of life, and stood under the stars, free and strong.

Leah saw I was moved and held the silence with me. Then, in a quiet voice, she added, "'The light shines in the darkness, and the darkness has not overcome it.'"

"Amen," I said, thinking of how I and so many others have been sustained by that verse.

Leah was born at milking time to a family burdened by tragedy and poverty. She was raised in a church with a life-denying theology. But she received God's Word there. It came down like rain from heaven to a girl in a pasture. It is Leah's great gift of imaginative, lively faith that enables her to receive that life-imparting grace, even in seasons of drought.

Note

I. Isa 55:10–11.

27

Releasing the Parking Brake: Charles

The blessings of the visit to the monastery lingered, and in the last year I saw Charles for spiritual direction he discovered what his freed hands could do. Much of the work related to excavating desires that had been overshadowed and suffocated by the issue of marriage. Bit by bit, he faced long-denied desires. There was some elective surgery. His ears had protruded from his head since childhood (though not noticeably to me), and he wore his hair to hide his ears. Surgery moved his ears into a more flattering position. Increasing pain in his foot began to interfere with hiking and other pleasures, so he had surgery that allowed him to walk pain-free. The surgeries gave Charles greater freedom, as he no longer needed to be careful about combing his hair over his ears or concerned about how far he walked. Limiting self-consciousness and discomfort were shed.

He moved out of his garret. That decision was difficult because it affected his roommates, but they respected and accommodated his choice. Now he had a room to himself with no loud noises. He was able to engage in centering prayer in a place of solitude and peace. He noticed that contemplative life was leading to active change. He was not always sure it was okay.

"I'm thinking of leaving my church," Charles informed me one day. This is a church he had been active in for more than a decade, and it was his primary community. I was surprised, and he saw that.

"Yes. I know. I've been very involved. But all I do is serve there, and everyone else is part of a family. I always feel like a fifth wheel. Before I felt I had to stay there, and I prayed that God would put the right single woman there for me. That hasn't happened. I'm not happy there, so I'm thinking about looking around."

"That's a big change to consider. Do you know what you're looking for?" I asked.

"Partly I'm looking for more single people. I'm looking for people my age and hoping for ways of getting to know people that don't involve taking on leadership responsibilities. I'd also like to find a church where there's some centering or contemplative prayer," he listed his hopes with clarity and force.

"You've given this a lot of thought."

"Yes. But is it all right?"

"'All right?'" I asked.

"Is it all right to go looking instead of waiting on God to bring these things to me?" He inquired, his dark eyes looking at me earnestly.

"That sounds like an either-or question," I said. "'Does God do the work, or do I?' In my view, God's not just working in the external environment. God's also at work in your heart and mind. Your heart is opening to desires you didn't attend to before, and you've thought of ways to seek satisfaction for those desires. I think it's good to pray about it, listening for what God might tell you. And it's good to think things through ethically and practically—for instance, are there costs in such a move, for you and others?" His eyes moved to middistance, as though he were beginning to inventory the possible collateral effects of his decisions.

Wanting to encourage Charles's participation in his destiny, I ended our time together by saying, "I see no contradiction in God and you both being active. I haven't heard you say anything that seems unfaithful to God. You might want to talk with friends about this, too."

It was my strong impression that Charles was registering God's call and blessing in his life more and more fully as he prayed in a listening posture, integrating his experience of prayer with the whole of his life. He listened to what was deepest in his heart, and he attuned to God. His close friends affirmed the steps he was taking, and it seemed that his reflections on his life and decisions were intricately interwoven with the community of faith as well as with his own history and convictions. It wasn't an emancipatory reflection of the sort that radically extricates a person from the relationships and meanings of his life.[1] Rather, it was the movement of faithful growth in grace.

Seeing Charles follow his heart was like watching a plant send up shoots from the ground and slowly unfold toward the sky. I thought of that wide, low sky enfolding the monastery he had visited. The proverb that tells of unrealized hope making the heart bitter closes with the affirmation that "a desire fulfilled is a tree of life."[2] I felt I was seeing the sapling before me, life flowing up through him and eventually out into the world. The tree of life brings healing and grace into the world, and the steps Charles was taking seemed completely compatible with his long-standing desire to care for a family and serve the world.

Charles was doing what a psychiatrist friend of mine once described as "releasing the parking brake" so he could move forward, without reservation, toward his desire. In my friend's case, psychotherapeutic work helped him realize he had been trying to drive with the parking brake on. In Charles's life, he courageously set his heart to seek God, which enabled him to release impediments to growth and movement.

Early experiences of brutally dashed hopes teach us to shelter hope. Charles had suffered many dashed hopes as his parents' poverty and divorce forced unwanted change. He learned to shield hope from assault. There is wisdom in guarding against unrealistically high hopes, but we can become like the proverbial ostrich, thinking that our hopes are sheltered if we hide them.

By God's grace, Charles made a major existential shift. The parking brake was off, hope exposed, and action needed. His free hands enabled him to seize what he could reach: a new job, church, and home. As he made these changes, he strove to attend to God and felt a distant, watchful presence.

One day Charles announced, "I've decided to apply to law school. It will mean moving, probably, and it's a whole new direction to take professionally. I want to work in the civil rights arena, and a law degree will help me do it. I also am ready for a substantial change and challenge. And I'm sure you're wondering how I've sensed God in making this decision." Smiling broadly, he declared, "My sense is of God's provision. God is making it possible, putting it within my reach. He's not handing it to me, but he's essentially saying, 'If you want this, take it.'"

Charles spoke resolutely. He seemed strong and capable, determined and calm. The seething anger and resentment of earlier years were not evident. He was moving on with his life. I imagined that the hope for a mate was still held between his feet, and he would take it with him as he pursued other dreams. Over the next nine months, I met with Charles as he applied to law schools, was accepted by a fine one across the country, packed up, said his "goodbyes," and faced the future with hope.

As I regarded his calm face on the day he told me of his intention to go to law school, I thought about the Hebrew word "shalom," which means peace, but also connotes healing and wholeness. I no longer found Charles unreadable. He seemed open and spoke fluidly, feelings playing across his face as he spoke. Through prayer and risk, he had found a way to hold hope without being shackled by it. That was the shalom I saw. He had shed theology that rendered him paralyzed by tormenting desire. God had not materialized *ex machina* carrying a mate for Charles, but, rather, had given him "a wide place" in which to walk.[3]

Notes

1. See Hans-Georg Gadamer, *Philosophical Hermeneutics*, trans. and ed. David E. Linge (Berkeley: University of California Press, 1976), 42.
2. Prov 13:12.
3. Ps 18:36.

28

The Spirit's Dwelling
Place: Ruth

Sometimes a spiritual direction relationship ends with stunning finality.
That was the case with Ruth.

For a year after Ruth stopped coming to my office for spiritual direction, we stayed in touch through notes, e-mails, and occasional spiritual
direction sessions on the phone. She had an inquiring mind about everything Christian, and I learned to prepare for our phone conversations by
having a Bible and concordance (index to the Bible) at hand. She would ask
me what certain biblical passages meant and what particular words indicated. She was reading several translations of Scripture and having conversation with friends who spanned the spiritual spectrum. Ruth lapped up the
information and was excited about learning more. Sometimes she alluded
to the fact that it was preparing her for what she was going to encounter
when she died. She wrote to her cousin: "The most comforting thing to
me these days is to know a God who chose to suffer with his creatures both
emotionally and physically. That, and that alone, makes me feel that my
small suffering is held in something so much larger and more meaningful
than I can see when I am stuck in a depressive pit."

At the time of what turned out to be her last Easter, Ruth sent me a
card. On it she wrote:

I thought about you often this Easter, remembering your kindness in taking me to the church service. To think that at the time I didn't know if I'd see another Easter! But I'm still here, and this Easter has been deeply meaningful to me in unexpected ways. Christ told me to turn over the healing of my body and soul to him, and I have. . . . I would like to make an appointment with you to talk about it. I may even feel well enough to climb the stairs to your office! I hope the beautiful spring and Easter's arising are bringing you much joy. . . . I think of you so often and remember being in church with you last Easter.

Ruth wrote that she was painting, had joined a choir, and that the cancer was still progressing—"a strenuous test of faith."

She kept reminding herself "that God's perfect plan doesn't necessarily mean I'll be living as long as I'd like to. But I'm still working at it!" She closed by sending me "much love and prayers for your happiness."

Two weeks later, Ruth sent an e-mail saying she was feeling lousy, looked forward to talking with me when she felt better, and hoped I was enjoying the beautiful weather. Two weeks after that e-mail, I received a call from our mutual friend saying that Ruth was dying and wanted to see me. She was being cared for at home by friends and intended to die there.

For the second time in our relationship, I drove the long way to her home by the water. It was just a little more than a year since that Easter trip, and I felt immense sadness. I had grown to love Ruth. She had taught me about living and dying and had included me in her large embrace. She'd pushed me to the edges of my comprehension and the boundaries of what I felt I was capable of as a spiritual director. Now I was driving to see her, carrying with me a Bible, the Book of Common Prayer, consecrated oil I had from a retreat I'd participated in, and Communion elements I'd created out of wine and bread in my kitchen as my husband and son watched with curiosity. I was saying to God, "I'm not a priest. I don't know how to pray with a person who's dying. I'm scared." I didn't hear from God, but I could imagine Ruth chuckling and saying, "Is this a little strange for you, sweetie?" Yes. Yes, it was.

Arriving at Ruth's house, I encountered a physician friend of hers leaving. He shook his head and said it wouldn't be long, maybe a few hours more. Women friends spoke in hushed voices in the kitchen, and Ruth lay asleep on a reclining chair in the living room facing a large window that looked out at the water. Tubes were attached to her, but she looked beautiful. Her skin was luminous and creamy, and her body looked fit in the sundress she was wearing. Her pale hair had grown back, and I longed for it to have time to keep growing.

A friend of hers escorted me to her bedside and invited me to sit down. I did. I watched Ruth breathe, and I prayed silently. My mind wandered back to all our meetings. I'd seen her in more places than I'd ever seen a directee. I'd seen her dance and I'd seen her in a hospital gown. I'd met friends of hers and become a link in an e-mail prayer chain. She'd clung to my arm as we walked together on Easter Sunday, and she'd brought her paintings and family photos to my office. We had grown entwined.

As I registered the sweet pain of that, I saw that she was looking at me and smiling. Her eyes telegraphed their usual amused delight, and I knew she was still with me. She might be dying, but she was doing so fully conscious. She reached for my hand and said, "So good to see you, dearie. It's come to this. I'm on the edge between life and death. My doctors lovingly and regretfully told me their treatments are no longer of much use to me. I'm amazed at how calm and cheerful I feel, though. I'm accepting it as part of God's plan for me. I'm going to move ahead and find out what is next for me."

I could not speak. She smiled and spoke, and I cried. I had been with people as they died, but never had them speak to me so clearly. Her liveliness contrasted gruesomely with the nearness of death, giving the situation the feeling of an execution. The inexorable approach of fate was nearly unbearable. For me. It did not seem so for her. I needed, therefore, to surrender to God as she was doing. As I prayed, I felt warmth in me, coming up through my body into my hands and face. The sick feeling left my stomach, and I was able to hold Ruth's hands in my warmed ones.

I told her what I had brought with me and said I would be happy to read Scripture to her, give her Communion, and/or anoint her with oil. She replied, "I want it all. First, I'd like to hear you read the Twenty-Third Psalm. It has that bit in it about eating and anointing. How apropos." Indeed.

I read to her:

The Lord is my shepherd, I shall not want.
He makes me lie down in green pastures; he leads me
    beside still waters;
he restores my soul.
He leads me in right paths for his name's sake.

Even though I walk through the darkest valley, I fear no evil;
for you are with me; your rod and your staff—they comfort me.

You prepare a table before me in the midst of my enemies;
you anoint my head with oil; my cup overflows.
Surely goodness and mercy shall follow me all the days
    of my life,
and I shall dwell in the house of the Lord my whole life long.

I saw that Ruth had closed her eyes, so I waited. A tear welled up under her eyelid. She was squeezing my hand hard. Taking a deep breath, she repeated, "Surely I shall dwell in the house of the Lord my whole life long. Amen." When she opened her eyes, they were sad. She declared, "I don't fear. My cup does overflow. I trust. But I grieve, too."

"And so do I," I confessed.

"I know you do," she said kindly. "That's why you can be here. Now, let's get to the eating and anointing."

I read the words of institution for Communion and served her the elements. Amazingly, she was able to swallow the wine and bread. Then from the Book of Common Prayer I prayed, "'Sanctify, we beseech thee, O Lord, the sickness of this thy servant; that the sense of her weakness may add strength to her faith, and seriousness to her repentance; and grant that she may dwell with thee in life everlasting; through Jesus Christ our Lord. Amen.'"[1] Then, marking the Cross on her forehead with oil, I said, "I anoint you with oil, Ruth, in the name of the Father, and of the Son, and of the Holy Spirit. Amen."

Ruth's skin under my hand on her forehead was dry and cool. I kept my hand there as she whispered "Amen" and lay on the pillow, her eyes shut. I watched blood throb in a vessel in her neck and wondered at this mingling of life and death. Such powerful mysteries. I was grateful for those words passed down through the centuries, read by millions of grieving people at the bedsides of those they loved. The communion of saints seemed close, hovering near as Ruth's breath mingled with mine.

Never one to let an unanswered question go by, Ruth opened her eyes and asked, "What does 'repentance' mean?"

I answered as best I knew, that repentance means turning again toward God, often involving confession and accepting forgiveness. "I like that," she affirmed. "I am turning again toward God. My life has been a long turning, and a series of turnings toward God. He leads me in right paths. I am past regretting all the dead-ends I explored, and the meandering and traipsing I did in getting here. It's all part of the path I was on, and I know now that Christ was with me on it. He restores my soul. Part of that restoration is a shedding of regrets. I used to be riddled with regret. And with striving. I am forgiven. Now I feel at peace. I shall not want. I shall dwell with God."

As she spoke, Ruth's eyes slowly closed and her speech grew faint. Those were the last words she spoke to me. I heard her speak to others, but I was not alone with her again. I stayed for a few hours, during which she dozed and then roused to conversation, then dozed again. At all times she was held in a circle of love that she had woven with women friends. Philosophers write about "a good death." Ruth's death struck me as beautiful.

Ruth died in the company of friends who honored her wishes by holding a wake. I did not return for that. I savored the last moments I had alone with her. Like the psalmist and Ruth, I felt that God restored my soul. Stillness had come into me and continued to calm and warm me. I trust that it was God's Spirit, and that it was an experience Ruth and I shared. In inviting me into the liminal space with her between life and death, Ruth had granted me that peace. Death seemed more palpable and awesome than I'd known before. Her courage enabled me to be in its presence, and, I pray, will help me be in its presence when it is my turn to follow the Good Shepherd into new pastures.

Ruth died wishing people much love and saying prayers for our happiness. Those she loved created an atmosphere of beauty and grace around her death, and at its center was Ruth, shining, smiling, greeting people, asking about us, laughing and touching, then drifting to sleep. For a couple of years, I felt as though I stood inside and felt the force of the embrace Ruth and Jesus shared. Jesus was God's love incarnate, and love was Ruth's religion. When we held her memorial service several months after her death, it felt as though she, in her embrace with Jesus, continued to be a shining sun holding us in her orbit.

One of her final poems contains these words:

> He will crack open my heart
> to make of it an open vessel
> for the effulgence of God's love. . . .
> [D]eath will make of me
> an unused candle
> to be kindled by
> the Light of God's great love.

Although Ruth is no longer visible, I feel her radiant heat.

Note

I. "Visitation of the Sick," *Book of Common Prayer* (New York: Seabury, 1953), 310.

29

Fruit in
Lent: Carl

Carl contacted me about nine months after he settled into his new home beside the picturesque New England campus of the college that had hired him. It was the perfect place for him, we both felt. Top-notch academically, yet small enough to feel at home. His family was nearby, and he loved the white winters and dramatic fall foliage. All was going well with him, but he hadn't been able to find a spiritual director to his liking in his new community. Would I be willing to work with him over the phone? I was delighted to try, but not sure how well it would work. We began experimentally.

When he called at the appointed hour and after we exchanged greetings, I asked, "Shall I light the candle to remind us that God is with us?"

I heard Carl's encouraging, "Sure," and invited him to do the same at his end. During the ensuing moments of silent prayer, I watched the day start to darken in my home looking out toward the San Francisco Bay and imagined him in his home long after sunset.

After a minute or so, Carl said "Amen" and began to tell me about life in his new town and college. He was a five-minute walk from his office. Colleagues lived on his street. His parents and two brothers were within an hour's drive, and the family cabin within two hours. He loved his classes and research lab. One of his projects had been in the news recently, so he had a part-time job handling the media interest in it, which included some travel. Life was perking along.

I had always admired Carl's integrity. There was even integrity in the way he ordered our spiritual direction sessions, something I noticed more when we met together on the telephone, having only his voice to attend to. He almost always began a session with thanksgiving. "I'm grateful for the classes I'm teaching. The students are really sharp and are engaging the material in a very satisfying way." Or "I just received confirmation of a grant that will allow me to keep the staff I've hired for my research project. I'm so glad to be able to keep them. It's a terrific team." Most often, Carl's thanksgiving began with the workplace.

But sometimes it started with his home, especially if he was calling me from there. In the warm months he might call from his backyard. Gentleman that he is, he would identify for me the sounds I was hearing, "That was a hooded warbler. There seem to be two of them in a tall tree in the back of my lot. I'm sitting on my back porch looking across the garden. The sun is just setting. The light is magical, long horizontal rays casting a mellow light on the trees and neighboring houses." I would imagine him at rest in his own place. It seemed a realization of his heart's desire, and, noticing that, I felt in me something like that mellow glow he was describing.

From expressions of thanksgiving, Carl usually moved to speaking about aspects of life he considers central to his faith: prayer, worship, community. With his intelligence and willpower, Carl has been more able than some to adopt and persist in spiritual disciplines. He's kept journals in different seasons of his life and often has had a daily devotional practice with prayer and Bible reading. He likes to be in a weekday Bible study group, and he's committed to worship, though finding the right place for worship was a challenge in his new home. As a professor, he wanted to find a group of Christian colleagues for fellowship, and felt a desire to make himself available to campus Christian groups as a faculty advisor. He felt both a responsibility to do the latter and great eagerness for it. He had truly discovered his vocation. He felt that God had placed him where his deep gladness was meeting the world's hunger, as manifested in his students' eagerness to know him as a professor and as a Christian.

The final segment of our hours together often focused on a salient issue, something Carl was wrestling with. Sometimes it had to do with family relations, sometimes with a friend, and often with his as-yet-unrealized desire to meet the woman he would marry. It was a testimony to his discipline that he would strive to leave the big issue until after he had expressed thanks and checked in about ways he was nurturing his relationship with God. Every once in a while, the issue would leapfrog to the forefront because of his intense feelings about it, but usually, even when extremely distracted by a concern, he would follow his established practice. It gave the spiritual direction sessions a sort of order of worship, and I found it comfortable to rest in that order, my heart accompanying him through the different movements.

When Carl called from the east that first spring evening, he was in the midst of a discernment crisis involving a woman. In keeping with his pattern, he didn't mention this until well into the session. It turned out that, soon after his arrival in New England, a friend had invited him to meet a Christian woman who lived in the next town. She was a committed Christian, bright, attractive, and kind. Carl grew to like her very much, and she him. In fact, she fell in love with him. We spent many subsequent sessions discussing the situation and his distress over not having reciprocating feelings for this woman. Was there some block in him to a deep relationship with a woman? Had he not fully healed from the relationship with Sarah? Was it legitimate to keep seeing this woman when he knew he was not in love with her and had told her so as kindly as possible?

The hope in spiritual direction is to aid discernment. It is often in the light of God's truth and grace that we are able to see what we need to see to take the next step. Carl was practiced with this, and I had seen him faithfully discern about career options. This situation was harder because of another person's feelings, and it cut closer to the bone with him. Marriage is something he longs for, and there are no set paths to follow in order to secure it. Keeping courage through the ordeal of the job search was a challenge, but there was a map, of sorts, for that journey. Not so for this.

We talked about the possibility of Carl seeing a psychotherapist to work on the issue, and even about him and his friend seeing one together. In the end he worked on the issue in spiritual direction with me and in long conversations with friends. The work of Ignatius of Loyola has shaped my (and many others') understanding of discernment in spiritual direction, and it helped Carl. Ignatius advised his followers to engage in the prayer of the *Examen*, sometimes called an *Examen* of conscience or consciousness.[1] This prayer was intended as both: a way to notice when one is and is not obedient to God, and an aid to notice, consciously, God's presence in all of daily life.

Ignatius's followers, the Jesuits, engage in that prayer regularly, as a spiritual discipline of the highest order. When they were busy attending doctrinal meetings at the Council of Trent in the mid-1500s, some Jesuits begged permission to drop their regular practices. Ignatius's response was that if they dropped some, they should be sure not to drop the *Examen*.[2]

As I teach the practice, it involves a simple retrospective look at the past day. In prayer, one remembers the day backwards. Doing so backwards interrupts the normal narrative thrust of our lives. Our emotional drive toward conclusion fades with the breaking of the story line. We're able to remember isolated moments that catch our attention and remember the thoughts, feelings, sensations, and images that accompany them. Moving back in time systematically causes us to accord each hour the same amount of attention, even if some hours were more eventful than others, and notice the meaning embedded in the memory.

After prayerfully reviewing the past twenty-four hours, one reviews this time again, specifically looking for the sense of God's presence, any fruits of the Spirit, or any sensations one has come to associate with the holy. Also, one notices the opposite: a failure to attend to the holy, a sense of being turned from God, or just insensitivity to things of the Spirit. What one notices may evoke confessions or thanksgiving. After such prayer, it is good to rest in contemplation with God, savoring what has happened in the light of God's grace.

The prayer of the *Examen* is a user-friendly, portable, adaptable practice that has blessed Jesuits and many others the world over throughout the centuries. As a spiritual discipline engaged in with regularity, it helps you learn your spiritual make-up. For instance, you notice that you're more inclined to be aware of God when you're alone or when you're outside. Maybe art or music awakens your spiritual appetite. Perhaps certain kinds of activity are apt to deaden those spiritual inclinations. To notice such connections is the foundation of spiritual discernment. Once you have noticed, you can make choices and take action. For instance, Carl discovered he was best able to discuss energy-consuming issues after he took time to notice what he was thankful for. That awareness shaped our work together.

The *Examen* can also be taken up for a season of discernment, and that is how Carl engaged it. He prayed with his experience of the relationship, noticing the thoughts, images, feelings, inclinations, and sensations it evoked in him. He imagined himself moving deeper in the relationship and noticed what that stirred; then he imagined himself distant from it and noticed that as well. He scrupulously examined his heart and conscience and, as gently as possible, spoke honestly to the woman of what he knew. She, too, was honest.

It was interesting to discover that I was engaged in Carl's process of discernment, but that I had no sense of what the right outcome would be. Nor did I feel any need to know. It wasn't for me to discern. This is a different experience than I, and I think many of us, have with friends in similar circumstances. We often have opinions of what would be good, or better, or best for our friend. With Carl, I listened for what was going on with him and God.

What I heard about from Carl was God's gentleness. No direct instructions, invitations, or warnings came to clarify the decision Carl was approaching. But he had a strong sense of God's presence and the assurance that his decision must not be based on fear: fear that he would never get married if he let this opportunity go, and fear that he would be plagued with guilt if he broke off the relationship. For Carl, there was an opportunity for hope in the midst of pain and loss.

The clarity was of the Serenity Prayer kind: the serenity to accept what he couldn't change, the courage to change what he could, and the wisdom to know the difference.[3] Part of what he couldn't change was his continued sense that this was not the person he could marry. It took great courage to stand by that truth and care for himself and for the woman through the end of their dating relationship. Another truth was that he couldn't spare her or himself pain. There was no pain-free resolution in sight. Being true to himself meant he couldn't cut and run, but must remain a supportive friend for a time. It also meant he couldn't pretend and stay in the relationship after he knew it was not the one he sought.

The word "examen" is Latin and refers to the tongue or weight indicator on a balance or scale, that part of the scale that points to the weight value. The word conveys the idea of an accurate assessment of the situation. It usually takes awhile after weights are put on the scale for the swinging to settle and the *examen* to point steadily to the true value. So it was with Carl. But, in time, the prayer practice helped him find the course that was true for him, and as he followed it, he felt God with him.

The relationship had begun early after his move east and muted the loneliness of arriving in a new community. Thus, its end left Carl exposed to the chill of solitary evenings, meals and outings by himself, few people calling to chat, and even fewer stopping by. The house that had felt so right, now felt quite empty. Holidays were especially hard, even though family members lived near.

"I don't like being alone so much of the time. Living alone when I was in a relationship is very different from being alone without one. There's the sense that I'm not accompanied in thought. No one's thinking, 'I wonder what Carl's doing. Maybe I'll give him a call.' Sure, friends and family sometimes think like that, but it's not the same. And I'm not thinking that way about anyone either. It creates a kind of vacuum. I feel it intensely as Christmas approaches. Do I even bother to decorate the house?"

Carl went into triage mode with the holidays. He took definite, well-considered measures to ensure his well-being. Instead of spending time alone at the family cabin, he traveled back to the West Coast to visit special friends. He spent Christmas Eve and Day with his brother, who has young children. They sledded and made snow castles. He played.

He also worshiped. He attended services at several of the churches he'd been visiting. He decided he needed to commit and so joined a small group at the Lutheran church he was attending. A few people from his college were there, and he liked the church. There were few single people his age, so he got to know a young doctoral student, a man who had sought him as a mentor. He went to a concert with an elderly widow in the congregation who shared his taste in music. Carl took his nieces skiing. At home, he immersed himself in beautiful music and hung little white lights at the windows. He wrote cards to friends around the world and knew the joy of receiving responses. All the while he maintained his devotional practices and prayed. But he didn't feel God close at hand.

Carl survived Christmas and entered the new semester with vigor. His research was engrossing, and he spent more time at the lab. When he came home late at night, he would eat in front of the television, exhausted from the long day at work. One night as he explored sites on the Internet, he discovered an article I had written. It's about ways our culture pushes us toward desolation, away from what is most satisfying to ourselves on a deep level. As a result we are in constant motion, our attention fragmented by multiple demands. In times of rest, the culture plies us with junk food for the soul (enervating activities like television watching, web-surfing, mall trolling, and so on).[4] Of course, the paper itself benefited in its inception from what I've learned from directees, including Carl, so, although I was surprised to find my article a part of our conversation, I wasn't surprised that he resonated with the ideas in it.

After reading my article, Carl resolved to give up television for Lent. When we next spoke by telephone, he had spent a week without TV. "I think television watching leaves me numb and empty inside. It isn't the kind of activity that's refreshing, and I turn it on only because I'm so exhausted after work. Well, that's not the whole truth. I turn it on, too, because it fills the silence of my empty house."

"So with the television off, you might encounter that emptiness," I wondered.

"I do encounter that emptiness. I find myself not looking forward to the silent evening. But there's also a sense of anticipation to it," Carl said.

"Tell me about the anticipation," I encouraged, eager to hear.

"The ultimate goal of Lent is to know Jesus more fully. Not being able to watch television makes me think about God's presence. In the absence, there is presence, even if I don't experience it with my senses. It's an affirmation. It's kind of a quiet affirmation, so if the television were on I wouldn't notice it," he explained.

"A quiet affirmation," I repeated.

"Yes. Kind of like the psalm says, 'Be still and know that I am God.' The stillness comes when I remove the things that were filling up the space. Even little projects can fill up that space. It's not just clearing the space of noise, it's also holding the space open." I invited Carl to say more about that. "I can hold it open with certain reminders of God. One is a photo I have of my cabin. I love that place. I used to spend summers there as a boy, and I have taken everyone important to me there. It's rustic, and my family built it by hand over several generations. It's probably more home to me than any other place. I meet myself at every age when I'm there."

"I love hearing about it. And you say a photo of that reminds you of God?" I asked, returning to that reminder of God.

"Yes. The photo was taken on a dark night from outside looking into the cabin. The interior is filled with golden light from the lanterns and the fireplace. The window is made of panes of glass that are separated by wood, and in the photo the wood crosspieces of the window form a cross. So it's as though I'm looking into my home through the Cross." He said "cross" in such a way that I heard the capital C. "I think of it as the window on my soul. The shape of Jesus' Cross is imprinted on my soul, and my soul is a home in the shadow of that Cross."

"Powerful image, Carl."

"It goes to the core of me," he said, with feeling reverberating in his voice. "It's an altar for me. It serves the same function as the candle you light. It reminds me that God is here with me."

"'A quiet affirmation.'"

"It is," he whispered. We sat in that quiet. I imagined him looking at the photo. I can see it in my mind's eye, the warm light behind the cruciform lines, the dark Cross embracing and enveloped by the reddish-amber color. Like the pulse of human life.

Carl cleared his throat, and I asked him what he'd been experiencing. He replied, "Well, I was looking at the photo, and I felt rested, calm. Transported out of the daily concerns of my life. I feel more whole, more in touch with my whole self."

I asked if this is his usual experience with the photo. "Yes, it is. And I can rest in that state for a long time. Sometimes I listen to music, like Bach's *B Minor Mass*, and I feel cared for."

I felt joyful as I listened to Carl. He then spoke about how the Lenten evenings are infusing his days. "This time at night helps me the next day. That sense of being rested and restored lingers. I feel more whole."

"It stays with you as you go to work?" I asked.

"It does," he affirmed. "I don't get so stressed out. I'm less apt to move to anxiety. When something pushes my buttons, I have more ballast. I don't get knocked off balance. I feel the push, but I re-right myself quickly, like one of those standing punching bags," he said, laughing.

"That sounds like a great feeling. You say you're 'more whole,' and hearing that I get a sense of heft and integration," I offered.

"Yes, and you mention integration, which is exactly what I've been thinking about, but in a different sense," Carl said. As I expressed interest, he continued: "You know I've been praying for Christian community here. And I have committed to the church I've been attending. I've also joined a small group and now mentor a doctoral student. There's also a class at church I've started attending, so my week is saturated with Christian community, from Sunday through Saturday. More and more I now see people in town and on campus from these different contexts, and it feels as though I'm a part of this place. I'm known. Not just my face and my job, but the deepest desire of my heart—to follow Jesus—is known. It's known by people I see drive past me as I walk home, and known by people I bump into at the grocery store." That last image made us both laugh.

"I'm really struck by your saying you're known in such a deep way. I know how important integration is to you. It's a way in which you're not alone, too."

"I'm known, and I'm not alone. But it reminds me of the deeper way I'm not alone. Each time I see someone I've seen in worship or Bible study, it reminds me of the fundamental way in which God is with me. So it's a double reminder."

"Another 'quiet affirmation?'" I asked.

"Yes." He answered softly. "Another quiet affirmation. God is the one 'in whom we live and move and have our being.'"

In the article Carl read, I described the experience of consolation as like being planted and rooted in the garden. Carl told me he felt it was a season of "fruition" for him. It was moving to hear him embrace that gift in the midst of singleness. He embraced the consolation he received, instead of rejecting it as a "consolation prize." It was fruitfulness in the season of Lent, the hearth glow in the shadow of the Cross.

I could tell that this was Carl's authentic experience, rather than a principled stance to which he was holding himself. He saw ways in which the communities he'd been a part of in the past were, at some level, intertwined through him with the new community that was forming. Things were converging: past and present, day and night, Sunday worship and midweek living. His home was becoming a place of hospitality for students and faculty, friends and family. The word that came to mind was "maturity." There was a depth gained by faithful living, season after season, year by year, and that depth helped Carl weather droughts and other unsought vagaries of life's existential climate. He was planted by streams of living water and bearing good fruit for the world.

Notes

1. I recommend Ignatius of Loyola's *Spiritual Exercises* (of which there are many translations) as well as the following books about the *Examen*: William A. Barry, *Finding God in All Things: A Companion to the Spiritual Exercises of St. Ignatius* (Notre Dame, Ind.: Ave Maria Press, 1991); Katherine Dyckman, Mary Garvin, and Elizabeth Liebert, *The Spiritual Exercises Reclaimed: Uncovering Liberating Possibilities for Women* (New York / Mahwah, N.J.: Paulist Press, 2001); and Dennis Linn, Sheila Fabricant Linn, and Matthew Linn, *Sleeping with Bread: Holding What Gives You Life* (New York / Mahwah, N.J.: Paulist Press, 1992).

2. Linns, *Sleeping with Bread*, 19.

3. The Serenity Prayer is attributed to Reinhold Niebuhr, and is best known as the prayer central to the work of Twelve-Step groups.

4. Phillips, "Garden or Circus: Christian Care in the Face of Contemporary Pressures," *Transformation: An International Dialogue on Mission and Ethics* 22, no. 3 (July 2005): 158–65.

30

"But I Trusted in Your Steadfast Love": Melissa

I've had five surgeries on my back, and infections have developed that they aren't able to culture and combat." As she talked to me, Melissa leaned over her knees in her wheelchair. She was thinner than when I had last seen her, months ago before the surgeries.

We had spoken briefly and occasionally during the intervening months. Once when she was in the hospital, her mother answered when I called Melissa's cell phone. She told me that Melissa would try to return my call. More often than not it seemed she was in the hospital, having surgery, or fighting infection. Always there was pain. Medication covered the pain, but left her in a fog. Another time I called her home and her husband answered, saying, "This isn't a good time to talk. Friends are here praying with Melissa." Once I received a voice message from her, saying she had thought we had an appointment, a message that encouraged me with the thought that I might see her again and rattled me with the knowledge that she thought I had stood her up for an appointment.

Finally, to see Melissa was piercing. No amount of imagining her situation and praying for her had prepared me for the surge of emotion I felt as I listened to her and watched her. Melissa asserted that she wanted our time together to be spiritual direction. I had told her I would visit her and pray with her, even if we no longer had a spiritual direction relationship, and I would do so gladly and without charge. In Antoine de Sainte-Exupery's book *The Little Prince*, the fox, who has allowed the little prince to become his friend, says at their parting, "You become responsible, forever, for what you have tamed."[1] When I teach spiritual direction, I read that to my students because a similarly sacred trust is established in spiritual direction. It is akin to taming, without the patronizing connotations, in that another has trusted their vulnerable underbelly to the director, who is a person of some authority and professional power. We are forever responsible for the other's intimate self-disclosure, which has implications not only for confidentiality, but also for our comportment in the world. On rare occasions, as with Ruth and Melissa, it means that the responsibility reaches into a new relationship, beyond the dissolving of the formal spiritual direction relationship, and that is something discerned through prayer and examination of the heart. My heart told me I was committed to Melissa, come what might.

After her husband had adjusted her in her chair and given her water to drink, all done with affectionate strokes and words, I lighted the candle and we prayed silently. Melissa sat up abruptly, as she said, "Amen."

"It's been confusing," she began. "I've been in a fog, with opioids and other medications, and feel I'm just now coming out of that fog. I've been caught between pain and fog, neither state being comfortable. Both hard."

"Yes. Very, very hard. I'm very sorry you've been suffering so much."

"Thanks. I try to figure out what I've done wrong," Melissa confided. I wasn't sure I was hearing correctly and so echoed what I thought she'd said, as a question, and told her my hearing hadn't improved any since I'd last seen her.

She laughed and commiserated, saying that her voice hadn't improved either. Then she repeated, "I'm trying to figure out what I've done wrong. I want to confess everything to God." Melissa gave me a sharp look, as though watching how I registered what she said.

"You're trying to come clean with God about things you've done wrong?" I asked. "Tell me more about what you're trying to accomplish with that. I know you've said before that you thought you made some bad surgical decisions when you were young, and think perhaps those decisions are related to your pain now."

"That's right," she said. "But it's not just that. There are other things."
Melissa told me of other sins that were on her mind, that she had confessed to her husband, pastor, and friends. I asked how they had responded.
She answered with a smile of affection for them, "Oh, they all thought
they were small, no big deal. They forgive me and are sure God forgives
me, too."

"Tell me about your sense of God in this," I invited.

Silence ensued. Eventually, Melissa repeated, "I just keep trying to figure out what my sins are, so I can confess them. It seems endless."

"Insult to injury," I thought, wishing I could free her from that tread-
mill. True confession sets us free and reorients us to God's love, but many
of us get caught from time to time in what we think is confession, yet has
the effect of binding rather than freeing us. What I said to Melissa was, "It
sounds oppressive. You say, 'endless.' You're trying to do this for what reason? To what end?"

Another long silence, and she curled her head down. "I think it's magical thinking." Melissa smiled at me from her hunched position as she
spoke.

"Magical thinking," I reiterated, grateful for her ability to view what
trapped her and for her smile, inviting me to share her perception. "So if
you confess everything—every sin you've committed—and come clean with
God, then God will heal you?"

"I hope so. But it's never-ending. There's always more sin. Even new
ones." I felt her eyes imploring me, as I prayed to speak truth with love.

"Melissa, it makes perfect sense that you would try what you're calling
'magical thinking.' Of course. If you can find a way to ease the pain, you're
going to try it. You've worked so hard in physical therapy and endured multiple surgeries. Of course you're going to try every avenue you can think of.

"Your situation of continued terrible pain is something we who love
you, and you, too, very much want to see changed. It's wrong that you're suffering so much. It's just plain wrong."

She was crying, and I prayed I wasn't inflicting more pain. I was voic-
ing the cry I had made to God time and again on her behalf, and it would
not be suppressed. My tears came as I watched her body heave with sobs

and her hands wipe the tears from her face. The words of Psalm Thirteen drifted through my mind: "How long must I bear pain in my soul, and have sorrow in my heart all day long? How long shall my enemy be exalted over me?"[2] My thoughts screamed, "How long must Melissa bear this pain, Lord? How long? How long!"

The psalmist eventually recalled God's "steadfast love" in which he trusted.[3] I asked myself about that and whether I, too, trust that. Confronted with Melissa's suffering, I found this to be a challenge. Writing about suffering is one thing; witnessing it, another. Melissa had borne paralysis and pain for most of her life. Now she was in acute agony, and intense, chronic pain is a destructive force.[4]

In the midst of her pain and as we spoke, an atmosphere of calm came over Melissa. She looked at me through wet lashes, her face open and trusting, momentarily free from the twists of pain. I continued speaking to her from my heart: "I believe that your suffering is terrible, Melissa, and unjust. It makes me yell at God to explain it and change it. In the midst of that, though, I also believe that God *is* loving. That God loves you." She was nodding. "I'm wondering what it's like for you when you take all of this to God."

Melissa straightened up and closed her eyes. I was trying to get out of the way. Part of me had doubts about God in this whole business, and I felt a great urgency to summon up wisdom. Pushing that "ever ready to take charge" part of me out of the way was an act of submission, submission to the One who calls us to trust and abide in that steadfast love. Slowly I felt that something was released in me, leaving me more naked and empty-handed. In that relinquishment, I waited to see what Melissa would say. I felt I had nothing to offer but my waiting prayers.

When she opened her eyes, Melissa's face was somber, and she let me in on her experience in prayer. "It feels like a relief. There's a relief from the self-condemnation." I nodded. Then she said something I didn't understand. I thought her words were, "I felt a hand," meaning God's hand. I leapt at that, and echoed it for confirmation. She shook her head, vehemently asserting, "No. I said, 'It felt sad.'"

"I'm sorry, Melissa, for not hearing that right. Yes, it is sad. Very sad. And you say there's relief, too?"

"Yes. There's a sense of relief. I see how I get caught up in obsessing about my sins. It helps to see that. And in the absence of that, I just feel terribly sad." A tear rolled down her face as she looked at the candle flame.

I felt a heavy peace descend. We both stared at the candle. It was not a happy sense of peace. It was more an absence of struggle and anguish. It was a contemplative space of regarding the harsh truth in the light of grace.

The hour was not finished, and we didn't remain at peace. Melissa lurched as though a giant claw raked her back. Her face contorted. I put my hand on her foot to signal that I was with her, and waited. Pain, the tormentor, seized Melissa, and I felt as though she had been dragged behind enemy lines. Her body's taut movements were a silent scream.

Eventually, exhausted by the agony, she seemed to doze off. When her eyes reopened, I saw what looked like woundedness in them. She gestured toward a small cup on the table beside the candle and asked for the pills it contained. I asked if she wanted me to put them in her mouth, and she nodded. I did that and then put the straw of the water bottle in her mouth for her to drink from.

As I sat back down, I was aware of the sensations on my hand. First, there was the remembered heat of the candle flame as I had reached over it to the pill cup, searing the fine hair on my wrist. Then, the softness of her lips brushing my fingers as I placed the pills on her tongue. Something about the joining of the scorching flame with the pliant lips on the surface of my hand held my attention.

After a moment, Melissa began talking again. The pills were the first line of defense against pain, and we both wished we had a greater and more effective arsenal. She told me, "It's painful to move to that place of compassion for myself. It doesn't feel right. It somehow feels like the easy way out or like a resignation to this situation. My situation is hurting people who love me. They suffer because of me. It's costly for them, too. For my husband, my friends, my family, my church. They pray for healing, and I don't heal." The tears were flowing again, and she mopped her face.

I asked about these people who love her, and she claimed it's through them that she most profoundly feels God's love. They have been saints to her, faithful and sacrificial. Yet she worries that she has failed them because she hasn't been healed. She bears responsibility to them for her lack of healing.

"It sounds as though you see the love these people show to you and the work they do for your sake. You're grateful, and you feel indebted." Melissa nodded. "It sounds as though you think the way you can repay or thank them is by healing."

"Yes," she said.

Our time was coming to a close, so I pushed an alternate view. "I wonder about another kind of work you do that is significant and challenging."

Looking curious, she inquired, "What's that?"

I answered, "What you just did a few minutes ago. The work of telling God how you really feel about what you're going through. The pain, the sadness, the anger. Being vulnerable. Trusting God with that vulnerability. Especially hard when God, who is all powerful, isn't healing you. At least not yet. I can't even imagine how you do it. But I see that you do. You courageously live your hard truth in the context of a relationship with God. It's what David did in the Psalms. He trusted God's love enough to shout at God and to keep on loving God in the midst of suffering and enemies. Just now, when you did that, you said you felt relief and sadness."

Melissa watched me as I spoke. She replied slowly and thoughtfully, "Yes. It was a relief from self-condemnation and that magical thinking, *and* it was sad. The magical thinking in a way was a distraction from the sadness. That kind of thinking was tripping me up, and I see that."

I asked Melissa about the sadness, and she said, looking down, "I wonder where God is in all of this. So much pain. Pain for me, and pain for those who love me. It's sad."

I just kept nodding as tears filled my eyes. Taking a deep breath and looking straight at me, Melissa declared, "That is what I bring before God. I bring sadness and pain. And questions about this mess and God's place in it. I bring those things to God, even though I wonder where God is. I bring all of that. . . . And I bring hope for healing." She smiled, and my throat contracted with emotion.

We sat silently.

"I'd like you to come back. I'd like more times of spiritual direction with you," Melissa said, almost shyly. I told her I'd like that and asked if it would be all right if I ended our time together by praying out loud. "Sure. I'd like that."

My voice breaking, I prayed: "O Lord, I am angry and sad to see Melissa suffering so much. I am amazed by her faithfulness to you and her love for others, in the midst of such agony. For me, Melissa is a light of grace and integrity in the world. I'm grateful for the people who love and care for her. Bless her, and all of us who love her, by healing her. In the name of your son Jesus, who taught us to pray in the midst of suffering. Amen."

Leaving Melissa's apartment, I felt limp and frayed. I had tried to go into the reality of Melissa's agony, keeping my eyes on Jesus as I went. Nothing had seemed clear or straightforward. Melissa—and I trying to stay with her—were tossed by the violent currents of her suffering.

You might wonder why this story is in a part of this book called "Fruition." It certainly doesn't end in a tidy, platitudinous way. There's no epiphany moment that holds the tragedy at bay, no theological point that miraculously creates order out of the messiness. It's like Jesus, God's son, born in the manger while other newborn boys were slaughtered by Herod's soldiers. How can one make sense of that? To try to explain it is to step back from the horror. Horror and injustice are present, but so are grace and love.

Melissa teaches me about how to stay with the truth, awful as it sometimes is. "Staying with" can be like riding an angry bull. There are moments of seeming balance and peace, but then the bucking begins again. The bucking can be the sheer physical agony that racks her body, depletes it, tortures it day and night. It can be the human cost: career decapitated, loved ones caring in costly ways, simple pleasures like sleeping, eating, and moving diminished. And, as surfaces in spiritual direction conversations (my own with my director as well as those with my directees), the bucking can be the compulsion to strike a deal with God, to do the right thing in order to be free of pain, to pray in such a way that this cup must be removed from our lips. Of course. We are told to choose life, and we try. As best we can discern what life is, we strive for it. Melissa does so day after day. She prays even in unbearable circumstances. She reminds me of a few others who have inspired me by doing the same. One of those is Etty Hillesum.

Etty Hillesum died in Auschwitz in 1943, yet her spirit has enlivened the world for decades. The journal of her final years tells about her life as a young Jewish woman in the Netherlands, suffering increasing restrictions and terror. Before being deported, she wrote:

I JULY [1942] 3:45 IN THE AFTERNOON. Sun on the balcony and a light breeze through the jasmine. . . .

    I can't take in how beautiful this jasmine is. But there is no need to. It is enough simply to believe in miracles in the twentieth century. And I do, even though the lice will be eating me up in Poland before long.

    It is possible to suffer with dignity and without. . . . I am in Poland every day, on the battlefields, if that's what one can call them. I often see visions of poisonous green smoke; I am with the hungry, with the ill-treated and the dying, every day, but I am also with the jasmine and that bit of sky beyond my window; there is room for everything in a single life. For belief in God and for a miserable end. When I say: I have come to terms with life, I don't mean I have lost hope. What I feel is not hope-lessness, far from it. I have lived this life a thousand times over already, and I have died a thousand deaths. Am I blasé then? No. It is a question of living life from minute to minute and taking suffering into the bar-gain. And it is certainly no small bargain these days. . . . I think . . . of many, many worried people, and I know it all, everything, every moment and I sometimes bow my head under the great burden that weighs down on me, but even as I bow my head I also feel the need, almost mechani-cally, to fold my hands.[5]

That is what I saw in front of me as I sat with Melissa, her head bowed under the weight, yet hands folded before the candle's light, entering prayer and spiritual direction.

The day when I finally saw Melissa after that long break was the Sat-urday before the third Sunday in Lent. Lent is the season in the Christian year when we remember Jesus' suffering and death. The word "Lent" is associated with cognates meaning long and slow. It is a season when the earth awaits the spring, the days lengthen, seeds stir and sprout in the late winter darkness, and our hearts are filled with longing. In this long, slow season, our desire deepens into yearning as we come face to face with the yearning that constitutes our faith. I felt it as I sat with Melissa. She yearned toward God, life, and healing. I yearned also. An aching, hungering feeling.

The next morning I read aloud the Scripture lesson in my church's wor-ship service. It was Isaiah, chapter fifty-two, verses two through nine, a passage about God's people at long last being released from bondage in strange lands. "Shake yourself from the dust, rise up, O captive Jerusalem; loose the bonds from your neck, O captive daughter Zion. . . . Break forth together into singing, you ruins of Jerusalem; for the Lord has comforted his people, he has redeemed Jerusalem." Jews and Christians have received comfort and hope from these words as well as from Isaiah's words about the suffering servant sent by our God, who promises that "with everlasting love I will have compassion on you."[6]

As I read about this God who comforts those who know enslavement and ruin, I prayed for Melissa. Between me and the congregation on a low altar table was a long tray of sand and rocks. In the middle of it stood a tall white candle, its flame flickering. Throughout the service, from every part of the sanctuary, people came alone and in pairs to light smaller candles from the tall Christ candle and then plant them in the sand to shed their own light. I watched the faces as they came down the aisles, as they held their candles up to the flame, and then as they planted their small sturdy candles in the sand. Sorrow, hope, fear, and faith mingled in their expressions. Almost always their mouths opened as they reached the wicks of their candles into the large flame. I felt on my hand again the scorch of the candle in Melissa's apartment and the brush of her lips. Something turned inside me. My heart opened again. With the lamenting psalmist I could say, "But I trusted in your steadfast love." Faith is in that coordinating conjunction "but."

Christian Scripture ends with a bracing pivot of faith: "Even so, come, Lord Jesus!"[7] Faith is the movement of turning, reorienting, hoping to turn again even among these rocks, this pain, the everything of a single life. And Melissa continues to turn to God and open her heart to hope, even as she suffers. Like the attendants who help her each day, I learn about faith from her.

Notes

1. de Sainte-Exupery, *The Little Prince*, trans. Katherine Woods (New York: Harcourt, Brace & World, 1943), 71.

2. V 2.

3. V 5.

4. Sociologist Jonathan Cole in his in-depth study of twelve people with spinal cord injuries writes, "Chronic pain . . . can wreck someone's life more than paralysis." Cole, *Still Lives: Narratives of Spinal Cord Injury* (Cambridge, Mass.: MIT Press, 2004), 286.

5. Hillesum, *An Interrupted Life: The Diaries of Etty Hillesum 1941–1943*, trans. J. G. Gaarlandt (New York: Washington Square Press, 1981), 158–60.

6. Isa 54:8.

7. Rev 22:20, *Holy Bible: Authorized King James Version*, ed. C. I. Scofield (New York: Oxford University Press, 1967).

Conclusion: God's Holy Habitation

Scholars write that spirituality is "self-implicating." Our knowledge is informed by who we are and what we see, and who we are and what we see are informed by the understandings we develop. Spiritual work is not a lab science or armchair philosophy. I am being shaped by my work with and love for my directees. They enable me to see more of who God is as I watch them pray, in all kinds of circumstances. As the dance of our work begins, journeys continue, and fruit is borne, I bear witness to God's transforming grace. We are clay in the Potter's hands. There is no end to the turning. We turn again and again on the wheel as we are shaped again and again, turning our hearts toward God. Many words in Scripture begin with "re-," again. Return, repent, refresh, renew, restore. This is God's call to individuals and to peoples.

We each come before the living God bringing our own heart and life. There is truth in the perspective that we come to God as solitary selves. However, we live in a culture that is far more individualistic than other cultures have been, and today's spiritual direction is strikingly privatized and personalized.

Yet even we in the twenty-first century are shaped by the "holy habitation" in which Scripture claims we dwell. Not only are we each a dwelling place for God's Spirit, but, perhaps even more mysteriously, our community is God's habitation.[1] In George Herbert's poem about prayer, the first phrase conveying the meaning of prayer is "the Church's banquet."[2] Is this true in our churches today? Do we come together and feast on prayer?

The biblical view is that we are to be joined together and grow as a dwelling place for God. This is what is to happen within and outside my office. While God's holy habitation is shaped by social and cultural forces external to it, the church ought to be a gift to the community and to the world. So, too, spiritual direction is to be sacramental in bringing God's truth and love into the world. The grace cultivated within it, ideally, spills out into the world, transforming relationships, inspiring charity, motivating worship, and, one hopes, aiding in the repair of the world.[3] I have seen this as I have practiced the art of spiritual direction.

Dwelling and Engrafted

Each person who sees me for spiritual direction is part of the communion of saints and sheds light in the world. I believe that, and I've seen it. St. Paul wrote that people of faith "shine like stars in the universe as you hold out the word of life. . . ."[4] One word in the Greek text conveys the sense of holding onto and holding out, another way of representing the uninterrupted flow of grace characterized by the prophets as the well-watered garden.

Fruition is not only personal flourishing or radiance. The fruit of the garden enters the world, as starlight pierces the cosmos. George Herbert called prayer "the land of spices."[5] Spices are sought-after and travel the globe, surprising and delighting us with their pungent flavors and aromatic fragrance. They season, preserve, and add zest. Perhaps the spiritual maturity that develops through spiritual direction contributes spice to the world, infusing the tree whose leaves "are for the healing of the nations."[6] Certainly my own healing and seasoning have been cultivated by the lives of my directees, and I see the salutary effects of their faithfulness ripple outward into the world. God's grace not only nourishes—it spices life up.

Being engrafted onto the vine of God enables and requires fruit-bearing. Love begets love. As we are cared for, so are we able to care. The word "adult" comes from a Latin word that indicates "having reached the stage of one who now nourishes (*allere*) what he bears and produces."[7] In being nourished, we become adults who are able to nourish others. This truth is found in all religions and is increasingly studied and documented by scientists who see that those who have received love are those who can give it.

For example, in 2004 at the encouragement of the Dalai Lama, Tibetan Buddhist monks submitted themselves to functional magnetic-resonance imaging of their brains as they practiced a form of meditation aimed at experiencing compassion for all living beings. Novice meditators had scans much like those of ordinary people. But the seasoned monks, who had spent more than ten thousand hours in meditation, showed striking differences. The part of the brain that registers joy (the left prefrontal cortex) was filled with activity, in contrast to the part of the brain that registers anxiety (the right prefrontal cortex). The part of the brain that directs planned motion also exhibited increased activity, as though, wrote journalist Sharon Begley, "the monks' brains were itching to go to the aid of those in distress."[8] Immersion in loving prayer engenders loving action toward others. God's calls to *caritas* (love) and *communitas* (community) exist interdependently.

My work as a spiritual director depends on my own prayer life, and on my participation in a community of people who care about listening for the holy through the practice of spiritual direction. I meet regularly with a spiritual director, and with a consultant who helps me with my work as a spiritual director. I'm privileged to live in a community where there are quite a few spiritual directors and professors of spirituality. Many have been active in this work for decades. Some are steeped in the literature of spirituality, the lives of people of faith throughout history, and the practices of religious people of all kinds. Their lives and words teach me, and the thickness of my community is reflected in the acknowledgments at the beginning of this book. This community undergirds my caring practice.

As it is in prayer, so communication is crucial to life in community. In my extended Christian community, we don't all speak the same language. Community, like culture, is deeply linguistic. While expressing myself authentically, I have to be careful not to use language that makes some feel excluded—or worse. For example, in my church community people easily refer to God as "Father," yet for many in my larger spiritual community that designation is restrictive. I agree that God is beyond gender and do my

best to avoid using limiting pronouns for God. But I can also get myself
into convoluted grammatical binds trying to avoid gender identifiers, such
as "God reveals God's self." How can our language aid our knowing and not
hinder it? How can our prayers constitute communication and not become
empty forms? Listening to responses from God and from others shapes our
engraftment in the whole reign of God. Response to God generates community, and community calls for responsibility. From contemplation flows
action, which, in turn, affects contemplation.

Thriving in Community

Some of us who are spiritual directors in the San Francisco Bay Area come
together twice a year at the home of a woman who makes a beautiful, calm
space for us, with candles and rocks, flower arrangements and cups of tea.
We make presentations to one another on issues related to the practice we
share. One night the presentation had to do with doing spiritual direction in
a postmodern age. We discussed features of postmodernity that affect spiritual direction: individualism, freedom of choice, release from traditions and
from many of the obligations of relationships, along with a tendency to oper-
ate as autonomous consumers with respect to our spiritual lives. Conversations like this are rare, yet it is essential that spiritual directors wrestle with
questions about spirituality and community in the context of our culture.

   Those studying our society in recent years have sounded an alarm: We
are in the midst of a social recession in the United States. People are "bowling alone," neighborhood associations are in steep decline, and for many
Christians, the shift is from a search for group identity and belonging to a
quest for authentic inner life and personhood.[9] Experiences of community
have been less than ideal for many people, and today the political outlook
of some American Christians is not at all a view that invites some other
Christians into community with them. Many Christians are not active par-
ticipants in community life, but rather are spectators to a supposedly faith-
influenced political process and performance-based worship, some of which
can be accessed remotely and passively by radio, television, and the Internet.

   Those who see me for spiritual direction assume a variety of different
stances toward community. Some are retreating from it. Many people come

to spiritual direction to recover from unpleasant experiences, from judgmental, seemingly uncaring communities with harsh theologies. Community for them has not been a source of emotional or spiritual strength to draw on during hardship. Rather it has been intrusive and prescriptive, sometimes foisting unhelpful theodicies on them. Yet they still have faith in God and a desire to share that faith with others. They would like to participate in a community in which they are able to grow in intimacy in a context of compassion. They are not averse to challenge and healthy conflict, but they desire appropriate shaping and even pruning, not stunting, amputating, or engulfing engagement. In this book we have seen how Leah in childhood and some others, in different ways and to varying degrees, have been exposed to harsh Christian community.

Others come to see me feeling dissatisfied with community. They may come from communities that they love and are committed to, but that have left them hungering for conversation about their deepest longings and joys. Such communities are often fine at focusing on teaching and social action, but are less articulate about spirituality. Prayer is not the banquet they serve. As a result, many learn to consider their spiritual experiences private and seldom talk about them. One Christian activist said to me that after having lunch with a Christian friend, she was walking alone down the street and passed two African Americans. She, a European American, overheard the word "God" in their conversation. That encounter made her think about the fact that she and her friend (also European American) had not mentioned God once during their lunch conversation. The only times God is discussed in her life is in formally religious contexts, like spiritual direction, Bible studies and classes, and church. Why, she wondered, is the core relationship in her life so seldom on her lips? Is she part of a Christian subculture, she wondered, that suppresses conversation about God in daily life? Her reflections led her to initiate changes in her church. Others with whom I've worked have left communities and found others that enable them to be more in touch with the flow of God's grace to and through them.

There are people who come to spiritual direction longing for community. Some have been part of communities in the past, are no longer part of them, and long for that experience again. Many talk to me about worshiping as children, kneeling alongside their parents in pews, singing hymns with a congregation, not remembering what was said in sermons but remembering that people were together listening and worshiping. They have left their parents' churches, no longer are theologically comfortable in their childhood faith communities, but have tasted the flavor of spiritual community and are seeking it again. Jim was able to take an ember of spiritual light from his childhood and find a place in adulthood where it could grow and be nurturing to others.

Others have never been part of Christian community, and they long for it. They have no real vision for finding or creating community, but sharply feel the desire for it. Some are suffering from the general mobility of our society and no longer live near family and longtime friends. They also suffer from our general cultural ignorance about how to create or enter community and feel they lack time to invest in it.[10] In working with people with these feelings and experiences, I have seen how their increased attunement to God leads them to seek Christian community.

Quite a few people I've worked with—like Melissa, Carl, and others in this book—testify to being nourished by community. Some come with a rich experience of communal spirituality that whets their appetite for more. One man said, "When I can't pray, I rest in the prayers around me in the sanctuary, as though I clip onto the clothesline being pulled over my head toward God." A woman said, "I think I don't believe in God, and then I sit in church, am enfolded in the singing and prayers of others, and sense God moving in my heart." Another said, "I feel that being with my church community in worship or at meals amplifies my knowledge of God." Many of these people still have no friend with whom they can talk in depth about matters of faith, but they grasp the meaning of joining together with others for worship and table fellowship. Spiritual directors pay attention to directees' experiences of community.

Prayer and Worship

Understandings of discipleship have changed in the United States. Despite an amorphous longing for community, the typical Christian spiritual seeker isn't necessarily looking to be a disciple. This means that the person is exposed not only to loneliness, but to the danger that in isolation he or she will be vulnerable to forces of persuasion and imagination unchecked by the broader evaluation and reflective distance a community can offer.

"Spirituality" has become a good word, and "religion," a negative one, which is in part an anti-institutional stance. That accords with our fantasy of individualism as well as the hegemony of our socioeconomic milieu that infects our spirituality with consumerist concepts and practices. Even scholarly conversations about the restoration of community and spirituality resort to economic terms like "social and spiritual capital," as though these blessings can be accumulated, multiplied, depleted, exchanged, and deployed.[11]

This is a serious concern in spiritual direction. Christianity affirms the Body of Christ, the gathered community, the temple of the Holy Spirit. We are aware of the community even in solitude, just as were the Desert Fathers and Mothers of the third century, the Russian *poustinikki* (people who lived like desert hermits, but in villages) of the nineteenth and early twentieth centuries, and modern-day Christian hermits who pray for the world. Making this point about Christian community being present even in isolation, Tilden Edwards wrote that the Russian word for solitude carries theological freight and means "being with everybody."[12] In spiritual direction before the candle, we, director and directee, experience *zweieinsamkeit*, a German word also freighted with theology, which connotes the grace-filled dual solitude of two gathered together.[13] In that dual solitude, we are part of the Body of Christ.

Ronald Rolheiser claims that "community as a constitutive element of true worship" is one of four nonnegotiable essentials for any healthy Christian spirituality and, he claims, it is prescribed by Jesus.[14] (The other three are private prayer and private morality, social justice, and mellowness of heart and spirit.) Church community strips us of false freedom, humbles us, expands our ethical horizons, moves us to live the confronted (rather than the unconfronted) life, and holds us responsible. Rolheiser cites Jesus' two Great Commandments, affirming that love of God and love of neighbor are inseparable. Because love of the other is fundamental to worship and prayer, spiritual directors attend to the flow of grace that moves out into the world in acts of truth and compassion.[15]

Rolheiser emphasizes community's significance for "true worship." Not only is community of moral, psychological, and practical import, it is essential for our relationship with God. My directees who remarked about feeling lifted toward God or held in prayer by the worshiping community are experiencing what Rolheiser describes. Worship and love meet in the Body of Christ. This is related to the mystery of the triune God: Communion is fundamental to the nature of God. In Genesis we see Abraham welcome the God, manifested as three persons, under the trees of Mamre.[16] In Christ we are told that the Word, which was with God in the beginning and is God, was made flesh.[17] The resurrected Jesus said to his disciples, "Receive the Holy Spirit," and breathed that Spirit into them.[18] Mystery. As theologian Jurgen Moltmann writes, "God's word and his spirit belong together, like God's breathing and his speaking."[19] In shared worship we experience that breathing and speaking.

Recently, I participated in my church's Tenebrae service, the ancient Good Friday service of growing darkness as Jesus' death is remembered. It was a service of Scripture, hymns, and prayer. As I prayed among the several hundred other worshipers, I thought about the magnitude of Good Friday. Only a community can hold that suffering, just as our own personal suffering is best borne in community. As we sang familiar hymns, I noticed the freedom that came in our union. We could rest in the song. When one person was moved to tears and unable to sing, the others carried the song. When one hit a false note, it blended and streamed into the whole. Low and high voices met in the harmony, the loud and soft weaving and dancing. I could rest on the flow of music that surrounded and penetrated me. It was a living, breathing, holy habitation of God.

Community fails when it becomes judgmental, doctrinaire, or conventional. It loses life. Just as personal faith is a matter of living relationship, so is faith held in community. The relationship between spiritual director and directee is a small instance of God's holy habitation and may serve as a gateway to fuller experience of the Body of Christ. Our most personal experience of communion with God is bodied into words and gestures, laughter and tears, into the vitality of real relationship. The director listens the other into speech. The directee trusts and explores the mystery, as "in the Spirit, personhood and sociality come into being simultaneously, and are complementary." [20] True worship is experienced as we listen for God by the light of the candle.

Seeing through a Glass Darkly

Willingness to encounter and explore holy mystery entails what John Keats called "negative capability." This is a quality he claimed to discern in great poets, and one that I witness in spiritual fruition. In a December 1817 letter to his brothers, Keats wrote that negative capability is "when a man is capable of being in uncertainties, mysteries, doubts, without any irritable reaching after fact & reason."[21] This capability is essential for communities of faith as well as for individuals. We see through a glass darkly. Contentment with this half-knowledge is necessary for faith and for the perception of beauty.

Experiences of prayer and worship rely on the capability to enter mystery and perceive beauty, without explaining or justifying, resolving or finalizing. It is not a matter of drawing on carefully accumulated "spiritual capital" in the calculated way current theories suggest. It is, rather, a matter of faith. Over time I have seen people's negative capabilities expand through the work of spiritual direction. They explore mystery and beauty, sometimes in circumstances of suffering.

In postmodern Christianity, we are still captivated by images of the self-made man, the liberated woman, the rugged individualist, each caught in the "solitude of [our] own heart[s]."[22] We have lost our communal imagination. At times we are able to identify with the lost sheep, the Good Samaritan, even the Suffering Servant, but we turn from images of the flock, the field of lilies, and the Body of Christ. The shared prayer of spiritual direction helps resuscitate communal imagination as we come together as companions on the journey.

My own capacity for both mystery and clarity has been expanded, stretched, and challenged through the practice of spiritual direction. My sense of beauty has also grown, and, as I've witnessed beauty, I've grown in love. This has been a result of the practice, not a result of intention alone. Like leg muscles strengthening on a long trek, so my love has grown like a muscle unconsciously exercised in a particular pursuit. In this case the pursuit is care of another's soul. Some degree of love of God and for others allowed me to take up that pursuit, but, amazingly, that love has gradually and mysteriously been amplified over time.

In the face of divine mystery and inescapable uncertainties, it is love that matters in the caring art of spiritual direction. As Ruth affirmed while facing her death, "love never ends."[23] Prophecies will cease, tongues will fail, and knowledge will pass away. At any time, we see through a glass darkly. We have confidence that this is not final: "Now I know only in part; then I will know fully, even as I have been fully known."[24] Faith and hope depend on love.

"I am fully known" is the basic trust underlying this work. Both of us in the room are fully known by the ultimate Director, as fully known as in what we jokingly call "the biblical sense." This is a loving intimacy we can barely comprehend even by way of analogy to our most intimate human relations. It is no wonder that spiritual direction moves us to tears time and time again. It seems miraculous that two acquaintances with minimal contact outside one-hour meetings in an office are, in fact, the dwelling place of God, an instance of loving communion.

While there is mystery, there is also clarity. Though we see through a glass darkly, we do see. George Herbert's poem about prayer ends by calling prayer "something understood."[25] We begin to understand when we begin to see. In large part what I see is beauty. That beauty shines in Ruth's clear-eyed meeting with death. It's there in Carl's willingness to extend hospitality and grasp consolation in the face of unfulfilled prayer. There is beauty in Charles's courage to dismantle idols in order to choose life, and in Leah's and John's willingness to trust that God is present in all places: pastures, fascist countries, classrooms, businesses. Dark beauty glows in Melissa's suffering faithfulness and Grant's turn toward the Cross. Jim and David shed their robes of divinity in order to feel the breath of God's Spirit on their skin.

All are being refined, pruned, fed, and engrafted into the vine of Christ by our gardening God.[26] The vine is communal and love, its lifeblood. I sense its pulse in those I watch in the chair across from me and in the answering throb within me.

This is mystery and clarity, a reality simultaneously indisputable and immeasurable. The pile of tissues in my wastepaper basket and the smoke from the extinguished candle are artifacts of our hearts being touched and stretched by Love. Sometimes I return to my chair after a directee departs and savor the time we've shared. Too often I plunge back into the work of the office. When I leave for the day, I replenish the candle and notice the third chair. It's always there, reminding me that God is always present with me and with those for whom I pray. The chair and candle have become icons pointing to the One by whom I am fully known, whom I glimpse by candlelight in my brothers' and sisters' lives.

Notes

1. Eph 2:19–21.

2. Herbert, "Prayer (1)," *The Temple: The Poetry of George Herbert*, ed. Henry L. Carrigan Jr. (Brewster, Mass.: Paraclete, 2001), 45.

3. In Jewish theology and social action, this is the call of faith expressed by the Hebrew words *tikkun olam*.

4. Phil 2:15–16, *NIV Study Bible* (Grand Rapids, Mich.: Zondervan, 2002).

5. Herbert, "Prayer (1)," *The Temple*, 45.

6. Rev 22:2.

7. Erik H. Erikson, "Dr. Borg's Life Cycle," *Adulthood* (New York: W. W. Norton and Company, 1978), 20.

8. Sharon Begley's report in *The Wall Street Journal* was quoted by Jim Holt in "Of Two Minds," *New York Times Magazine*, May 8, 2005, 12.

9. See Robert E. Webber, *The Younger Evangelicals: Facing the Challenges of the New World* (Grand Rapids, Mich.: Baker Books, 2002), in which the author refers to the research of Wade Clark Roof.

10. Americans have the longest work year (49 1/2 weeks, with the Japanese working 46 weeks, the British, 43, and the Germans, 37) of all industrial nations. These statistics were found in Steven Greenhouse's article, "Report Shows Americans Have More 'Labor Days,'" *New York Times*, September 1, 2001, and quoted in my article "Garden or Circus: Christian Care in the Face of Contemporary Pressures," *Transformation: An International Dialogue on Mission and Ethics* 22, no. 3 (July 2005): 158–65.

11. For well-articulated theories on this subject, see the writings of sociologist Robert Putnam and economist Robert Fogel.

12. Edwards, *Spiritual Director, Spiritual Companion: Guide to Tending the Soul* (New York: Paulist Press, 2001), 13.

13. This word was introduced to me by Tom Reiss in *The Orientalist: Solving the Mystery of a Strange and Dangerous Life* (New York: Random House, 2005), 275.

14. Rohlhiser, *Holy Longing: The Search for a Christian Spirituality* (New York: Doubleday, 1999), 53.

15. My pastor and friend Mark Labberton has written a fine book on the subject of worship and justice, *The Dangerous Act of Worship: Living God's Call to Justice* (Downer's Grove, Ill.: InterVarsity Press, 2007)

16. Gen 18.

17. John 1.

18. John 20:22.

19. Moltmann, *The Source of Life: The Holy Spirit and the Theology of Life*, trans. Margaret Kohl (London: SCM Press, 1997), 93.

20. Rohlheiser, *Holy Longing*, 92.

21. http://www.mrbauld.com/negcap.html.

22. Alexis de Tocqueville [1835], "Of Individualism in Democratic Countries," *Democracy in America*, bk. 2, ed. Richard D. Hefner (New York: Mentor, 1956), 194.

23. I Cor 13: 8.

24. I Cor 13:12.

25. Herbert, "Prayer (I)," *The Temple*, 45.

26. John 15:1–17.

About the Author

Susan S. Phillips, Ph.D., is Executive Director and Professor of Sociology and Christianity at New College Berkeley, an affiliate of Berkeley's Graduate Theological Union. For many years she has been a spiritual director and supervisor, teaching courses in the fields of spiritual theology, the ethics of care, and spiritual direction at Fuller Theological Seminary (Menlo Park, Calif.), San Francisco Theological Seminary, and Regent College (Vancouver, B.C.). She edited the award-winning *The Crisis of Care: Affirming and Restoring Caring Practices in the Helping Professions*, writes at the intersection of social science and practical theology, and serves on the editorial boards of *Radix* and *Presence* magazines.